MIKE ON CRIME:

TRUE TALES OF LAW & DISORDER

MIKE MCINTYRE

GREAT PLAINS
PUBLICATIONS

Copyright © 2014 Mike McIntyre

Great Plains Publications
233 Garfield Street
Winnipeg, MB R3G 2M1
www.greatplains.mb.ca

All rights reserved. No part of this publication may be reproduced or transmitted in any form or in any means, or stored in a database and retrieval system, without the prior written permission of Great Plains Publications, or, in the case of photocopying or other reprographic copying, a license from Access Copyright (Canadian Copyright Licensing Agency), 1 Yonge Street, Suite 1900, Toronto, Ontario, Canada, M5E 1E5.

Great Plains Publications gratefully acknowledges the financial support provided for its publishing program by the Government of Canada through the Canada Book Fund; the Canada Council for the Arts; the Province of Manitoba through the Book Publishing Tax Credit and the Book Publisher Marketing Assistance Program; and the Manitoba Arts Council.

Design & Typography by Relish New Brand Experience
Printed in Canada by Friesens

LIBRARY AND ARCHIVES CANADA CATALOGUING IN PUBLICATION

McIntyre, Mike, author
    Mike on crime : true tales of law and disorder / Mike McIntyre.

Issued in print and electronic formats.
ISBN 978-1-927855-06-5 (pbk.).--ISBN 978-1-927855-07-2 (epub).--
ISBN 978-1-927855-08-9 (mobi)

    1. Crime--Canada--History. 2. Criminals--Canada--History.
I. Title.

HV6804.M37 2014   364.971   C2014-903359-1
                                  C2014-903360-5

ENVIRONMENTAL BENEFITS STATEMENT

Great Plains Publications saved the following resources by printing the pages of this book on chlorine free paper made with 100% post-consumer waste.

TREES	WATER	ENERGY	SOLID WASTE	GREENHOUSE GASES
12	5,531	5	370	1,019
FULLY GROWN	GALLONS	MILLION BTUs	POUNDS	POUNDS

Environmental impact estimates were made using the Environmental Paper Network Paper Calculator 3.2. For more information visit www.papercalculator.org.

FSC
www.fsc.org
MIX
Paper from responsible sources
FSC® C016245

To Chassity, Parker and Isabella

INTRODUCTION 7
1. "BEEPER" 11
2. A DREAM LIFE SHATTERED 33
3. DRIVING THEM CRAZY 45
4. THE BLANCHARD CRIMINAL ORGANIZATION 71
5. PHOENIX 90
6. THE LOBSTERMAN 117
7. THE FINAL GOODBYE 131
8. LIFE OR DEATH 151
9. JUSTICE WASN'T SERVED 178
10. A HEARTLESS ACT 206
11. LEGAL LOTTO 219
12. THE MASTER MANIPULATOR 247
13. THE LOST SOULS 271
14. HORROR ON THE GREYHOUND 283
15. COLD WINTER, WARM HEART 315
16. TJ'S GIFT 325

INTRODUCTION

Teacher. Meteorologist. Winnipeg Jets play-by-play voice. Accountant. Professional wrestler. Like most kids growing up, I wasn't really sure what I wanted to be when I "grew up." But I certainly had plenty of ideas, some of which were admittedly far-fetched. I mean, an accountant?? C'mon!

It wasn't until late in my final year of high school that things began to come into focus, thanks largely to a meeting with a guidance counsellor. He helpfully suggested some of my interests and skills might be suited for the communications industry and pointed out a local post-secondary program that might be right up my alley. The rest, as they say, is history. Wonderful, memorable history.

I was accepted that year, at the tender age of 18, into the Red River College Creative Communications program. It is there I first developed a love for writing, especially of the non-fiction variety. Local news especially piqued my interest. Much of this was fostered by my incredible journalism instructor, Donald Benham. He helped chart a course for future success—one that included a fantastic work placement at the *Interlake Spectator* newspaper following completion of my first year of college. I covered it all that summer—local politics, crime, feature stories and all kinds of quirky tales about local residents. As I returned for my second year, my focus was clear. And the planets began to align in a way that I still look back and thank my lucky stars over. A three-week stint at the *Winnipeg Sun* would prove to be my big chance. They happened to have a job opening and offered it to me as I neared graduation in the spring of 1995, barely 20 years old. Incredibly, they weren't just offering me a job. They were offering me their prized beat—covering cops and crime. Here I was, a wide-eyed kid who grew up on the not-so-mean streets of North Kildonan in Winnipeg, about to immerse myself in a crazy world I knew very little about. But like everything in life, I jumped in with both feet. And what resulted has been a wild, 20-year journey that I still find hard to believe at times.

I left the *Winnipeg Sun* after two-and-a-half years, taking a job opportunity at the *Winnipeg Free Press* to remain on the crime trail. I moved to the justice beat in 1999, parking myself down at the downtown Winnipeg Law Courts where I've remained ever since. I have a daily front row seat to some of the worst society has to offer. But I remain proud and passionate about my hometown. Whether it's sitting down with a grieving victim's family or staring down a criminal behind bars at Stony Mountain, I've always strived to get all sides of the story.

Preparing for this, my sixth true crime book, was an emotional experience. It required many long nights of going through old story archives, re-living many of the notorious cases I've covered and drudging up long-buried memories. All of what you will read in these pages is based on interviews conducted by me and colleagues, sworn testimony, first-person accounts from the courtroom, documents and exhibits filed in the hearings, parole documents and previously published newspaper stories and columns with full credit and attribution. No dialogue or scenarios have been improvised, assumed or re-created.

There are so many people to thank for the first 20 years of my career: Former teachers, editors and my extremely talented colleagues. Staff at the courthouse who have helped me in so many ways. Lawyers, judges and yes, even those criminals who have permitted me access. And all of those victims of crime—the survivors, the grieving family members—who have opened their lives to share their stories.

And, finally, my incredible supportive family. My parents, my wife and my two amazing children.

I believe the stories you are about to read are important ones which have helped shape the fabric of our community. It is a trip down memory lane well worth taking. Thank you for joining me on my journey.

Mike McIntyre
www.mikeoncrime.com
www.twitter.com/mikeoncrime

CHAPTER 1

"BEEPER"

It was one of the first signs that Winnipeg had a major street gang problem. And it made headlines across Canada while sparking calls for tougher penalties for young offenders and tougher laws for organized crime members. But what I'll remember most about the following story is this: The sight of a lifeless boy on the pavement, the sounds of screaming and the utter chaos in the night air. Joseph Spence was the first dead body I'd ever seen in my life.

I arrived at the scene within minutes of his shooting, having been monitoring the police scanner along with another young reporter, Nadia Moharib, and photographer Chris Procaylo. All three of us were relatively new employees at the Winnipeg Sun *and were keen to make a good impression on our bosses. And so we would often hang out at night, rushing to major calls to get first-person witness accounts and photographs. We were just a couple blocks away when this one was broadcast over the airwaves. But I was not prepared for what I saw that night. And the vivid memory of it continues to haunt me to this day.*

SUNDAY JULY 23, 1995

Joseph Spence had spent the night playing video games with friends at his grandparents' residence. Now the 13-year-old Winnipeg boy, known to everyone as "Beeper", was on his way to a nearby relative's home.

It was 2:30 a.m. As he pedaled his bicycle through the city's gritty North End neighbourhood, Beeper and a small group of friends who were with him didn't seem to notice the blue van approaching from behind. Inside were three young strangers hell-bent on revenge.

As they approached the intersection of Flora Avenue and Robinson Street, one of the strangers put on a pair of gloves and then picked up a sawed-off shotgun. He wiped down the weapon several times, then picked up a shotgun shell and did the same. The van rolled up beside Beeper and his buddies. The window came down. The man with the gun yelled for them to come closer. Before anyone knew what was happening, he raised the firearm and pulled the trigger. The result was catastrophic—for the young victim, the shell-shocked neighbourhood and the city at large.

It was an image Dale Wiltshire would never be able to forget. The 24-year-old off-duty Winnipeg police constable just happened to be driving down Flora Avenue, on her way to visit a friend, when she witnessed the sort of horrific event that no amount of training could have prepared her for. Beeper Spence had just been shot in front of her.

"It was the most horrible thing I've ever seen in my life," Wiltshire would later tell colleagues. "I saw him fall—it was so close and so forceful it lifted him up in the air."

She had only graduated into the police service one month earlier, but Wiltshire's instincts immediately kicked in as soon as the shot rang out and the victim went down. She jumped out of her vehicle. Her first thought was to reach for her firearm. But she wasn't in uniform, of course. She was unarmed. And scared. The suspect's vehicle had sped away, leaving behind a scene of utter chaos. Several of the victim's friends were screaming. Neighbours who heard the incident had come rushing outside. Sirens could be heard in the distance as police and paramedics rushed to the scene.

Wiltshire ran to the victim, instantly checking for a pulse. The damage from the shotgun blast was enormous. But the boy had briefly gasped for air, giving her some hope. Then the boy's breathing suddenly stopped. Wiltshire turned him over on his back and began giving him CPR. Her boyfriend, who had been with her in the vehicle at the time, helped as well. But all their efforts would be for naught. Beeper was dead.

They called him the "question boy"—an ode to the inquisitive nature of the Grade 7 student at David Livingstone School. But now those who knew and loved Beeper Spence were the ones asking questions. Why would someone kill the popular teen in cold blood?

The initial theory being looked at by police was gangs. Winnipeg was struggling to cope with an emerging street crime scene that had seen the formation of several factions in recent years. While highly disorganized, there was no disputing just how dangerous some of these individuals could be. So-called "turf wars" were beginning to develop, with each group trying to stake their claim of the lucrative drug trade. The result was a growing amount of violence, including numerous acts that weren't being reported to police but rather being dealt with by a form of street justice.

There were rumours circulating that Beeper himself was a member of the Indian Posse gang, which had quickly established itself as Winnipeg's biggest with more than 100 members. However, those closest to Beeper knew the truth: While he certainly knew members of the gang, he wasn't a member. But police believed those responsible for his death didn't know that. They were suspected members of the Deuces gang, which was known as the main rival of the Indian Posse. They were much smaller, with only about 30 known members. Several Deuces members had been attacked in recent weeks. And word on the street was that they were looking to settle some scores with the Indian Posse.

"This was retaliation," one neighbourhood resident told the *Winnipeg Free Press*. She had witnessed the ugly aftermath of the shooting after being awakened by the shotgun blast just outside her front window. "You know it's not going to stop here. There's going to be more killings," she predicted.

Beeper himself had expressed concerns about gangs in the area, specifically about guilt by association. Beeper was living with his grandparents on Sinclair Street but would spend weekends with his father and aunt, who lived near the scene of the shooting. His grandfather, Nick Grisdale, recalled how members of the Deuces had harassed the boy in the past, believing him to be a rival. Now it appeared they had done a lot more than just harass him. Beeper had been caught in the crossfire, the victim of a tragic case of mistaken identity.

Bright. Chatty. Happy-go-lucky. These were some of the terms being used to describe Beeper Spence in the wake of his tragic shooting death.

Rick Johnston was the coach of Beeper's peewee baseball team, called the Indian and Metis Friendship Centre Eagles. And he was now mourning the loss of a second player to violence. Last year, his star pitcher, Trevor Sanderson, was gunned down in a gang-related shooting, and now Beeper, another young hurler, had his promising life cut short. "It's maddening," Johnston told the *Winnipeg Free Press*. "There's another one gone." He said these types of senseless incidents were making him more determined than ever to get kids off the streets and into positive environments such as team sports. "It makes me want to fight even harder… I'm not throwing in any towels."

Meanwhile, one of Beeper's former teachers was speaking out as well, saying this type of deadly attack was her worst type of fear come true. "I'm worried sick when the end of June comes. At least when they are at school, you know the kids are safe," Anastasia Yereniuk told the *Free Press*. "I was just sick when I heard [about Beeper]. He was a nice kid, full of life." She described the culture of violence that had seemingly taken over many of the youth she taught. "I can't say I'm surprised this happened," she said. "They all hang around gangs here. It's a sign of the times in this area. The gang problems have never seemed as bad as they are now."

MONDAY JULY 24, 1995

They gathered close together, more than 100 strong, as the sun began to set on another hot summer's day. It had been less than 48 hours since Beeper Spence was shot dead at this intersection. Now the boy's photo, pasted to a large piece of cardboard, rested against the tree. Mourners, many of them in tears, signed their names after touching the image of the slain boy. A blue blanket adorned with his photo and a flowery cross of tissue paper was also nailed to the tree. A Catholic priest said prayers followed by eulogies by three of the boy's friends.

"We just did it to show our love for him," Beeper's mother, Nancy Flett, told the *Winnipeg Free Press*. She repeated the family's strong denials that Beeper had any kind of gang involvement: "The only colours he wore was the yellow T-shirt and baseball cap for the Winnipeg Boys and Girls Club."

Meanwhile, police had made their first arrest. A teenage boy was picked up earlier in the day while walking down a North End street. He was now charged with first-degree murder, indicating justice officials believed this was a planned, pre-meditated act. Three more arrests would soon follow. And police admitted they were bracing for more potential violence. "We're kind of holding our breath and hoping for the best," police spokesman Eric Turner told reporters. "There is definite concern we're in the midst of a very serious situation."

Police were beefing up enforcement, and the 15 members of the street gang unit would be working overtime as they tried to keep a lid on any fallout or retaliation. "We'll be keeping an ear to the ground to see which way the winds are blowing," said Staff Sgt. Caron.

"Moms and dads, where are your kids."

Ken Biener was growing frustrated at what he felt was the lack of accountability being shown by many Winnipeg parents. And so the inspector of the police youth division was speaking out in the wake of Beeper's slaying, suggesting that allowing your young teen to roam the streets at all hours of the night was a bad idea. "I'm satisfied this is happening all over. But it's the element of risk for kids that is different. Let's face it, there are a lot of crusty things happening in the core area after dark," Biener told the *Winnipeg Free Press*.

Beeper's family members were stinging at allegations on radio call-in shows and newspaper letters-to-the-editor that they must not have cared about the young boy. "It was just a short walk to his auntie's," Nancy Flett explained. She repeated the story of how he and friends had been at his grandmother's, but then was asked to leave because it was getting late and they were making too much noise. So they were on their way to Beeper's nearby aunt's home.

She and husband Stanley Spence split when Beeper was four. But that didn't mean he was from what most people think of as a broken home, she said. "He was very well looked after, and he was well-loved by everyone," said Flett. Meanwhile, she was now worried about the safety of her two other children, daughters aged 10 and 12, fearing there could be more violence to come.

"TIME FOR ACTION"
Editorial published in The Winnipeg Free Press, *Tuesday July 25, 1995*

> The weekend shooting of 13-year-old Joseph Spence and the escalation of street gang violence in general raises the inevitable question: Can anything be done about it?

The answer is yes. The solutions aren't simple, nor do they necessarily entail the expenditure of vast sums of money on new programs or the hiring of civil servants to run them. They do, however, require leadership and commitment on the part of some politicians and community leaders—the kind of leadership that has been lacking over the last few years.

Winnipeg has experienced a dramatic rise in youth related crime—particularly violent crime—since the start of the decade. Car thefts, purse snatchings, muggings and assaults are all up substantially over the numbers recorded just a few years ago.

Police attribute most of this increase to the growth and evolution of youth gangs in the inner city.

Indeed, police no longer refer to them as youth gangs; they're now called street gangs. The police say these gangs have become more organized and actually control federal and provincial jails in Manitoba.

And what were city and provincial government officials doing while the youth gang problem worsened?

Well, Justice Minister Rosemary Vodrey held a youth crime summit a few years ago and decided the solution was to talk about harsher sentences, boot camps and cancelling drivers' licenses of young offenders. The city, meanwhile, has done even less. As noted on this page last week, city council has given Mayor Susan Thompson a budget to hold conferences on youth crime, but nothing to help people actually do something about the problem.

In other words, the two levels of government closest to the issue have done virtually nothing.

Everyone knows why Winnipeg has a gang problem. Kids in the inner city—mostly native—are growing up in poverty, sometimes without strong parental support and often with a sense of alienation and hopelessness.

Short-term solutions are obvious. The city and the province have to make youth crime a priority and develop and fund the kinds of programs—like sports and recreation centres—that can give community workers a fighting chance to reach kids before they get into trouble.

In the long term, the Filmon government has to address the underlying causes of youth crime. It has to develop programs that reduce child poverty and make these kids believe they can have a future. That means making sure they have an opportunity to get an education that will lead to a decent job. It also means building a society that is tolerant and open, one where native youths can feel included rather than excluded. If not, the problems of the inner city will continue to grow—and spread.

TUESDAY FEBRUARY 23, 1996

He hadn't pulled the trigger. But a Winnipeg teen would still have to pay for his role in the killing of Beeper Spence. The 16-year-old pleaded guilty to a charge of being an accessory after the fact to murder, admitting he hid the shotgun and spent cartridge that had been used to gun down the teen less than a year earlier. Judge Philip Ashdown gave the youth one year of jail in addition to six-months of time already served. He was also placed on 18 months of supervised probation. His name could not be published.

"You've taken my only son away from me. You sit here like it was nothing," Nancy Flett said in a victim impact statement she read aloud. "[Beeper] can never sit with us around the Christmas tree, he can never go to school… still, you can do these things. Nobody said you guys could go out there and play God."

Crown attorney Cathy Everett said a strong message needed to be sent to anyone considering getting involved in this type of "brutal, tragic, cold-blooded offence." Defence lawyer Jim Macdonald told court his client was an otherwise law-abiding young man who was on the honour roll in grades 7 and 8 and got pressured into helping hide the weapon other gang-involved peers. "He is not a gang member, but lives in a neighborhood riddled with gang members," Macdonald said.

The judge questioned why all of these young people, including Beeper, were out so late at night. "One has to ask what happened to the parenting that night," said Ashdown.

THURSDAY APRIL 24, 1997

They sat in the prisoner's box, trading jokes and giggling as if they were in the back row of their high school classroom. Perhaps they were laughing at the justice system, which was about to give them a sweetheart deal. The three Winnipeg teenagers charged with first-degree murder in the drive-by shooting of Beeper

Spence had all struck plea bargains to reduced charges. Conrad Johnson, now 17, who fired the fatal shot, admitted to second-degree murder. Kami Pozniak, now 18, and Fabian Torres, now 19, entered pleas to manslaughter. All three would be given adult sentences, meaning their names could now be published. Lawyers on both sides refused to discuss details of the last-minute resolution, which came just as the jury was about to be picked for the start of their six-week trial.

Crown attorney Sid Lerner gave a brief outline of the facts they were pleading guilty to. He described how Beeper was shot in the back as he was biking home. And he told court of a "celebratory" mood amongst his killers, who traded high-fives and literally patted Johnson on the back for pulling the trigger. He said Johnson was bent on revenge that night because he had found out his friend had been badly beaten by rival gang members. Beeper had nothing to do with that, of course. But that didn't matter. After obtaining the sawed-off shotgun from a friend, the trio talked about payback. And so as they snaked their way through the North End, they spotted Beeper and decided his life would end at their hands. It was a cowardly act, one that simply could not be rationally explained. Now the killers would pay. But at a greatly reduced price.

FRIDAY MAY 23 1997

It was an emotional ending to a case that had sparked plenty of anger and sadness. The mother of Beeper Spence lashed out at her son's killers as they appeared in court to be sentenced. Nancy Flett aimed much of her rage at Queen's Bench Justice Sid Schwartz after he spared a jail sentence to one of the accused. Fabian Torres was given a one-year conditional sentence to be served in the community. The Crown was seeking prison and would eventually get their way on appeal, when the penalty would be increased to three-and-a-half years.

"You might as well do the same thing for the other fucking ones," shouted Flett as the judge handed down his surprising sentence. She then turned her attention to Torres's father, who was also in the courtroom. "You have your son Mr. Torres. I don't have mine," Flett said before storming out of court.

Kami Pozniak was given two years behind bars for her role after admitting to manslaughter. Conrad Johnson was given a mandatory life sentence with no chance of parole for six-and-a-half years after pleading guilty to second-degree murder. There was no guarantee of ever being released, but he wouldn't have to wait too long before he could apply. Schwartz told court he wasn't going to bow to public pressure and dish out "high sentences on children."

"Mr. Torres will go through life knowing he helped Mr. Johnson in the killing. Someday I hope [Torres] has a son and every time he looks at him, he will wonder if his son is at risk. That's pretty heavy," the judge said.

Torres was the first of the killers to apologize for his actions: "First of all I would like to express remorse and tell the family how sorry I am," he said. "It's one thing for me to talk to the priest and tell him how sorry I feel about what happened and what I did and my involvement in this, but it's a different story facing the family altogether." According to the Crown, Torres had urged Johnson to shoot Beeper, telling him to "bust a cap in his ass." Pozniak also addressed the court, but by then Flett and her family had exited. "If the Spence family were here, I'd want to say I'm sorry again," she said. Her lawyer, Evan Roitenberg said she is "not a monster" and simply got herself into a terrible situation through her peers. Johnson chose to remain silent.

JULY 2000

A service was held on the five-year anniversary of his killing. Nancy Flett helped organize the event at a local drop-in centre that bore his name, which drew children from the neighbourhood and included face-painting and traditional native dancers.

"I want to show kids the good way of life," Flett told the *Winnipeg Free Press*. "To bring people together and to show the youth there is more to life than hanging around on street corners and getting into trouble." Sadly, she said, the gang and violence situation in the city only seemed to be getting worse. And she thought the weak-kneed justice system was partially responsible. "I do not like this at all. They should have gotten life. They all played a part. I try to be strong for my girls, and I think I'm doing good for how far I've come. But every day I really wish my son was still alive."

2008

It appeared Canada's catch-and-release justice system was alive and well. Despite being convicted for their roles in a notorious Manitoba murder more than a decade earlier, parole documents revealed just how little time the three killers served behind bars and how their downward spirals had continued.

The man who gunned down Beeper Spence at the age of 15 walked out of a federal penitentiary in late January 2008, less than 10 years after he began serving a life sentence. It marked the second time the National Parole Board decided to take a gamble on Conrad Johnson's freedom. His first bid at day parole didn't work out so well. Johnson was first released in July 2006 but failed a drug test weeks later. He was displaying what parole officials called "deteriorating" social behaviour including throwing temper tantrums and lying. However, Johnson was given several additional chances to succeed. Parole officials didn't revoke his release until February 2007 after several more drug test failures and increasingly problematic behaviour. Back behind bars, Johnson admitted his mistakes and blamed them on being given too much, too fast.

"You believed you had to catch up on your lost youth and began hanging out with people who had no goals or values," the parole board wrote. "You started smoking pot in an attempt to fit in with your peers. You then began lying to your support network because you were scared to go back to prison." Parole officials, in their January 2008 decision, felt Johnson had learned from his mistakes and was ready for another chance: "You have come to realize that being back in jail was a waste of your life… and that prison is not the place you want to be," they wrote. "You stated that this was an experience you needed to awaken you. You now state that you are motivated to change your lifestyle and have taken positive steps in reaching this goal."

Johnson had remained silent at his sentencing but was now discussing Beeper's killing in some detail, admitting he mistakenly thought the 13-year-old was a rival gang member who'd assaulted one of his friends. He said he smoked marijuana and took LSD just prior to pulling the trigger on the sawed-off shotgun.

"You admit during the first several years of your incarceration you cared about little, gave no thought to the future and thought little about the crime you committed," the parole board wrote. "You have [now] displayed what the board believes to be sincere emotional empathy for the victim. You compared the loss this family must have suffered to the loss you felt when your mother passed."

The parole board applauded Johnson for taking steps to address his many problems, including drug abuse, poor relationship choices and anger management, by taking jailhouse treatment and programming. But they also cited his less than stellar track record behind bars as grounds for concern. He'd been hit with dozens of institutional charges, mainly for assaulting fellow inmates, being caught abusing contraband drugs, associating with gang members and abusing staff. Johnson also survived a brush with death after being stabbed in prison, then lashed out after his mother died and he couldn't attend her funeral. Family, friends and associates had been caught several times trying to smuggle drugs to him during visits. However, since 2003 Johnson had showed "steady improvement" as his security status went from maximum to medium to low, where it currently stood.

Johnson was raised in a home "plagued with violence and abuse," the parole board wrote. He became a habitual runaway by the age of 10. He only completed grade six. He began using drugs by 11, drinking excessively by 12. He started selling drugs as a young teen to support his addiction, then found a "surrogate family" in the form of a street gang.

The parole board rejected Johnson's bid for full parole in January 2008, meaning he had to still report each night to a halfway house. They called a full release "premature at this point." But they said he was on the right path, provided he avoided falling back into the same poor lifestyle choices that have seen him waste most of his life to date.

Despite being given numerous breaks by the system and cracks at freedom, Fabian Torres kept finding a way to land back in prison. Yet a forgiving parole board had ensured his stints didn't last long. Torres's first break may have been when he was convicted of manslaughter instead of second-degree murder for his role in the killing of Beeper Spence. He was originally given a 12-month conditional sentence, increased to three-and-a-half years in prison on Crown appeal. Still, Torres dodged a bullet and was back on the streets after serving only one-third of that penalty.

But he quickly went back to the gang and criminal lifestyle, culminating in an August 1998 home invasion. The victims were several adults and children. Torres and three co-accused, clad in masks, looted the home and stole the family's van. They were nabbed after a brief chase with police. Torres's parole was revoked, and he eventually received an additional 11 years in prison for the violent robbery.

Just six years later, Torres was back out. He was given day parole, which eventually turned into full parole in the fall of 2005. At the time, parole officials said Torres had made great progress in dealing with his demons, which stemmed from an abusive childhood, drug addiction and poor peer choices. But success was short-lived once again. On December 9, 2006, police stopped a speeding car. Torres was behind the wheel, the smell of marijuana in the air. Torres was arrested, but his parole was allowed to continue with a condition that he live at a community residential facility until his condition "stabilized." Torres was allowed to go home a few weeks later. But he failed to appear in court on the drug charges and a warrant was issued for his arrest. He was nabbed by police on Valentine's Day 2007 after being caught driving without a licence. The parole board gave him yet another chance. But Torres blew it when he failed to meet with his parole officer in early March 2007.

Another warrant was issued and this time, parole was revoked. A drug test found Torres provided a false urine sample by using a device to store "clean" urine. He failed to say what drug he had been using. Torres spent two months in prison before the parole board decided to give him yet another chance in the summer of 2007. They said his breaches were serious but his risk "did not rise to an unmanageable level." Torres was ordered to live at a halfway house and continue getting psychological counselling.

"It does not appear you have learned from your mistakes and you are indeed fortunate that you have not been revoked and returned to jail," the parole board wrote. "Your impulsivity, poor decision-making and your inability to follow the conditions of your parole over the long term suggests you have a well-entrenched criminal mindset and values. Your behaviour suggests that you continue to require the structure, monitoring and controls of a halfway house."

Kami Pozniak just couldn't stay out of trouble. Court records show Pozniak had been convicted of 11 separate offences—including drugs, prostitution and failing to comply with court orders—since 2003 alone. Pozniak had been in and out of custody for much of that time, often getting released on bail only to be re-arrested on breach allegations or new substantive criminal charges.

During her sentencing for manslaughter, it was suggested Pozniak had just been in the wrong place at the wrong time and made poor choices about her peers and lifestyle. Hope was expressed that some time behind bars would give her the chance to escape the past and move forward to a brighter future. Yet the sentencing judge heard Pozniak had not been making very good use of the time. Instead of focusing on treatment and programming, she was getting into violent disputes with other inmates and guards that landed her in segregation. She eventually got out—but like her co-accused Johnson and Torres, the revolving door of justice kept on swinging. In 2000, Pozniak appeared before a parliamentary standing committee in Ottawa that was exploring possible changes to the Youth Criminal Justice Act. One of the big issues then was whether youth criminals who were raised to adult court should be named in public, as Pozniak was.

"Every day when I go out, lots of people recognize my name when I get introduced to people. I have a hard time getting a job. When I attended school, the teachers knew who I was, and my law teacher knew who I was," Pozniak told federal lawmakers, including Peter MacKay. "I find it very difficult to be known just as [a convicted criminal] instead of being known as me, being known as something I was labelled for in the past. It still reflects in my face every day I live out in the community."

Kim Pate, executive director of the Elizabeth Fry Society, described Pozniak at the time as a "young aboriginal woman who is struggling to complete school... is basically struggling to get back on her feet after that." She told the committee that Pozniak had attempted suicide on multiple occasions and frequently found herself in segregation. "She unfortunately has had some of the worst experiences of our system and some of the worst experiences of the current system."

Pozniak also told government officials she hoped to one day meet with Beeper's family: "I've always wanted to meet with them. At my sentencing I apologized to the family for my responsibility in taking part in it. But the family isn't ready for me, I guess, so I'm just waiting until that perspective comes."

Kami Pozniak died in February 2011 at the age of 32. She was survived by two children. An official cause of death was never released publicly but those close to her told me it was linked to the various vices she'd spent her life fighting. She never did get that meeting with Beeper's family that she had talked of wanting.

Fabian Torres has seemingly stayed out of trouble. Perhaps he finally got the fresh start in life his family predicted he would upon his release.

Conrad Johnson has continued to go through the revolving door of justice. After his second shot at freedom in 2008, he fled from a halfway house in Winnipeg in July 2009 and spent 15 months on the run. Officers caught up with Johnson in October 2010, finding him in a city hotel room with several high-ranking gang members and a large quantity of marijuana. Johnson was not charged for the drugs but did get slapped with being unlawfully at large.

He claimed he ran away because he wanted to see his newborn baby and knew he'd be in trouble for smoking pot. His day parole was cancelled. He spent a couple of years in remand custody before being returned to federal custody in December 2012. He enrolled in several substance-abuse programs, demonstrated model behaviour and was given a third shot in October 2013 when he was granted unescorted temporary absences for up to 72 hours of freedom per month. These came despite ongoing concerns about his risk to the public. They were supposed to be for "personal development" and included both family and social time. He claimed he was going to use the time to "participate in community activities such as church services, cultural ceremonies, and shopping centres" during which he would be in the company of his common-law wife. But parole documents show those privileges were revoked in the summer of 2014 after he got caught lying to parole board officials about how he was spending his free time.

Parole board officials say they received a tip Johnson was going around bragging to others about how he'd pulled the wool over their eyes. Specifically, his absences allowed him to attend weekly Narcotics Anonymous meetings to help deal with outstanding addictions issues. Yet Johnson was skipping out—a fact confirmed when federal officials did a surprise check-in and he was nowhere to be found.

"You initially acted as if there were no concerns," the parole board wrote in their latest decision. "Then you claimed you missed your bus and became disoriented." The parole board members said they could no longer trust him, especially considering his less-than-stellar track record. "You continue to have difficulties following the rules," they wrote.

Meanwhile, I still hear occasionally from Beeper's family. They are, understandably, outraged at the state of the youth justice system, the violent street gang scene in Winnipeg. Unfortunately there have been countless other young victims just like Beeper who have had their lives cut short in the nearly 20 years which have passed. Like him, several were the victim of mistaken identity, gunned down for simply wearing the wrong colours or walking through the wrong neighbourhood.

In 2013, a veteran staff sergeant in the community relations unit penned a very eloquent column in the Winnipeg Free Press *that described how Beeper's death wasn't the wake-up call that it should have been:*

"Unfortunately, Winnipeg's gang situation has not improved since then. Aboriginal gangs aren't the only ones to have taken hold in Winnipeg. But they certainly deserve special attention because of the harm they cause on their ancestral lands and the harm they cause to their communities," Andy Golebioski wrote.

"In Winnipeg, several gangs exist, but a few really stand out as having a particularly destructive effect, not just because of their crimes, but because they claim a perverted sense of aboriginal identity. I'm talking

about the Manitoba Warriors, the Native Syndicate and the Indian Posse. These gangs make a mockery of the words Indian, native and especially warrior. Their ancestors would be embarrassed."

Golebioski called on local Aboriginal leaders to take a stand and work closely with law enforcement. "We, as the police, do our best to combat street gangs. However, it will take much more than just our enforcement and prevention efforts to eliminate their influence. Our entire community must rally around this cause and end it once and for all," he wrote. "As a police service, our wish is to stand with aboriginal leadership as they publicly and privately condemn these gangs. We just need them to give us that opportunity."

CHAPTER 2

A DREAM LIFE SHATTERED

Sometimes the most incredible stories can be found in places you might not expect. Such as the obituary section. Like most justice reporters, I've long made a practice of scanning the daily death notices. As ghoulish as that might sound, they can often be a means of learning more about a victim of crime we might be writing about. Or finding contact information for family members and close friends who might wish to speak out. And they can also alert us to potential newsworthy tales that might otherwise go unnoticed to the general public.

Such was the case back in July 2005, when a particular bulletin caught my eye. The lengthy, well-written obituary told the tale of a beloved Winnipeg family man who had died "suddenly" following a lengthy struggle with a disease I admittedly knew very little about. Several passages left me wanting to know more, including the following: "The last few years he showed an incredible strength to fight a disease which only a few experience in such severity. He was a true fighter and had the courage to keep going. In his deepest, darkest moments he always wanted the best for his family. He wanted them to be happy."

I knew this might be a delicate situation with the family, given what I was reading. I would have to tread very carefully. I waited a few weeks before following up, tracking down the man's wife and calling her to introduce myself. I explained what I knew—including some information I had obtained independently by this point—and asked her if the family might be willing to talk about the tragedy. Somewhat surprisingly, she said yes. I was invited to the family home, where I was given a window into what truly seemed like something out of a Hitchcock movie.

Bob was living the dream life. A rock-solid 23-year marriage, three beautiful children, a spacious home in an upscale Winnipeg neighbourhood, a relaxing summer cottage, an important job he loved, financial security and an extensive network of good friends and family.

"You've got it all," co-workers would often tell the 47-year-old man. He was living proof that good things do indeed happen to good people. Yet for the past 18 months, Bob's storybook life was literally being drowned out by a seemingly demonic force straight out of Edgar Allan Poe's spine-tingling *The Tell-Tale Heart*. Every second of every minute of every day, Bob's head was haunted by an overpowering, high-pitched ringing noise from which there was no escape. There was a clinical name for this bizarre ailment—tinnitus. There was also no known cure. Bob often described it as his "worst nightmare."

"I wish I had terminal cancer instead," he told his wife, Liz, on several occasions.

"I just don't understand. How come you guys can't just go into my head and turn off the ringing? Just shut it off," he asked several doctors.

Bob had read up on his condition, but the facts did nothing to offer any comfort. A man who loved nothing more than the peaceful tranquility of watching a morning sunrise at his Manitoba cottage was now being held hostage by his own ringing head. "He always loved silence, especially at the lake. But that was gone forever," said Liz.

It was literally driving her husband mad. First came the anxiety, a feeling that Bob had totally lost control of his life, that his world was crashing and burning around him. Next came the panic attacks, which were often mistaken for heart attacks and resulted in several trips to Winnipeg emergency rooms. Finally, the depression set in. Medication, repeated talks with psychiatrists and other doctors, several admissions to hospital and even a radical brain treatment failed to ease his constant suffering. Bob sunk deeper as he became resigned to his fate, yet nobody who knew and loved him could have predicted the unspeakable horror that was to come.

THURSDAY JULY 14, 2005, 7 A.M.

It started off like any other day. Bob woke up and got ready to head to his job with a major Canadian company, where he had worked for 29 years, the past few in a supervisory capacity. The morning was uneventful. It was around 1 p.m. when he called his wife and said he was heading to Elma, Manitoba to deliver supplies. There was nothing unusual about the phone call, and Bob's mood on this day seemed to be better than it had been earlier in the week but Liz couldn't help but wonder what kind of impact Bob's appointment with his psychiatrist the previous day was having on his mind. She worried that what he'd been told might have been enough to drive him over the edge.

Liz, as she always did, had gone with Bob for moral support to his medical appointment, and also to ensure the doctor was aware of his recent mental state. It had been a rollercoaster few days, beginning with Bob going off his antidepressant medication a couple weeks earlier to attend a holistic retreat in Saskatchewan. Bob was desperate for improvement, and had thought a more natural approach might help. He'd returned home in early July, but the ringing in his head was just as loud, and his mood just as low.

Bob had frightened his wife a week ago when he suggested that he might harm himself. Liz managed to talk him through the crisis. The past weekend had offered little improvement, and the new week started off with Bob driving himself home from work on Monday after speaking with a work counsellor. The situation looked bleak.

"He wasn't sure he was going to make it home safely," Liz told the psychiatrist two days later. "He is totally done right now. He has no more energy to fight this disease, and I am scared for his safety."

The doctor had suggested several options. They could try a new medication. Bob could be re-admitted to the Victoria General Hospital, where he'd spent several weeks in January undergoing a radical treatment for depression that involved electric currents being zapped into his head. Or they could start the paperwork to get Bob placed in a mental health institution.

Bob had heard enough, focusing squarely on the worst-case scenario. He and his wife left the doctor's office and returned home. Bob took a few tranquilizers and went to sleep. It was several hours later, now into Wednesday evening, that Liz woke her husband up. "I've got something special for you," she said. Bob got up, and Liz led him outside where they both got on their bicycles and took a short ride to the nearby Fort Whyte Centre, which was a beloved spot for the couple.

"I led him around a path to a lake, and we took our shoes off and dipped out feet in the water. Bob always loved it there, and I said to him, 'Look at all the natural beauty out here,'" said Liz. Bob mentioned how the scene reminded him of his favourite painting, which hung in their home. Back at home and in bed that night, Liz took Bob's hand, sensing he was not doing well. She asked him to list the fears in his life.

Losing his family, being fired from his job, being passed over for career opportunities and advancement, and never escaping from his affliction were his answers. Bob then stressed the positives in his life— three wonderful children, a great wife, nice cottage, good job and the company of good friends and family, he said. Eventually, the couple stopped talking and said goodnight. As usual, both struggled to fall asleep. For Liz, it was the constant worrying that kept her awake. For Bob, it was the noise in his head, which only grew louder as night fell.

THURSDAY JULY 14, 4:15 P.M.

Don Giesbrecht, a trained paramedic from Whitemouth, was off-duty as he drove his 1998 Chevrolet down Highway 15 near Elma when he came across a horrific scene. Smoke and flames were pouring into the air, the result of a violent two-vehicle crash between a large truck that had apparently slammed into the side of a semi-trailer.

Giesbrecht rushed over to help and found a dazed man stumbling away from the burning truck he appeared to have been driving. He led the man to the side of the highway, looked him over and then sat him down on the ground so he could check on the status of the semi driver. As Giesbrecht made his way over to the other man, who appeared shaken but uninjured, he turned around to see his own green car speeding away from the scene. Behind the wheel was the injured man he'd just led away from the fire.

THURSDAY JULY 14, 5:15 P.M.
"Bob, phone me."

Liz hadn't heard from her husband in several hours and was growing concerned. It wasn't like him to take more than a few minutes to return a message on his cellular phone. Her anxiety intensified when one of Bob's co-workers pulled into her driveway.

"What has happened?" she asked, desperation clearly in her voice.

"Bob's been in an accident. He's OK ... but he's missing," said the man, who had been notified about the highway crash near Elma involving Bob's company vehicle.

Liz knew to fear the worst. She grabbed the telephone again and frantically dialed her husband. No answer. "Bob, it's OK, it's OK. I love you, it's OK. Just phone me," she pleaded in her message. As the minutes stretched into hours, there was still no returned call.

Bob's workplace quickly organized an intensive search, which included renting two helicopters to fly over the area near the crash scene. An all-terrain vehicle was also being used to search through the thick brush and forest. The RCMP also began looking for Bob, who was seen as both an injured person and a suspect in a vehicle theft. Most people worried that Bob might have suffered a head injury in the crash and wasn't thinking straight. Liz figured her husband was probably thinking quite clearly. And so it came as no real shock when searchers made a horrific discovery the following afternoon, about two kilometres from the crash scene.

Bob had hanged himself in the woods.

"I don't believe Bob deliberately crashed into the side of the semi. I think that was probably an accident, but it would have totally set him off. He would have thought, in his state, he was going to lose his job, his family, everything he loved," Liz recalled, months after her husband's death.

Suicide is often seen as taboo to discuss, but Liz didn't shy away from it while giving a heart-wrenching tribute to her husband at his funeral service. She now wanted to help educate others on tinnitus, anxiety and depression. She had already done a presentation at Red River College and planned to do more.

"Bob had so much to live for, but he couldn't accept his suffering," she said. "He gave us 23 wonderful years. He did what he had to do under the circumstances."

As compelling as this story was, it almost never saw the light of day. Just days before it was set to go to print, the grieving widow emailed me to say the family was now having second thoughts. She was still very much in favour of publication, as were her children, to educate others about what they had gone through in the hopes of preventing future tragedies. But other extended members didn't see it quite the same way. They had expressed concerns about the publicity that was sure to follow. They just weren't comfortable with it. The end result was a compromise: The story would still run, but the family's full names would be removed, and no photographs of them would be published.

I'm glad we found a way to get it out there. This story generated more response from the public than probably 98 per cent of what I've written during my career. So many people contacted me—by telephone, by email, by snail mail—wanting to weigh in. Some just wanted to express how much the story impacted them. Others wanted to know how to send their condolences or whether they could make a charitable donation. Some were directed straight at the family. And many had their own stories of struggling with tinnitus, expressing a sense of relief that this long-hidden issue was now out in the public domain. Here are just a few:

> *"Two weeks ago, I was working with a guy out of Winnipeg who told me about a friend and co-worker of his who had killed himself by driving in front of a semi near Winnipeg. He said this fellow suffered from a condition which caused a constant loud ringing in his ears that he couldn't get relief from. Three days after this conversation, a friend and former co-worker of mine, who just retired this spring, laid down on the tracks in front of a train in Brandon. Everyone who knew him was shocked, as he too seemed to have the perfect*

life. At his funeral in Brandon last Saturday, 975 people showed up. It was the saddest funeral I've ever been to mostly because we were all trying to understand what drove him to take his own life. Then on Tuesday, I found out that he too suffered from Tinnitus and had kept it a secret. This has definitely helped myself and hopefully a lot of other people to cope with our friend's death."

"My husband & I have lived through some of the same things. We were in a car accident 23 years ago and his injuries have caused him to be completely disabled for the last five years. The pain was so intense that he was only able to get out of bed to see the doctors. He was on antidepressant medication and high levels of Oxycodone. There were four times that he almost ended his life. These were very hard times with little understanding from others. I applaud you for telling your story and for sharing a very difficult time in your life. It is through the sharing of your pain that you will help others going through they own tragedy. "

"I have been suffering from Tinnitus for years (more than 10) and have the same high-pitched ringing in my ears 24/7 – 365 days a year. You learn to live with it but it is not easy. For example, I cannot hear birds chirping, or the rustle of leaves in the wind and many more noises because they are drowned out by this high-pitched noise. The most frustrating problem is that I do not hear the initial word spoken to me on most occasions because of this noise and concentrating on some other things that I am hearing at the time. My *wife says I need a hearing aid because I never hear what she says. This is not true; I hear what she says, but not the first words spoken because I may be listening to something else at the time. I can turn down the volume of the radio or TV fairly low and still hear everything if I concentrate on that one item only. I have obtained information on Tinnitus from a number of sources, but there is no cure, you live with it, frustrating as that is."*

"I went through the same problem four years ago. It started with an awful pressure in my ears, and ended with the sound of a fire engine in my head for three months, I couldn't sleep, work, think. I went to emergency departments, ear specialists, counsellors for help, both medical and emotional, and all the websites I could find, even phoning people in Calgary who specialized in tinnitus. I totally relate to this man and his family, it was a living hell. There were times that I thought how can I live with this for the rest of my life? And no one really understands. I still have it, but nowhere near as bad. I got dependent on sleeping pills, and eventually got off them. Unfortunately no one can help you. My sympathies to his family, hopefully someday someone will do research on how to help people afflicted with this problem."

"I know it is hard to deal with because I have had tinnitus since March 1995; non-stop noise, never lets up. I have dealt with it by not dwelling on it. I have practiced tai chi for 16 years and find that when I am practicing I do not hear the noise. I find that when I am absorbed in an activity it

does not tend to bother me. The worst time is at night when the house is quiet. When all you want to hear is silence and there is none. I know there are support groups for tinnitus but to me being in a support group and talking about it all the time would only make it worse by keeping it in your thoughts constantly. It is better not to dwell on it and just get on with things, as difficult as that is. I have had relief from the noise (lessening of the noise slightly but it never goes away), with acupuncture and tai chi, a wonderful chiropractor who lives in St. Rose near Montreal, and staying mentally and physically active. I appreciate that the man's wife wants to bring this to people's attention as apparently there is no cure and they can only guess at the cause and anyone who does not have this noise in their head cannot possibly know how annoying, and lonely, it is. All I pray for is silence."

SOME FACTS ABOUT TINNITUS

* Defined as a chronic ringing or other distressing noise in the ears or head, tinnitus can affect anyone at any age. It can range from mild to severe. It can be constant, or intermittent.

* More than 360,000 Canadians suffering from an "annoying form," with about 150,000 of those finding the quality of their lives seriously impaired.

* At least 50 different types of noises have been identified, including hissing, sizzling, buzzing, chirping, thumping, engine-like roaring, and a pulsing noise that tends to be in constant rhythm with one's heartbeat.

* Common causes include a blow to the head, severe ear infection, exposure to loud noise, whiplash or any kind of emotional or physical stress or shock.

* Treatment varies. Relaxation techniques such as yoga, therapeutic massage and even hypnosis have been successful for some people. Others lessen their ringing with sound-generating devices that produce a "white sound" in the ear.

* About 50 per cent of people suffering from tinnitus develop some form of depression.

—Tinnitus Association of Canada

CHAPTER 3

DRIVING THEM CRAZY

He has been a constant thorn in the side of justice and medical officials for more than a decade. And he is, without a doubt, one of the most interesting characters I've ever covered in my career. At times cold and calculated, at others times charming and engaging, Joey Wiebe is a man of many faces. There have been so many twists and turns with his story over the years that pretty much nothing surprises me about him any longer. His life could be a movie. Only, some might pan the plot at being too unrealistic.

MONDAY DECEMBER 3, 2001
Was he a crazed killer or a cunning con artist who had carried out his plan to perfection? That was the key question facing a Manitoba judge as a high-profile murder trial got underway. This was no whodunit. There was absolutely no doubt Joey Wiebe strangled his stepmother, slashed her throat with a knife and then tried to burn their house down. But whether the young Niverville, Manitoba man was criminally responsible for the May 2000 killing of Candis Moizer was yet to be decided.

Wiebe, 19, was being portrayed as a tortured teenager who once harboured a fascination for Adolf Hitler and Satan and left disturbing clues of his many troubles behind in a school locker. Police seized a number of bizarre poems and writings that offered a glimpse inside his mind. Including:

> *Sorrow, grief, and loneliness.*
> *Mindless, covert, and hopeless despair.*
> *Hatred and animosity, mindless mess.*
> *Searing passion. A human love.*
> *Shame and Embarrassment.*
> *And the hatred grows.*
> *Divine love, my heart won't accept.*
> *Lust,*
> *Infatuation.*
> *Hear my heart roar!*
> *Whhhhhhy!*
> *Confusion, relentless frustration.*
> *If only, if only, if only*
> *My heart does not stop repeating.*
> *When will my passion turn into action!*
> *Coward!*
> *I despise my own behaviour!*
> *When will my hate raise my fist!*
> *And I cry.*

Among the several hundred pages of material filed at trial were written transcripts of Wiebe's confession and explanation of the murder to RCMP officers who repeatedly tried, but failed, to obtain a motive. Wiebe, who had been living with his 40-year-old stepmother, biological father and stepsister since 1998, claimed he awoke at 4 a.m. on May 2, 2000, feeling something was terribly wrong.

"I didn't feel like myself at all. I woke up shaking very hard. I was just confused and frustrated," the teen, who was 17 at the time but had now been raised to adult court, said in an interview with police. Wiebe told police he walked into his stepmother's room, where she was sleeping alone, and began to choke her when she woke up and asked what was wrong. Wiebe's father was away on business, and his stepsister was asleep in the basement. "She was starting to pass out... I wanted to stop but I knew she was going to die anyways. I kept on telling her I was sorry. I didn't know what I was doing," said Wiebe. He said he retreated to the kitchen, grabbed a small knife and then returned upstairs where he slashed Moizer's throat.

Wiebe told police he then grabbed his father's rifle, which he used to shoot out the smoke detector in the home. He then wrote a letter to loved ones explaining his actions before dousing his stepmother's bed and bedroom with gasoline and setting it on fire. "I didn't want anybody to see her like that. I was just so disgusted," he said. Wiebe claimed he then cut the phone lines in the house, and woke his stepsister to get her out of the burning home. Wiebe said he confessed to killing their mother as he drove his stepsister to their grandmother's house in his father's truck. He said he apologized for what he'd done and told the young girl he loved her, for the first time in his life. "He said... that God loved me and that he was always going to take care of me," Cherylynn Moizer told police.

Wiebe called his biological mother from a gas station pay phone and confessed to his sins. The transcript of his phone call was tendered in court: "Hi Mom, it's Joey. I've done something terrible. I have to turn myself into the police. Um, I just want to tell you that I'm ex... I'm sorry for what I did to hurt you guys.

I love you all. I've got to turn myself in. Goodbye," he told his mother. Wiebe then flagged down a police officer and confessed. During a lengthy period of questioning, investigators repeatedly asked him why he'd done it. His only explanation was that "some evil forces were at work there."

Wiebe told police how he'd become a "Nazi" during his Grade 10 year at Niverville Collegiate, including shaving his head, and had begun to read up on Satanism. His stepsister said he often began speaking German in their home and told her he'd "marry her off to a German soldier" when he would "be able to get the power to be ruler of the world, like Hitler." She said he also spoke of hatred for Jews and said he would "do like Hitler did and kill them all."

Police later searched his locker at the school and found dozens of disturbing poems and writings he'd made, along with a series of lists which include references to the Mafia and mob terms. His principal, Howard Witty, told police he'd been concerned about Wiebe's conduct in school and had spoken with his father and stepmother, who shrugged it off by saying "they were just glad he was interested in something."

"He was a teenaged boy we were sometimes trying to figure out. He would turn in an essay to a teacher and it would be on whatever—farming. And right in the middle of it would be an outline or drawing of a Ku Klux Klan hood or hooded person," said Witty in a statement tendered by lawyers in the case. Witty said he took away Wiebe's computer privileges and forced him to remove offensive material from his locker, including posters he'd drawn of people with swords stuck in their heads and blood dripping down.

Wiebe, who said he only wanted to "belong to something," told police he'd put his Nazi beliefs behind him once he reached Grade 11 but admitted to having thoughts of killing someone only weeks before he carried out the act. By then, he was regularly attending church on Sundays and briefly thought about speaking to his pastor about his problems but changed his mind. He said he had a decent relationship with his stepmother but found she was too authoritative at times, including forcing him to do homework. He admitted to a history of problems with his biological father because of years of abuse he'd witnessed him causing to his mother. "I love everybody I know. I just hate what they do," said Wiebe.

Police also seized a handwritten note Wiebe had left behind for other family members: "To all of those that I have hurt: Please forgive me, I have gone mad, Max. May God forgive me. My sweet mother, I grieve you so. May Candis's soul be saved in heaven. Cherylynn forgive me. Dad forgive me. Why have I done this? Mom, forgive me of this selfish action I'm about to commit. I love you all and am so sorry, especially you mom and Cherylynn. Lord save me."

TUESDAY DECEMBER 4, 2001

They had spent months in a dark and disturbing place—the mind of a troubled teen killer. And they had come to the same conclusion: There's no way Joey Wiebe should be held criminally responsible for failing to control what they called a "catastrophic rage" that fueled his violent actions.

Dr. Eric Ellis, a Winnipeg psychologist who has testified for the defence in more than 200 trials across the country, said Wiebe suffered an uncontrollable "meltdown and eruption" when he attacked Moizer without provocation while she slept. "At the time of the killing, he had almost no capacity for judgment. He reports being in a trance-like state, where his body was present but his mind was not. There was almost nothing going through his mind," he said. "At various times he can describe it to me as if he was standing next to himself, observing himself [kill his mother]."

Those actions were consistent with borderline personality disorder and post-traumatic stress disorder, which Ellis said had been caused by Wiebe's horrific childhood which was filled with spousal abuse and parental neglect. "He could no longer control the rage that had been building up since the first years of his life," said Ellis, who said the only reason his stepmother was murdered was because she was the closest person to him. "This is an event which had nothing to do with the person who was the subject of it. It could have been anybody in the bed that night," he told court.

Dr. Robert Hill, an Ontario psychiatrist, agreed with the diagnosis and said the illness could manifest itself "in bizarre or severe forms of behaviour." "There is clear evidence [Wiebe] wasn't able to distinguish between right and wrong. He didn't have the mental capacity," Hill testified. "Unfortunately and tragically, he was not able to change or stop his behaviour because it wasn't as if he was carrying out the act. Some other force or power had consumed him."

The Crown asked both doctors if Wiebe could be faking his symptoms, but they said the evidence was overwhelming and foolproof that his mental illness was legitimate. Both doctors said Wiebe told them his father regularly abused his biological mother in his early childhood years, both physically and verbally.

"He was overwhelmed and scared and terrorized by the life threatening violence he witnessed against his mother. He was so close to her that he was practically experiencing the terror himself," said Ellis.

Dr. Fred Shane, a forensic psychiatrist, said the young man's mental illness acted like a powerful narcotic which rendered him helpless: "It was as though in a sense he had been given a drug, like LSD or cocaine ... which caused the psychotic episode with catastrophic results." He said Wiebe's traumatic upbringing, which included years of witnessing his father abuse his biological mother, left him unable to cope in society. "In his head, he had a Columbine sort of fantasy for his school," said Shane, adding any number of people could have become victim to his rage.

THURSDAY DECEMBER 6, 2001

The verdict was in: Joey Wiebe would not be going to prison. Wiebe gave a weak smile towards his weeping biological mother as Justice Brenda Keyser took only two minutes to deliver her verdict—not criminally responsible for second-degree murder due to mental illness.

Defence lawyer Greg Brodsky hailed the decision as potentially groundbreaking in law, saying the courts had finally recognized the emotional devastation felt by children who witness domestic abuse. He said the troubling case was the first in Canada in which the issue of being a battered child had been used as part of a successful defence. A similar defence of "battered wife's syndrome" had been used in courtrooms across the country, but the effects on children are usually lost, he said. "I hope there will now be a recognition that children should be treated too, and not just beaten-up wives," said Brodsky. "This shows that children of abusers can grow up to become abusers themselves. A little child who sees the abuse doesn't have the coping mechanisms and that becomes the world he sees, the world he knows."

Keyser said this was the only logical conclusion, especially since the Crown called no evidence casting doubt on three defence experts who examined Wiebe. "The evidence is overwhelming and uncontradicted that Earl Joey Wiebe was at the time suffering a mental disorder," Keyser said. A mental health review board would now convene within three months to decide where the teenager should be sent for long-term treatment and monitoring.

The family of murder victim Candis Moizer wasn't buying it. They believed her teenage stepson had gotten away with murder by fooling medical authorities and a judge into believing he is mentally ill.

"It's the biggest crock I've seen in my life. He put on a really good show, and we flat out don't believe he belongs in a mental hospital. We believe he belongs in a penitentiary," Lorne Hodge, Moizer's brother, said outside court. Along with his elderly parents, Hodge took issue with the three doctors who testified the teen could not distinguish between right and wrong. Two of the doctors admitted they had read the findings of their colleagues. "How can these doctors spend a few hours with Joey and then come to a fair conclusion when they all get to read each other's reports? It was very frustrating to sit through and listen," said Hodge.

The family had known the teen since Candis Moizer began a relationship with his father, Earl Sr., nearly 16 years ago. At the time, he was estranged from Wiebe's mother. Many of Wiebe's mental problems stemmed from years of violent abuse of his mother he witnessed at a young age, court was told. Moizer was aware of the resentment Wiebe felt towards his father but always tried to reach out to the troubled teen, Hodge said. She often stood up for him against his father and mother, and saw to it that he got a car on his 16th birthday. "Candis would have gone to the end of the earth for him, and that makes this even more tragic," he said. The family now feared that mental health officials would put too much stock in Wiebe's traumatic background and release him too quickly back into society.

MONDAY FEBRUARY 10, 2003

Manitoba's only long-term mental health facility wanted nothing to do with Joey Wiebe. And yet, due to a court ruling, they had no choice but to accept him into their care—despite taking the position they didn't think he was truly mentally ill. Dr. Jim Willows, a psychiatrist with the Selkirk Mental Health Facility, said Wiebe posed an imminent danger to patients and staff, along with residents of the community. He said staff could no longer treat Wiebe, who he believed tricked the courts into believing he was not criminally responsible. Willows believed the now 20-year-old should be jailed indefinitely. "He should be held responsible for what he has done. He doesn't have an illness, and

I don't agree with the decision of the court," Willows told a review board hearing at the downtown Law Courts. The hearing came after Wiebe was removed from the Selkirk mental facility by police days earlier and charged with threatening to bring a gun into the facility. He was also accused of threatening and extorting from patients, and was being detained at the Remand Centre. The hearing was to determine Wiebe's immediate future.

The family of Wiebe's victim was in court and said the legal system should be ashamed. "It is pretty sad that somebody like that can manipulate the justice system," said Lorne Hodge. "As time goes on, the truth is slowly coming out."

Hodge was sickened to hear Willow testify how Wiebe had recently admitted to attempting to rape his stepmother before he viciously attacked her with a knife and his hands. That disclosure of evidence was never made by Wiebe during the trial.

Defence lawyer Greg Brodsky called allegations that his client faked being mentally ill "the theatre of the absurd." "It's absolutely inappropriate for us to retry this case," he said. Brodsky said Wiebe was willing to say and do just about anything to get out of Selkirk, where he was spending most of his days locked in a small room by himself. The only medical treatment he was receiving was a daily sleeping pill, said Brodsky. He wanted Wiebe transferred to a facility in Ontario or British Columbia, but the waiting lists were long.

Willows said there was good reason Wiebe wasn't being treated more extensively: "He has no symptoms of psychosis, no symptoms of post-traumatic stress disorder. Whether the court found [a mental illness] or not, I don't see it and I can't treat it," he said bluntly. He blasted Crown and defence lawyers in the trial for relying on evidence from doctors commissioned by Brodsky to examine Wiebe. "I find that very tragic," said Willows.

WEDNESDAY SEPTEMBER 27, 2006
This wasn't the way the Selkirk Mental Health Centre wanted to get rid of Joey Wiebe. The mentally ill killer was now a wanted fugitive. Wiebe, now 23, had somehow managed to shake two escorts during what was supposed to be a routine medical appointment in Winnipeg.

Selkirk's CEO, Ken Nattrass, said Wiebe and the two male staff members had just walked into the main doors of the Health Sciences Centre entrance when Wiebe suddenly turned and ran. Wiebe had not been wearing handcuffs or leg shackles. "He just turned and bolted out the door and ran as fast as he could," Nattrass said. He said the escorts chased Wiebe, but "he outran them and was out of their sight."

Wiebe's lawyer, Greg Brodsky, appealed for him to surrender to police right away so that he could get the psychiatric help he needed: "He needs to turn himself in. The best thing for him is to pursue his treatment options. He can't do that on the outside."

THURSDAY SEPTEMBER 28, 2006
There was still no sign of Wiebe, more than 24 hours after he bolted into the community. He was on the run. And, family members feared, looking to kill again.

Wiebe had earlier threatened to escape and murder his stepfather, according to newly released court documents. "My stepfather is a real asshole. Once I get out of here I will go and kill him," Wiebe once said, according to a report by a review board overseeing his care.

Meanwhile, Selkirk officials were reviewing whether security should be beefed up for high-risk patients being escorted to appointments or hearings.

"Anything that's put in place is better than what appears to be now," said provincial Tory justice critic Kelvin Goertzen upon hearing of the incident.

Selkirk Mental Health Centre CEO Ken Nattrass said his staff were following the security guideline for Wiebe as outlined by the review board. "He was not a prisoner. He's a patient. This is a hospital. It is not a jail," Nattrass said. "We don't use restraints. We do not treat ourselves as a security detail."

Yet serious concerns had been raised in a February 2005 report issued by the Criminal Code Review Board of Manitoba, which was tasked with supervising the care and custody of Wiebe and others who have been found not criminally responsible for their actions.

"Clearly Mr. Wiebe requires close supervision due to the unpredictability of his behaviour," the review board wrote in its decision to keep him locked up and under tight security. "Mr. Wiebe represents a significant threat and is a danger to himself and others." The board said Wiebe had been resistant to treatment, aggressive with other patients, depressed, suicidal and often exhibiting "childlike acting-out."

Leslie Finlay, a juvenile counsellor who had worked with Wiebe, expressed grave concern about his potential for violence: "He has been unpredictable, volatile, defensive and defiant of staff directions and authority and has, on occasion, exhibited behaviour of extreme anger and rage," she said.

FRIDAY SEPTEMBER 29, 2006

They were on high alert. Nervous days had been spent looking over shoulders and peering out windows, sleepless nights had been spent jumping at sounds and shadows. The family of Candis Moizer were sharing their fears and outrage that Joey Wiebe was allowed to escape from custody and remained at large.

"The people associated with this ought to be ashamed of themselves," said Lorne Hodge. "It's disgusting what's happened. Someone has dropped the ball here. Someone is going to pay."

Hodge and his elderly parents, Charles and Cecilia, feared that it might be an innocent member of the public who suffered the most. "Joey doesn't like being out in the world, being around people. If he encounters a stranger right now and the person says the wrong thing, brushes him off or slams a door in his face, there's going to be trouble," Hodge warned. He noted that Wiebe didn't want to be at Selkirk and only way to get himself behind bars now would be to commit a new crime. "In his head, I worry he feels he's got to do something to get himself to prison," Hodge said. "Who's he going to hurt or kill to earn himself a ticket to Stony Mountain?"

Wiebe's lawyer shared the concern, saying the escape was only going to make a bad situation worse. "His running away now means... he's got a life sentence now," said Greg Brodsky.

Family members believe they could also be in Wiebe's sights. After all, the killer once got caught in high school with a "hit list" of people he wanted dead. Candis Moizer, her brother and parents were all named.

"We are very, very concerned for ourselves and our family," Cecilia Hodge said.

"He has a bit of a hatred on for a few of us in the family," her son added. "If he does come here, we'll do what we have to do to defend ourselves."

However, Wiebe's biological father insisted his son was not a danger to others. Earl Wiebe—who was living common-law with Moizer at the time she was killed—said he felt Joey didn't want to hurt anyone, since he wanted to avoid getting into more trouble. "Joey's main thing is he wants his freedom," Wiebe said from his Niverville home. He also believed his son would turn himself in to police so he could go back to Selkirk.

Family members also blasted Selkirk officials for not taking greater precaution with Wiebe: "Where the hell was the sheriff's department to escort him? Those [nursing assistants] had no business being there," Lorne Hodge said.

Following the escape, changes were made to ensure sheriff's officers were brought in to escort dangerous patients like Wiebe to appointments outside the facility. But it was too late to make a difference here. "They say this guy is so dangerous and yet they have no controls on him?" added Charles Hodge.

WEDNESDAY OCTOBER 4, 2006

Joey Wiebe stole a pack of cigarettes from a convenience store when he was 15, only to be overcome by a guilty conscience that led him to return them along with a handwritten apology to the owner. "Mom, I did something really bad," he told Alma Brown at the time. Now his mother was hoping Wiebe would have a similar appreciation for his actions and do the right thing by turning himself in after spending the past eight days on the run from police. She made a tearful plea for him to come out of hiding before he—or anyone else—got hurt.

"I'm hoping he sees this and reads this. He knows by now I'm worried sick. But the fact I haven't heard from him is starting to scare me," Brown said. "I'm hopeful he will give himself up soon. I miss him terribly."

Brown, wiping away tears while staring at a smiling high school class photo of her son taken just months before he killed Moizer, said she didn't believe he was capable of repeating such violence. She attributed it to a psychotic disorder that caused him to "snap." "I believe with all my heart he's not out there to hurt anyone else," she said. That would include her husband, who Wiebe previously told a doctor he would kill if ever given the chance.

"That's just Joey blowing off steam," said Brown.

Brown said her son had been upset recently but never hinted that something big was about to happen. She last spoke to Wiebe the day before he escaped. They discussed plans for her weekend visit to Selkirk, with Wiebe even requesting the kind of food he wanted her to bring out.

"We would talk every single day on the phone and he would often tell me 'I'm so lonely, Mom', but he never said he wanted to escape," said Brown. Looking back though, she now believed Wiebe may have been planning his escape for some time, based on the fact he'd eluded capture for so long. He had been allowed phone and computer access in Selkirk, which could have allowed him to make some arrangements ahead of time. "Joey's a very intelligent guy, and he tends to keep things to himself. I know he wasn't happy [at Selkirk]. He just wanted freedom. He's been locked up so long," she said.

Still, Brown insisted she hadn't heard from her son and had no idea where he was. Many theories had gone through her head—maybe he found someone to shelter him or take him out of the province, she said. "I've been racking my brain like crazy." Brown believed Wiebe only had about $20 in his pocket, plus the clothes on his back, when he escaped. "He's not going to get very far on $20," she said. Brown said her house was now being watched by officers anxious to bring Wiebe back into custody.

"I don't even understand how he could run away. He's got a bad foot and can barely run," she said, explaining Wiebe was run over by a riding lawnmower as a young child and suffered permanent injury. "Were these people even really watching him? Were they careless? I think they know they're in shit."

WEDNESDAY OCTOBER 11, 2006

The manhunt was over. Joey Wiebe was finally back in custody. He had somehow ended up in Victoria, British Columbia.

"We're surprised he was able to make it that far," said Winnipeg police Sgt. Daryl Anning. "We know he had a wish to see the mountains...He saw them." Wiebe told police he'd hitchhiked across Western

Canada and had been in the BC capital for more than a week, enjoying the coastal sights.

"He told me he met a bunch of new people and has just been hanging out, having fun, bird watching," said Alma Brown. She spoke with her son by telephone for about 10 minutes after he was taken into police custody. "He told me he never had any intention of staying away permanently. He just said he wanted to get away for a while. But I'll sleep a lot better tonight. There's tremendous relief he's OK," said Brown. "I don't know exactly how he made it out there or what he's been doing. But he didn't commit any other crimes."

Insp. Les Sylven of the Victoria Police Department said Wiebe wasn't living on the street, but was likely staying in a low-cost motel. "It looked like he was able to support himself while he was here," he said. Sylven said Wiebe turned himself in after calling his lawyer, Greg Brodsky. Brodsky in turn contacted Winnipeg police and Winnipeg police called Victoria police. Brodsky said his goal was to get Wiebe to surrender as quickly as possible: "I encouraged him to do it and he did."

Wiebe was following news reports about his escape and was aware of pleas from Brodsky and Brown to turn himself in, according to his mother. "He just decided it was time," Brown said.

Sylven said a Victoria police officer with the major crime unit met Wiebe at the corner of Dallas Road and Cook Street, a scenic beach area overlooking the Pacific Ocean, the Juan de Fuca Strait, and the Olympic Mountains in Washington state to the south. Wiebe was sitting on a log when the officer approached, and his run ended without incident. He was by himself and appeared in good health. "He told investigators he had hitchhiked west because he wanted to see the mountains," Sylven said. Sylven also said police believed Wiebe committed no crimes while in the BC capital.

Brodsky now admitted he heard from Wiebe "at least a dozen times" while police were frantically searching for him. Brodsky said he did everything he could to urge Wiebe to give up. "I was telling him, 'Joey, you can't serve a life sentence on the run. You have to come back and we can confront what's not fair,'" said Brodsky. Wiebe finally listened to him, with the main trigger for turning himself in being the avalanche of news reports painting him as dangerous, said Brodsky.

"He was very upset at all the awful things being said about him, hearing that schools were being watched and people were scared of him. He didn't want people to think of him as some ogre," Brodsky said. "He has shown everyone he's not violent, he's not dangerous. When he was out [on his escape], all he was doing was wondering how many skips his stones could make on the water in Victoria."

MONDAY OCTOBER 23, 2006

His escape was the final straw. Now Selkirk Mental Health officials were seeking to send Joey Wiebe to another province, saying they could no longer tolerate his aggressive behaviour and refusal to be treated. The request came during a Criminal Code Review Board annual hearing that included a heated exchange between Wiebe's doctor and lawyer and new revelations about how he spent two weeks on the run after his recent escape from custody.

"The treatment team is strongly in favour of him being transferred. He still acts grossly inappropriate at times," said Dr. Jim Willows, adding facilities in British Columbia and Ontario were options to consider.

Willows said Wiebe's disruptive actions over the past year included challenging staff members to fights, jumping up on tables and screaming and showing his fists while refusing to co-operate with counselling or treatment. He had also dared staff to "call the RCMP"—which Willows admitted he'd taken him up on out of fear that staff or other patients could be in jeopardy. That reaction prompted defence lawyer Greg Brodsky to accuse Willows of creating a "toxic" environment that Wiebe was desperate to get away from.

"I don't think you should be slandering me like that," an angry Willows told Brodsky in court. "It would be malpractice if I didn't respond the way that I did."

Wiebe now admitted he planned his flight and even received financial help from a source he refused to identify. Wiebe cut his hair short, dyed it and shaved off his moustache and goatee. He then headed to the west coast. He certainly didn't act like a frightened fugitive. He told police he spent two days sitting inside the British Columbia Superior Court while he was being sought on a Canada-wide warrant and also tried to pose for a picture with an officer he met at a rock concert.

"Could you speculate on why he'd put himself out like that in public?" Brodsky asked Dr. Leon Mowchun, another doctor who has briefly worked with Wiebe.

"It appears he wished to be caught," Mowchun told the Review Board.

Wiebe was charged with escaping lawful custody, but the Crown stayed the charge after it was confirmed he didn't commit any further crimes while on the loose—a fact Brodsky claimed proved Wiebe wasn't dangerous. The dropped criminal case meant that Wiebe would return to the custody of mental health officials rather than spend a short stint in jail.

Wiebe expressed relief after learning that Willows—who he'd repeatedly clashed with—would no longer be the treating psychologist at Selkirk. That job now fell to Dr. Steven Kremer, who had yet to meet with Wiebe. If Wiebe stayed in Manitoba it would be under far more stringent supervision, court was told.

Wiebe—who was led to court in hand and leg shackles—would only be allowed out of the locked Selkirk facility under the guard of sheriff's officers, said Willows. He had also been placed in the most secure part of the facility where only three other patients reside. "Any other security would be very dangerous. [The staff] would be putting themselves at risk and the public," said Willows.

Several doctors, including Willows, still believed Wiebe was a high risk to re-offend. Ken Nattrass, the CEO of SMHC, told court that history wouldn't be allowed to repeat itself. But Crown attorney Corrine Deegan said everyone who dealt with Wiebe must be vigilant. "He is a risk to escape. He obviously has the means and the street smarts to sustain himself in the community," she said.

MONDAY OCTOBER 5, 2009

He had managed to stay out of the headlines for the past three years, seemingly playing by the rules and being on his best behavior. But Joey Wiebe was back in a way that nobody could have imagined. Officials at Selkirk Mental Health Centre had caught Wiebe hiding a knife, drugs, alcohol, cash, cellular phone, laptop computer—and love letters from a female nurse—in the ceiling tiles of the facility in which he was believed to be planning another escape. The alarming discovery prompted several investigations and major security upgrades at Selkirk.

Wiebe was now facing numerous criminal charges after a security guard heard a noise coming from Wiebe's room in and discovered him accessing the stash. Wiebe assaulted and bit a guard during a subsequent scuffle. He was immediately removed from Selkirk and placed in the high-risk ward at the Winnipeg Remand Centre, where he remained on charges including assault, possession of a dangerous weapon and mischief.

Danah Bellehumeur, the chief executive officer of the Selkirk facility, confirmed numerous steps had been taken to prevent a repeat occurrence, including terminating the employee who wrote several lurid letters found in Wiebe's room. She immediately ordered increased searches of all patients and rooms inside the high-security forensic unit, where 14 patients deemed not criminally responsible by the courts currently resided. "We were already conducting searches, but now we are going to do them more frequently and extensively," said Bellehumeur.

Selkirk was also bringing in an outside agency to conduct a "risk assessment" of security in the unit and was applying for additional government funding to allow for three independent security guards on-site at all times. Currently, just one was stationed full-time in the building. "We want to ensure we're doing all we can. We take this as a learning opportunity," said Bellehumeur.

Police and Selkirk officials were continuing to probe how Wiebe was able to get the contraband inside his room. "Clearly this represents a gross breach of security. This causes us to profoundly reconsider how he's doing and where he's at," Dr. Steven Kraemer, Wiebe's treating psychiatrist, told his annual Criminal Code Review Board hearing.

Kraemer said Selkirk officials weren't prepared to welcome Wiebe back under any circumstances: "He has shown the ability to circumvent our security. We could not manage his return to our facility, even in the high-risk area," he said. Kraemer suggested maximum-security facilities in Saskatchewan and British Columbia would be better fits. Kraemer said the fact Wiebe struck up a relationship with an employee shows how manipulative he could be, adding there were other staff members who were "enamoured with him."

Wiebe appeared at the hearing without a lawyer and was allowed to cross-examine the two witnesses and make his own arguments. "I don't fear Selkirk. Selkirk fears me," Wiebe said bluntly.

Security was high in court, with five sheriff's officers guarding a handcuffed and shackled Wiebe. They refused Wiebe's request for a pen to take notes, issuing him a dull pencil instead.

"The conditions I've been subjected to are 90 per cent of the reason these incidents have transpired," said Wiebe. "There's a lot of lies and half-truths here."

Wiebe said marijuana was thrown over the fence to him at Selkirk by another patient on the outside. He claimed he obtained the knife and alcohol while on an escorted outing with the nurse he was later found to be involved with. Wiebe said he had help from at least one other patient at Selkirk Mental Health Centre who wasn't in the high-security area. He was never searched upon returning to the facility because their policy at the time didn't require it based on the fact he had been escorted, court was told.

Dr. Lawrence Ellerby, who had worked on Wiebe's case, said that Wiebe might be developing a feeling that "he's got nothing to lose" based on his ongoing frustrations and disciplinary issues. "He feels like he's not able to move forward with his life at all," said Ellerby.

MONDAY OCTOBER 19, 2009

She was a newlywed with an exciting new job and her whole future ahead of her. But everything changed when she met a dangerous, mentally ill killer she was supervising at the Selkirk Mental Health Centre. "I've basically ruined my whole life, my marriage, my job, my schooling and future career," the 33-year-old woman told a *Winnipeg Free Press* reporter at a downtown Winnipeg coffee shop. She agreed to speak out—and provide extensive details into the high-profile case—on the condition her name not be published.

The woman said she still had strong feelings for Joey Wiebe despite the damage she'd caused. "I still really care about him, and I believe that he does love me. I saw a different side of him. I do feel that he has a good, kind, gentle side and that I help bring that out in him," she said. "I really don't want to abandon him. But I don't see [an ongoing relationship] as being good for me."

Among items found in Wiebe's possession were two love letters that had been written to him by the nursing student, who was hired in May 2009 on a term position while in her third year of studies at the University of Winnipeg. "They weren't overly explicit, but they stated my feelings for him," said the woman. "I always worried about them being found during room searches, but Joey had told me they wouldn't be." Also seized from Wiebe's room was a cellular phone he had smuggled in—with her knowledge—and used to take about eight nude and semi-nude pictures of her.

"I know Joey wanted to protect me. I would always tell him I had a lot more to lose than he did," she said. The woman admits she had sex with Wiebe at least six times on the grounds of Selkirk beginning in July. "I knew it was wrong, that there was a possibility of getting caught. We were always careful, Joey knew a spot that was private, outside the view of the cameras," she said.

The woman was surprised to find out she'd immediately begin working in the forensic unit at Selkirk upon being hired the previous spring—and even more stunned when told she could begin escorting a handful of dangerous patients into the community within her first few days of work. Armed with only a cellular phone, the woman would take Wiebe and others on various excursions to movies, the mall, the library and restaurants. They were never shackled or handcuffed.

"I didn't think Joey would try to escape with me, I knew he wouldn't want to get me in trouble," she said.

The woman said she took a liking to Wiebe because she felt other staff members weren't treating him fairly based on his reputation as a troublemaker. She claimed to have no knowledge of how he got the contraband into the facility or of any plans he had on fleeing.

"He knew that he needed to be punished for what he did. But he felt staff weren't really advocating for him at all. All of the staff seemed to have a really negative view of him. I just always tried to be nice and helpful to everyone I worked with," she said. Wiebe surprised her one day by admitting he wanted a relationship with her.

"I was kind of taken aback. I was attracted to him, too. But I didn't really want to go there," she said. The woman had been married a year earlier but had been struggling with a deep depression. "I just wasn't in a good place," she said. She began confiding in Wiebe about personal issues in her life. "I was sharing things with him I probably shouldn't have. It ended up with him kind of supporting me. He really listened to me, and you don't meet a person that often that you can really talk to," she said. "This was just a combination of having this emptiness and having someone who filled it."

The woman said she was conflicted about what to do—but ultimately followed her heart despite knowing it was wrong. "I didn't want to break up my marriage, didn't want to hurt my husband. I was really confused all summer. I really loved Joey, but I really loved my husband. I couldn't hold onto both forever," she said. "Obviously there was no real future with Joey, but I didn't want to give up that connection."

She had no choice when her love letters were found and officials immediately fired her. The woman told her husband about the affair and was kicked out of the home. She was now living with her parents after spending two weeks in crisis stabilization in hospital.

She faced an uncertain future. "I am carrying a lot of guilt for what I did. Nobody needs to worry that I'm not being punished enough. I made some wrong choices and now I'm living with the consequences," she said.

Joey Wiebe and the Selkirk Mental Health Centre finally got the divorce they were seeking. It was anything but amicable. Wiebe was sentenced in October 2012 to five years in prison for charges stemming from yet another violent outburst that happened a few months earlier. He pleaded guilty to several offences including assault, mischief and uttering death threats, admitting he attacked a guard and caused more than $50,000 damage by setting off the hospital fire alarm and flooding some of the premises with the sprinkler system. It could have been worse, as the hospital doors were automatically unlocked during the emergency, raising the potential of escapes. Some patients were found wandering on the premises.

Once his sentence is complete, Wiebe will likely be sent to a psychiatric hospital out west. There's no way he's going back to Selkirk. If history is any indication, we likely haven't heard the last of him.

CHAPTER 4

THE BLANCHARD CRIMINAL ORGANIZATION

It was a case so wild and so juicy that even Oprah came calling. And while the Queen of all media never did end up getting the scoop—the key player refused her interview requests—I had a front-row seat to this utterly fascinating story. Gerald Blanchard is the most interesting criminal I've ever covered. I couldn't get enough of this story. Our readers couldn't get enough of this story.

There's no question the vast majority of crime cases we see are impulsive acts, often driven by addictions and/or intoxication. Which makes something like this so unique: A carefully planned, complex series of acts executed with brilliant precision, all in the name of getting filthy stinkin' rich. It's still hard to believe, all these years later.

2004

It was a seemingly innocent event in a Winnipeg parking lot—but one that caught the eye of an employee working at the nearby Wal-Mart. Two vehicles were parked outside the brand new Canadian Imperial Bank of Commerce on Empress Street in the city's West End, just days before it was set for its grand opening. Curious, the worker took a closer look. There seemed to be nobody around, just two empty cars. He jotted down the licence plate numbers before carrying on with his day. It would be years before anyone realized just how critical a move this was.

THURSDAY JANUARY 25, 2007

They had been dubbed the "Blanchard Criminal Organization"—a group of western Canadian con artists who shared a common goal: make as much money as humanly possible. While they may not have had the same instant name recognition of the Hells Angels, police believed members of the "BCO" had quietly stolen millions since they first formed in the fall of 1999.

A half-million-dollar heist from a series of automated bank machines in Winnipeg. Trafficking in counterfeit credit cards and related data. Defrauding the Royal Bank, CIBC and Bank of Nova Scotia in Vancouver and Winnipeg time and time again. Their high-tech crime spree, which spread as far as Europe and lasted for over seven years, involved taking some Canadian financial institutions to the cleaners and allowed for a jet-set lifestyle. Who were these criminal masterminds? And how had they managed to be so successful for so long, while staying beneath both the public and police radar?

Investigators in Manitoba were being tight-lipped about developments in the case, which involved the culmination of a three-year undercover investigation through a series of search warrants and arrests in Manitoba, Alberta and British Columbia. But court documents offered an introduction into what was expected to be one of the largest and most sophisticated cases of its kind ever uncovered in Canada.

"This is all quite unbelievable," said a justice source familiar with the investigation.

The eight accused, which included two women, were facing a total of 61 charges, including fraud, theft, conspiracy, credit card trafficking and participating in a criminal organization. According to court documents, the alleged leader of the group was a mystery man named Gerald Daniel Blanchard, 35. He was arrested in BC and was being held in custody, according to his Winnipeg-based lawyer, Danny Gunn.

"This is going to be a very interesting case," Gunn told the *Winnipeg Free Press* as news of the criminal enterprise began trickling out for the first time.

Blanchard was facing 27 charges, by far the most of any of the accused, and his name was on the figurative masthead of the criminal organization. He had previously lived in Winnipeg, but was most recently on the West Coast. He had also used other identities and was believed to own property around the world "He's a bit of an international man of mystery, a very interesting guy," a justice source said of Blanchard.

The police investigation began in Winnipeg following one of the biggest heists in recent local history. Winnipeg police were initially stumped and turned to Crime Stoppers to publicize the incident and offer a $2,000 reward for information on the May 2004 theft of at least $500,000 from the Polo Park-area CIBC mega-centre. Detectives believed someone broke into the branch at Empress Street and Ellice Avenue just days before its grand opening and emptied the cash out of eight ATMs. They had now identified two suspects, Blanchard and Winnipeg resident Aaron Syberg, as being responsible.

Investigators eventually got a major break in the case and began exploring the theory that the heist involved a well-organized plot involving several other accused and likely several other crimes in Ontario, Alberta and British Columbia. That put the Winnipeg Police Service's Criminal Investigations Bureau, the main city police detective office, front and centre in an investigation would eventually involve several other Canadian police agencies. And it would take them places they couldn't have imagined in their wildest dreams.

Gerald Blanchard was an international man-of-mystery —even to members of his own family. His father, Gerald Blanchard Sr., told the *Winnipeg Free Press* he was stunned to learn of his son's arrest and alleged involvement in a massive criminal organization.

"All he ever told me was that he buys and sells condominiums," Blanchard Sr. said in an interview from his home in Strathmore, Alberta. His adopted son, who often went by his middle name of Daniel, usually called each Christmas, but the two hadn't seen one another for years. "We talked just before Christmas and he said he'd call me again on my birthday," Blanchard Sr. said. "But he didn't. To tell you the truth, I wasn't surprised. I was always kind of suspicious things weren't on the up and up. I don't know why. I just wasn't."

His son was born in Canada but largely grew up in Nebraska. Blanchard was deported from the United States several years ago after serving a seven-year jail sentence for stealing a police uniform, gun and other property from the Council Bluffs Police Department in Iowa and a police car from the nearby Omaha Police

Department. In hindsight, the case offered up some insight into how cunning Blanchard could be.

Blanchard escaped custody from Council Bluffs April 27, 1993 after being arrested for car theft, according to a report in the *Omaha World-Herald*. When no one was looking, Blanchard hid behind a desk, then scaled a wall to hide above ceiling tile until the room was empty and he could leave. He then took with him a police badge, gun, holster, hand-held radio, police cap and coat and duffel bag. He hitched a ride back to Omaha on the back of a motorcycle while wearing the police cap. The next day police found him hiding in the attic of his mother's residence after the stolen police gear was recovered there.

But Blanchard wasn't done with his escape act. While wearing handcuffs, Blanchard stole the Omaha police cruiser from the Central Police Headquarters garage and fled yet again. The two officers who had transported Blanchard to the police garage got out of the car but left the keys in the ignition. As the officers were preparing to get Blanchard out of the back seat, he managed to wriggle his legs up through his handcuffs, putting his hands in front of him. He then slipped into the front seat, locked all four doors, and drove away. Police gave chase. It ended about 20 minutes later after Blanchard parked the police car outside a downtown Omaha steakhouse and fled on foot. He was caught moments later. But it wouldn't be long before Blanchard had authorities on the run once again.

TUESDAY JULY 10, 2007
It was the type of plot that wouldn't have been out of place in a James Bond movie. And now the public

was getting its first taste of the elaborate tale behind "Operation Kite", the complex Winnipeg police investigation which brought down the Blanchard Criminal Organization.

The biggest revelation of all? That the group was accused of stealing a jewel-encrusted broach—the Koechert Pearl Diamond, also known as the Sisi Star—from a castle in Vienna during a daylight robbery in 1998. The priceless heirloom once belonged to Queen Elisabeth, the Empress of Austria, during the 19th century and had been recently recovered by police in a Winnipeg home. You can imagine how this went over in a city more accustomed to hearing about their local gas bar or convenience store getting knocked over by thieves.

Court documents included a detailed list of hundreds of items found in houses, cars and business across British Columbia, Alberta and Manitoba when police executed 16 different search warrants at homes and business of the eight accused. In Winnipeg, police found plenty of electronic surveillance equipment inside an Olford Crescent home linked to co-accused Dale Fedoruk, who was working for Blanchard. On Ashland Avenue, in a home connected to family members of Aaron Syberg, they knocked over a marijuana grow operation. Drug charges against two relatives were now pending. Police searched Syberg's home on Bertrand Avenue and found boarding passes to Cancun and Edmonton, bus tickets to Calgary and Regina, numerous video cameras, handcuffs and a crossbow.

A search of four homes and storage unit linked to Blanchard had yielded a fairly incredible haul that was definitely not the typical starter kit for your everyday common criminal.

Among the more noteworthy items:
- Rocket propelled device
- 1,000 rounds of ammunition for a .39 mm handgun and .22-calibre rifle
- Airport x-ray film protector
- Several 'pin hole' cameras
- Cameras hidden in bird houses and garden lights
- Sonic ear enhancers
- Night vision goggles
- Underwater cameras
- Surveillance cameras
- Police scanners
- Paintball gun
- Air Pistol
- Egyptian Monkey statue
- Blood-stained towel with hotel key from UK
- Boxes of adult diapers
- More than $10,000 in Canadian money
- Egyptian and British currency
- Fireworks
- Wire cutters
- Black grappling hook with 60 feet of rope
- Several boxes of ammo

All of this was only enhancing the growing legend of Gerald Blanchard—both in criminal and police circles.

WEDNESDAY NOVEMBER 7, 2007

Cunning. Clever. Conniving. Creative. Crown attorney Sheila Leinburd needed just four words to sum up Gerald Blanchard and the high-tech criminal investigation he led.

Blanchard had just pleaded guilty to 16 charges and was given an eight-year prison term under a joint agreement between Crown and defence lawyers. He admitted he was the brains behind several sophisticated attacks on banks in Winnipeg, Edmonton and British Columbia that netted his group millions of dollars.

"Add some foreign intrigue and this is the stuff movies are made of," Leinburd told court. Specifically, Leinburd revealed how the Blanchard Criminal Organization was funding terrorism in Iraq by working under the control of a mysterious London-based leader and his group of Muslim extremists. She described how Winnipeg police were stunned to overhear a conversation with a man Blanchard called "The Boss"—who was based in England and appeared to be calling the shots. The man ordered Blanchard and his associates to fly to Cairo in November 2006 and begin stealing money from bank machines using counterfeit credit cards, said Leinburd. He also sent three of his own associates to meet with Blanchard in Egypt and make sure things were done right, she said.

The group spent 10 days in Egypt and stole several hundred thousand dollars. They all wore burkas —the traditional dress for Muslim women which had them covered head to toe—to avoid detection from surveillance cameras, said Leinburd. Blanchard stopped in England on his way home and met again with "The Boss" to give him his "cut." Blanchard cleared C$65,000 while the man kept the rest. Police later overheard a conversation in which Blanchard discussed what the money was being used for.

"It was to fuel terrorism," said Leinburd. She said Blanchard told his associates how "The Boss" was sending money to Kurdish fighters in northern Iraq, court was told.

"And Mr. Blanchard was aware of that?" Associate Chief Justice Jeffrey Oliphant asked.

"Yes, he was," said Leinburd.

The three Muslim associates tried to come to Canada last year to meet with Blanchard but immigration officials at the airport in Montreal turned them away for not having proper paperwork, she said.

Defence lawyer Danny Gunn said his client cut ties with "The Boss" once he learned of the terrorist connection. "It was at this point he realized he'd gotten himself involved in something pretty serious and with people who didn't abide by the same code as he did," he said.

Blanchard was briefly held as a "hostage" in England when one of the associates he'd brought with him stole $50,000 and 50 counterfeit credit cards and then fled to Africa.

"I guess it proves there's no honour among thieves," said Oliphant.

Police heard a frantic Blanchard making calls to get the man to return the goods. He was eventually allowed to return home to Canada unharmed.

Oliphant asked what became of "The Boss," whose identity was not disclosed in court or by lawyers outside of court.

"I don't know," said Leinburd. "The authorities in England have identified him, but they don't share information with us."

Blanchard was not charged with any terrorism-related crimes and Oliphant said it was clear he got in over his head. "I'm satisfied you really weren't aware of where the majority of money you were stealing was going. I guess this just says something about the world we now live in," he said.

Winnipeg police Insp. Tom Legge, who headed up the Project Kite task force that eventually caught Blanchard, admitted they were surprised at where the case led them. "We have no evidence [Blanchard] is a terrorist. But he is an opportunist," said Legge, adding the scope of his crimes was "something we've never seen before."

The Crown detailed how police first began investigating in 2004 following the theft of $510,000 from seven automatic banking machines inside a new CIBC branch on Empress Street just days before its grand opening. They would later learn Blanchard and associates had secretly installed a pinhole camera and two listening devices—including a baby monitor—inside the walls and roof of the bank while it was still under construction. That allowed him to monitor everything going on inside the branch from a remote location—and to know exactly when huge sums of money would be put inside the ABMs.

Leinburd told court it was ironic that such an elaborate criminal network was brought down by something pretty benign. Just days before the massive CIBC heist, a Wal-Mart employee took down the license plates of two suspicious vehicles parked near the bank property. His information proved invaluable for police, who traced the vehicles to Avis Rent-A-Car and Gerald Blanchard. Blanchard later dumped the vehicles—which the company had reported stolen when they weren't returned—and police found a fingerprint that matched. They also found two adult diapers inside that Blanchard apparently used during extensive surveillance he was conducting.

Oliphant was stunned to learn that Blanchard would have made such an amateurish mistake. "Pretty dumb leaving that car sitting there in your name," Oliphant said to laughs from the packed courtroom, which included all of the police officers who worked exhaustively to bring him down.

Blanchard admitted to a pair of similar heists in Edmonton that netted him over $60,000 in 2002. He would typically enter either by picking locks or crawling his slim frame through the air-conditioning ductwork. He'd rely on all kinds of electronic equipment, including night-vision goggles. He also became a master of disguise, and identity theft, repeatedly passing himself off as someone else. He often created bogus identification such as passports, driver's licences and even VIP passes which allowed him access to concerts and sporting events. He was set to try a similar robbery in early 2007 in Chilliwack, BC and believed he would be able to get at least $800,000, court was told. However, Blanchard somehow became aware police were monitoring his conversations and actions and called off the planned heist at the last minute.

The true "gem" of the police investigation involved recovering the Koechert Pearl Diamond from

Blanchard's grandmother's house in Winnipeg. He had told police about it, then led them directly to the basement, where it was hidden in a hollowed-out piece of Styrofoam. No one had been charged with the theft. Blanchard admitted to possession of stolen goods. Leinburd said the item was valued at about $10,000 but was priceless to Austrians because of its connection to royalty. "The police would not have been able to find the diamond if not for the co-operation of Mr. Blanchard," said Leinburd.

In subsequent interviews not admitted in court, Blanchard would give a detailed description of how he personally stole the jewel after getting into the castle while posing as a tourist. He spun an elaborate tale of parachuting out of a plane, landing on the grounds of the castle and then eventually defeating a sophisticated security system to snatch it. There were many who doubted his claims, which couldn't be independently verified. After all, this was a man who'd made quite the career out of lying and deceiving.

Blanchard's other crimes included using electronic "writers" and high-tech computer hardware to copy the data from existing credit and bank cards to make duplicate, usable replicas, court was told. Blanchard and his associates would also steal expensive electronics, then return them to stores using fake receipts they had created and make off with the cash in what is known as "rehashing."

Leinburd told court "this is a true plea negotiation" as a trial would have lasted at least a year and involved more than 60,000 documents. Police also made 120,000 telephone intercepts and would have had to call witnesses from across Canada and beyond.

"You're no hero Mr. Blanchard but you could have made this a lot more difficult," said Oliphant.

Blanchard agreed to liquidate his assets in BC, which would net around $500,000 and be paid to the banks he defrauded.

"He could have been a successful and lawful entrepreneur," said Leinburd. "Instead he chose this route. And now he must pay for it."

Blanchard was given two years of credit for his time already spent in custody, then sentenced to an additional six years in prison. He would be eligible for parole in two years. Seven co-accused remained before the courts, although Gunn hinted that many charges could be dropped now that Blanchard had taken responsibility.

Some were calling him Canada's version of Frank Abagnale, the legendary American con man portrayed by actor Leonardo DiCaprio in Hollywood's *Catch Me If You Can*. But Gerald Blanchard wanted to ensure that future high-tech criminals would be draw comparisons to him, not some relic from the past.

He had just ended his criminal case by cutting a deal with justice officials and pleading guilty and he was speaking out publicly for the first time, telling the *Winnipeg Free Press* he wanted to come clean to make up for all the pain he'd caused to loved ones while leading his globe-trotting double life. First up: Putting to rest any suspicions his family knew what he was doing. Blanchard said that was absolutely false, and he felt especially bad about dragging his Winnipeg grandmother into his mess. It was in her west Winnipeg basement that he stashed the Koechert Pearl Diamond.

Blanchard also claimed he'd had extensive chats with police and bank security officials about how he was able to defeat their ATM security systems.

"They [banks] should hire him and pay him a million dollars a year," Associate Chief Justice Jeffrey Oliphant had said upon being given the facts of the case.

"That has been discussed," replied Crown attorney Sheila Leinburd.

Winnipeg police had actually created a three-hour multimedia presentation based entirely on Blanchard that they showed to local security officials. "He's a very charming individual, not of the same ilk as a lot of other criminals we see," said police Insp. Tom Legge.

At his sentencing hearing, court was told Blanchard was diagnosed with dyslexia as a child, but as an adult had overcome that to develop an almost "encyclopedic" knowledge of electronics and surveillance. He was born in Winnipeg but immediately given up for adoption by his parents. He moved to the United States at the age of seven with his adoptive mother.

"His mother says that as a toddler, he could take anything apart," said defence lawyer Danny Gunn. He called his client a soft-spoken, highly intelligent and extremely polite man who has many layers—including a penchant for donating toys and other gifts to charities for children. "I'm not saying he's Robin Hood. But there's more to this complex and complicated individual," said Gunn.

As part of his plea bargain, Blanchard was hoping to be transferred to a minimum-security prison in British Columbia where he could be close to his girlfriend Lynette Tien, who was currently before the courts as a co-accused. Blanchard was actually charged earlier in the year with plotting to kill Tien while behind bars following his arrest—but the Crown dropped it based on a lack of evidence. Blanchard told the *Free Press* that so-called plot was cooked up by two inmates with whom he was in custody so they could get favourable treatment from the Crown on their own charges. "The police quickly realized it wasn't true," he said. Blanchard said he and Tien planned to marry while he was still in custody.

"He's looking forward to serving his time, putting this behind him and moving forward with his life," Gunn told court.

"I think you have a great future ahead of you if you wish to pursue an honest style of life," said Oliphant. "Although I'm not prepared to sign a letter of reference."

FRIDAY MARCH 7, 2008

The group had worn burkas to avoid detection from surveillance cameras. They had duped banks out of millions of dollars, held police at bay for years and used their electronic wizardry on victims around the globe. Yet the Canadian-based Blanchard criminal organization nearly came unglued thanks to the most unlikely of foes—the airline industry. A piece of luggage containing a king's ransom—$50,000 in cash, some diamonds and a few hundred stolen credit cards—somehow got lost when one of the accused was attempting to fly from Egypt to Africa.

The missing suitcase has never been found. The owner, Balume Kashongwe, pleaded guilty to fraud and participating in a criminal organization. He was the second accused to admit wrongdoing, following in the footsteps of his fearless leader, Gerald Blanchard. Kashongwe, 35, was sentenced to two years of time already spent in custody under a joint agreement between Crown and defence lawyers. He was set to be released from jail later in the day and planned to resume living in British Columbia, where a job in the forestry sector awaited. Kashongwe admitted he helped Blanchard steal an estimated $250,000 from several banks in Cairo in late 2006. The money was then funneled to the mysterious London-based man called "The Boss" and used to finance terrorism in the Middle East.

Blanchard, Kashongwe and four others spent 10 days in Egypt and used data from 633 stolen credit cards to access various bank accounts. Kashongwe was supposed to leave Cairo and go to Africa to continue the thefts, but stunned Blanchard when he called to report his suitcase had gone missing during his travels. The money and diamonds inside were destined for the British boss, forcing Blanchard to scramble and pay the man out of his own pocket.

Kashongwe met Blanchard in BC several years ago while they were neighbours, court was told. Kashongwe was a trusting man who came to Canada from the Congo in 1987 and was looking to make new friends. But he quickly got "in over his head" and didn't realize what Blanchard was involved with, his lawyer said. "He's now learned that if something sounds too good to be true, it probably is," Kathy Bueti told court.

Provincial court Judge Kelly Moar told Kashongwe the fact his criminal actions indirectly helped terrorist activities was a major concern. "When these attacks occur, innocent people die. That money being obtained by yourself and others was used to do that," Moar said.

WEDNESDAY SEPTEMBER 24, 2008

Lynette Tien had great taste in fashion. But the Vancouver woman apparently didn't have the same good sense when it came to men. Tien, 23, had just pleaded guilty in Winnipeg court for her role in the criminal operation run by her boyfriend, Gerald Blanchard. Tien admitted she helped Blanchard with some of his crimes—including returning stolen goods to electronic stores using bogus receipts—but wasn't considered a top player in the organization, court was told.

"She's learned a big lesson and is going to be a lot more careful with respect to what she does and who she becomes affiliated with," said defence lawyer Roberta Campbell. Tien would be allowed to serve her conditional sentence in BC, where she worked as a model and actress while also attending university.

Blanchard's cousin, Dale Fedoruk, had also pleaded guilty to his role and was given a 21-month conditional sentence. Fedoruk, 36, admitted to accepting a high-powered delivery from Blanchard that included an assault rifle, two handguns and 1,000 rounds of ammunition. Winnipeg police learned of the shipment through telephone wiretaps in late 2006 and early 2007, court was told. It's not clear what the weapons were intended for.

"You got yourself in quite a jackpot with your involvement with Mr. Blanchard," said provincial court Judge Kelly Moar.

WEDNESDAY APRIL 8, 2009
It started as a friendly relationship with a customer —and ended with his involvement in an elaborate international fraud ring. Now, Edmonton businessman Lance Ulmer had admitted to his role in the Blanchard Criminal Organization. He was the fifth accused to admit wrongdoing. Ulmer, 40, was given an 18-month conditional sentence following a joint recommendation between Crown and defence lawyers. He admitted to allowing his Edmonton mailing and shipping company to be used in a series of financial crimes committed across Canada and around the world.

Lawyers told court Ulmer was "seduced" into a world of crime by the charming and savvy Blanchard but never realized the scope of the criminal activity. "He has now learned to keep an arms-length from his clients... to be more suspicious of those who ask for his services, to ask more questions, and to sever relationships with clients he has suspicions about," said defence lawyer Shawn Beaver.

Ulmer was the final member of the "Blanchard Criminal Organization" to face the music. His guilty plea had closed book on one of Canada's most unusual crime cases, with all remaining charges being dropped by the Crown.

Gerald Blanchard's initial return to society was relatively short-lived. He was released on day parole in 2009, only to have prison officials revoke his freedom in 2010 and put him back behind bars. There were concerns Blanchard was on the road to getting re-involved in fraudulent financial activities. The parole board's decision highlighted concerns over Blanchard's history of falsifying documents, and the fact that he was "continuing to push the boundaries" of his supervision. They also noted he showed a "low level of remorse" for his actions. Blanchard had attempted to volunteer for the 2010 Vancouver Olympics, but was told he could not attend any Olympic venue, celebration or event after it was deemed risky due to his history of "manipulation for personal benefit."

In their original decision to grant him early release and allow him to live at a Vancouver halfway house, parole officials expressed hope that Blanchard was on the right path. They even noted he likely had a future as a security consultant, something that had been hinted at years earlier during his sentencing hearing.

Blanchard was given a second shot at freedom in April 2012. He's apparently taking this a bit more seriously, as there is no record of any breaches. He remains free in the community, living in British Columbia and keeping a relatively low profile. In documents, the parole board referred to what they called his "long-term positive plans." But they were keeping him on a relatively tight leash, restricting his access to computers and cellular phones and also requiring him to report all financial activity.

There was also mention of a possible movie in the works about his crime spree.

Pass the popcorn.

CHAPTER 5

PHOENIX

It is one of the most troubling cases I've ever covered. I can still close my eyes and see the basement where Phoenix Sinclair spent her final days. I got a tour of the property—courtesy of the new homeowner—only days after RCMP had wrapped up an extensive forensic examination. Few details about Phoenix's case had been released publicly at the time. All we knew is that she was presumed dead and that bad things were allegedly done to her in that basement.

I can still see the evidence markers that were stuck to the floor and the numerous holes in the walls. They are images I can never rid myself of, made all the more difficult by the revelations which would eventually emerge. Years later, I found myself sitting across a table with Phoenix's two killers in separate jailhouse interviews. It was hard to feel anything but pure rage, knowing what they had done to that poor little girl.

It was hard to fathom how anyone could be so evil.

TUESDAY MARCH 14, 2006

She hadn't been seen for nine months. Yet nobody—not her family, not her community, not the social services agency that was supposed to be looking out for her welfare—had apparently noticed that a five-year-old Manitoba girl had seemingly vanished into thin air. Or, if they had, they remained silent. And now it was too late. Phoenix Sinclair was dead. A search for her remains was expected to begin soon. Phoenix's mother, Samantha Kematch, was in custody. So was Kematch's boyfriend, Carl McKay.

"I don't have a clue why it took so long to discover this. Why didn't family members report this earlier or start asking questions earlier?" Fisher River resident Lloyd Cochrane wondered aloud as members of the media began arriving in his community, located about 200 kilometres north of Winnipeg. Police and justice officials were being tight-lipped.

McKay, 43, was charged with second-degree murder. Kematch, 24, was charged with assault with a weapon, aggravated assault, forcible confinement and failing to provide the necessities of life. Court documents indicated a broom handle was used as a weapon against Phoenix.

McKay and Kematch had moved out of their Fisher River home in November 2005. Police had spent more than 48 hours combing through it for evidence last week. "They told us we had to get out of here, and they would let us know when we could return," said Calvin Murdock, who moved into the home with his fiancée several months ago. There were numerous holes in the wall of the home when they took possession but Murdock said he never thought much of it. Police cut a hole in Murdock's kitchen wall, and also covered his basement floor with a bluish chemical, which still remained. Police also seized several items of clothing that McKay and Kematch had left behind. Evidence markers remained stuck to the basement floor.

According to information in her file, Phoenix was born in Winnipeg in April 2000. She was apprehended by Winnipeg CFS at birth and remained in care until September 2000, when she was reunited with her father, Steve Sinclair, and her mother, Kematch. In April 2001, Kematch had another baby girl, Echo, who died three months later as a result of pneumonia. While there was no record of Phoenix being apprehended again at this time, Kim Edwards—a friend of Sinclair's—took in Phoenix. Edwards said she cared for Phoenix on and off from that point until the child was three, when she went back to live with Sinclair.

In February 2003, Phoenix was treated at a Winnipeg hospital for an infection, at which point Winnipeg CFS reopened a file on the child and in June she was again apprehended from her parents' care. Phoenix returned to Edwards' home, but was removed by CFS within a couple of months after the child's parents signed an Authority Determination Plan. The ADP was a document that indicated the parents' wish that Phoenix's file should be transferred from Winnipeg CFS to a new, native-run agency. Phoenix—who was living with Sinclair—continued to visit occasionally with Edwards.

Edwards was now expressing shock upon learning the little girl she loved was presumed dead, her remains yet to be found. "How can it be that she's been gone this long and no one has known?" she asked. "This is just unbelievable."

WEDNESDAY MARCH 15, 2006

She was locked in an animal cage. Repeatedly shot with a BB gun. Deprived of food and water. Then, when her frail body finally couldn't take any more, Phoenix Sinclair was wrapped in plastic and buried near the

Fisher River garbage dump. The horrific allegations were beginning to emerge. And they were unlike anything justice officials had seen in years. And the entire case—the abuse, the torture, the killing and the cover-up—might have remained a secret if not for two brave young boys. Phoenix's 12-year-old and 15-year-old stepbrothers had come forward to police only days earlier, documenting what had gone on inside the house of horrors. RCMP then spoke to Kematch and McKay and were told that Phoenix was alive and well, in the custody of Child and Family Services. CFS quickly set the record straight, confirming she was not. Remarkably, Kematch then tried to pass off another little girl as Phoenix in a hastily-arranged meeting at a Winnipeg shopping mall. The ruse was over. The deadly secret had finally been exposed.

It didn't take long for what was quickly becoming one of Manitoba's most notorious criminal cases to be upgraded to a deliberate, cold-blooded act at. First-degree murder charges were now being laid against both McKay and Kematch, speaking to the fact justice officials believed this was a planned, pre-meditated killing. The decision was made despite not having the victim's body. The search was expected to be painstaking operation. The ground would have to be thawed, and police had to be careful not to disturb the remains or any potential evidence. The location where Phoenix was believed to be buried was in dense bush located about half a kilometre off a snow-packed logging road near the Fisher River garbage dump. Police had set up a wide perimeter to protect the scene. It would be early April when the tragic discovery was finally made.

WEDNESDAY NOVEMBER 5, 2008

It was the first time the public was getting to hear the full story of what happened to Phoenix Sinclair. Naturally, the opening day of the high-profile trial came with a warning from Crown attorney Rick Saull: The facts that were about to be presented in court were both "depressing and enraging. Saull urged jurors not to let emotions cloud their judgment when deciding the fate of Samantha Kematch and Karl McKay. Both had pleaded not guilty to first-degree murder.

Saull described how Phoenix was repeatedly confined and abused over a lengthy period of time while living with her mother and stepfather inside a home on the Fisher River reserve. "After the final blows were administered, she was left to die on a cold basement floor by both of them," Saull said in his opening statement, which included showing the 10-woman, two-man jury a picture of Phoenix. He said the couple made "feeble attempts" to revive Phoenix but never took her to a medical centre just a few kilometres away. Instead, they wrapped her tiny body in plastic, grabbed a shovel from a neighbour's home and then dug a hole near the local garbage dump and buried her "in the cold ground" in a remote, wooded area. The couple then carried on with their lives, even applying for welfare payments that listed Phoenix as a dependent, said Saull. They also scrubbed down the basement floor where Phoenix died and repainted it in an attempt to conceal evidence, he said.

Phoenix's death would remain secret until March 2006, when McKay's two young sons from another relationship told their mother what they'd seen and heard while spending time in the Fisher Branch home. She ultimately went to police.

Kematch and McKay differ from each other about what happened to Phoenix and why, said Saull. The pair were being represented by separate defence lawyers but sat in the same witness box, with some distance between them. "We say each of the accused were equally involved in the forcible confinement and abuse of Phoenix Sinclair," he said.

Samantha Kematch refused to let a Child and Family Services worker see her daughter during a home visit in March 2005—and the agency responded by quickly closing the little girl's file with no additional follow-up. It was just three months later that five-year-old Phoenix Sinclair was killed in the basement of her Fisher River home. An agreed statement of facts submitted by Crown and defence lawyers outlined CFS's ongoing involvement with Phoenix and her family in the time preceding her tragic death. The document confirmed CFS received a tip on March 5 that prompted them to visit the family's home four days later. They were met at the door by Kematch but denied entry.

"The worker spoke with Ms. Kematch but did not speak to Phoenix or access the residence as Samantha Kematch reported she had someone visiting," Crown attorney Rick Saull told jurors. The case worker did catch a glimpse of Kematch's other child, an infant named Rayne, "and decided there were no protection concerns despite not seeing Phoenix or the apartment," said Saull. No further details were provided to jurors about the tip that led CFS to the home.

Phoenix had a long history with the child welfare system prior to 2005, including two earlier occasions where her file was closed. The following history was provided to jurors:

APRIL 23, 2000: Phoenix is born to Kematch and the father, Stephen Sinclair. The couple "indicated they were not ready financially or emotionally" to care for their new baby and consented to a CFS placement. However, the couple changed their minds days later and asked for full custody. CFS obtained a three-month temporary order of guardianship and allowed the parents to have supervised visits.

SEPTEMBER 2000: Phoenix was returned to her family and found to be in good health. Kematch split from Sinclair months later and allowed him to have full custody of Phoenix.

MARCH 2002: CFS closed their file for the first time.

FEBRUARY, 2003: CFS reopened the file after Phoenix was taken to hospital with Styrofoam stuck in her nose.

JUNE 2003: Phoenix was apprehended by CFS because of concerns about her father's drug and alcohol abuse. Kematch then told the agency she wanted to try raising her daughter again.

AUGUST 2003: Phoenix was placed by CFS in the care of a Winnipeg couple who were friends of the father. Kematch agreed with the arrangement.

MAY 2004: Kematch told CFS she was once again caring for her daughter. CFS checked on Phoenix and found her to be in good health.

JULY 2004: CFS closed their file for a second time.

DECEMBER 2004: CFS learned Kematch had given birth to a baby girl and that the father was Karl McKay. No contact was made with the couple and the file remained closed. It wouldn't be reopened until the March 2005 tip that led them to visit Kematch but leave without seeing Phoenix.

WEDNESDAY NOVEMBER 12, 2008

It was unimaginable cruelty. Phoenix Sinclair had been deprived of food and forced to eat her own vomit in the days before she finally succumbed to a prolonged period of abuse and neglect that included being repeatedly shot with a pellet gun and choked unconscious.

"Some horrible things have happened to that little girl," a visibly distraught Cpl. Tara Clelland-Hall told the girl's mother, Samantha Kematch, near the end of a four-hour videotaped interview following her March 2006 arrest. "It absolutely breaks my heart the things that little girl went through in her short little life."

McKay's now 18-year-old son, who helped expose the killing to police, took the witness stand and pointed the finger of blame directly at McKay and Kematch, accusing them of countless violent and degrading acts and describing how Phoenix morphed from a "chubby" and happy child into a skinny child covered in cuts and bruises who would spend nearly every minute alone in her room without any food. He wiped away tears as he told court how he tried offering a helping hand to his stepsister, who had been kept a virtual prisoner in her own home. He described trying to feed a starving Phoenix some bread and water only to be caught and threatened by Kematch. "Samantha said what the fuck are you giving my daughter food for?" he said. "I'd feel sorry for her. She would say 'I'm hungry'."

He said McKay repeatedly played a "game" with Phoenix that he called "chicken" which involved picking her up by the throat, wrapping both hands around her neck and "choking her out." "Then he'd throw her to the ground," said the teen, noting visible finger marks would be left on her neck. "She'd make this weird scream. It was like someone had cut off her arm, like she was screaming to death."

McKay also liked to shoot Phoenix with a pellet gun, telling the girl to "run" and then shooting her repeatedly in the back and making her cry out in agony. "He'd shoot her for the fun of it," Phoenix's stepbrother said, noting the abuse would leave pellet marks all over her back. The teen said Kematch would often hit Phoenix with a metal bar and stool, especially when she'd urinate or defecate in her pants after Kematch refused to let her go to the washroom. Sometimes McKay and Kematch would throw Phoenix around, either to the ground or into furniture, he said. They also shaved the girl's head bald, court was told.

Kematch's lawyer, Roberta Campbell, suggested to the teen in cross-examination that it was McKay who was "most violent" with Phoenix. She also accused McKay of calling Phoenix degrading names like "fucking little baby" and "whore" while beating her.

"They were doing the same thing, equally," the teen replied.

"Isn't it true that sometimes he would hit Phoenix so much that she wouldn't even cry anymore?" asked Campbell.

"Yes," he answered.

McKay's lawyer, Mike Cook, suggested some of Phoenix's injuries could have been suffered during friendly "wrestling matches" that his client was having with the little girl. McKay's son said he believed the physical abuse was intentional, not accidental.

Earlier in the day, the 10-woman, two man jury watched Kematch's video statement in which she blamed McKay for Phoenix's death and said he refused to let her go to police to disclose what happened.

"I feel ashamed. I feel stupid. She didn't deserve anything like that. I think about it every day," she said. "I didn't want to see my kid like that. It hurt to see her like that. He wouldn't let me help her. He'd get mad at me." However, Kematch admitted to beating Phoenix at times for no clear reason. "I'd hit her because I'd get mad at her. I knew that wasn't right," she said.

Jurors heard how Phoenix spent her last hours naked, with an injury to her buttocks, lying on a cold basement floor. Kematch says McKay pushed her daughter violently to the ground, causing the child to bang her head on the concrete the day before her death. "I know it wasn't planned," Kematch said. "We didn't do it purposely. It was just something that got out of hand. An accident. This wasn't supposed to happen. I never wanted this to happen."

She said McKay asked her to bring him a garbage bag to wrap the child in when they discovered the next day she wasn't breathing. She said McKay put Phoenix in the trunk of a car and buried her in a hole in a wooded area near the dump at Fisher River reserve.

THURSDAY NOVEMBER 13, 2008

Her cries for help would keep him awake at night, an injured little girl pleading for food and water in an unheated basement filled with garbage and cobwebs. But it was the sound of silence that triggered a young boy to make a horrible discovery in his own home. The youngest stepbrother of Phoenix Sinclair told a Winnipeg jury how he found the five-year-old girl's body moments after she got what would be her final beating at the hands of her mother and stepfather. The boy, now 15, fought back tears as he described Phoenix's final moments alive in June 2005.

"I went downstairs and there was no answer from her. I just touched her back and it was all cold. Her eyes were open. I put my hand on her mouth... she wasn't even breathing," he said. His father, Karl McKay, and stepmother, Samantha Kematch, had been "taking turns" beating Phoenix, he said, and then left the Fisher River First Nation home to visit a relative. "They were passing her back and forth, punching her," said the boy.

After finding Phoenix's body, he called his grandfather looking for help. McKay and Kematch returned to the home, picked Phoenix up and placed her in a bathtub filled with warm water. "They weren't even crying or anything," the boy said. "I'd look at their faces. I saw no tears, nothing. They didn't even care what they were doing." The couple finished washing her body, then wrapped her up in a tarp, took it outside and placed it in the trunk of their vehicle, he said. "They said 'watch your baby sister, we're going to go to the dump and bury her.'"

That was the last time he saw Phoenix. He said McKay and Kematch told him not say a word about it. "They told me that if anybody asks, just say Phoenix went to Winnipeg to live with her dad," he said.

McKay's son told jurors how he watched helplessly as the couple repeatedly abused Phoenix "just for the hell of it." He said she was often forced to sleep in the "dark, cold" basement without any food or water. "It was dirty down there, you could see spider webs and garbage everywhere," he said. He awoke sometimes at night to the sound of Phoenix "sobbing through the vents." He would often go down to give her water and even tried to bring her a heater one night, only to be caught by his father and threatened. "She was just curled up in a little ball," he said. "The only time Samantha and [McKay] would go downstairs was to hit her."

He told jurors about beatings, including when McKay broke a metal broomstick over Phoenix's back and then used the broken end to cut her knuckles. "There was blood all over. It got infected," he said. McKay would also stomp on her and choke her to the point of unconsciousness, he said. "Her eyes would go back, her body would go limp and he'd just let her drop," he said. "He'd hit her so much that she wouldn't even cry anymore. She'd just take it."

MONDAY NOVEMBER 17, 2008
Karl McKay finally broke down under extensive police interrogation and agreed to lead officers to the body

of five-year-old Phoenix Sinclair in a decision he said proves he "has a heart." Jurors listened to a nine-hour audiotaped interview that began inside the Headingley jail and ended with McKay taking RCMP investigators to Phoenix's burial site. They heard how McKay initially refused to give any details beyond a vague map he drew for police despite repeated pleas for information.

"We're prepared to spend millions and millions of dollars to dig for Phoenix. We know she's out there, with no proper burial," Sgt. Norman Charett told McKay in the interview. "Phoenix didn't just walk away and start a life on her own. To have this girl sitting out there like she's trash... She's spent enough time out there."

Police continued to hammer away at McKay, telling him they wouldn't quit until the little girl's body was found. They also warned McKay that extensive media coverage would continue, noting the *Winnipeg Free Press* had identified McKay's 12-year-old son as a key witness against him. "There's going to be no closure for your boys," Charett said. "We'll continue to dig and dig and dig and dig. Trust me, there are unlimited funds."

Police then played on McKay's emotions, telling him he was not a "monster" and unlike notorious Canadian murderers such as convicted serial killer Robert Pickton of BC. "That guy doesn't care about anybody. But you have a chance here," Charett told McKay. "We need to put a rest to this once and for all, so that everyone can have some peace about this,"

At that point, McKay began to cry and blurted out: "OK, I'll do the right thing... I'll show you the exact spot." "I have a heart," he added. "I'm not just doing this to score brownie points." McKay then described his love for his other children, his fears about having them raised through the social welfare system and even told police about how he once saved the life of a choking baby by dislodging an item from his throat.

"It's sad when children die," said McKay, who asked officers if his first-degree murder charge might be reduced. "Maybe it will come down to second-degree or even criminal negligence," he said. Police said the directions to Phoenix's remains "puts a good light on you" but didn't make any promises.

McKay also spoke of being called "baby killer" by other inmates at the remand centre and his disgust at being housed in a cell with another man charged with killing a child. He also blamed his own abusive, alcoholic father for not setting him straight in life. "If it wasn't for alcohol, I'd have been an upstanding citizen. I wouldn't be sitting here," he said. McKay told police he loved his kids and knew first-hand what it was like to be the victim of the welfare system. "Yeah, I've had a hard life. I've been abused as a kid. I know what it's like to get a licking, stuff like that," McKay said.

McKay said he was one of 26 children his father had and called himself the "black sheep of the family" who lived in many foster homes.

"You get beat up lots?" asked Charett.

"Yeah, every day," said McKay.

Charett said he believed there was truth to a person being a "product of their environment."

"I'm not angry at the world," said McKay.

"The important thing is not to get caught in that vicious cycle where you're doing things that were done to you," replied Charett.

McKay had become emotional when he led police to Phoenix's final resting spot. "I'm sorry, you shouldn't be out here. Phoenix shouldn't be out here," McKay told RCMP officers who had driven him from Headingley jail to the makeshift gravesite at the Fisher River First Nation. A 17-minute video of McKay leading police to the burial location was shown to jurors. McKay and four officers went to the remote, wooded location by snowmobile, then trudged through deep snow before coming to an opening. Police used powerful lights to brighten the scene.

"It wasn't very far off the trail. I think it was just this spot here," McKay said before using his gloves to draw the spot in the crunchy snow. McKay insisted he was "99 per cent sure" they had the right spot, then recalled how he and Kematch used a spade to dig a hole for the little girl's body. "It was about eight inches in the ground," McKay said. "She'll be face up. I wrapped her in plastic with a yellow rain jacket. Her head will be here, her legs here."

Police asked if there would be anything else found in the grave.

"Just the dirt that she'll be covered with," McKay said.

He said Kematch insisted they pour pepper into the grave before covering it up to throw off police dogs that might sniff out the location. He said she got the idea from watching the television show Crime Scene Investigation. "It's a very sad thing that I've done, burying her out here," McKay told RCMP. "But at the spur of the moment, you're scared." McKay said he had borrowed the spade from a relative to dig a trench in his yard "and then this thing came up."

"I feel a lot better now that I've shown you this spot," McKay told police.

FRIDAY DECEMBER 5, 2008

She never stood a chance. Crown attorney Rick Saull told jurors Phoenix's fate was sealed by two heartless accused who worked together to kill her and then went to stunning lengths to cover up their crime. "Death here for this little girl was inevitable, given the course of conduct by these two accused," he said in his closing argument.

Saull said it was irrelevant how the abuse specifically broke down between Kematch and McKay. "Don't fall into that trap. Whether one went 10 or 20 punches more, or one used a weapon and one didn't, it doesn't matter," he said. "You just have to hold a small child in your arms once in your lifetime to know what a fragile life that is." Saull reminded jurors of the "absolutely mind-boggling" testimony they heard and said the verdict should be clear. "This is not normal parenting in any country in this world. That was an illegal domination of a child," he said. He singled out Kematch for continuing to collect social welfare cheques in Phoenix's name and trying to mislead investigators by passing off another young child as Phoenix.

Saull said it's obvious Phoenix was being confined in the home, which was an essential element to proving first-degree murder. There was evidence of exterior locks on doors and a makeshift wooden pen that was constructed for her in the basement. "This little girl wasn't going anywhere unless these two people let her," he said. "They are both guilty of first-degree murder. And that is justice for all of us."

Samantha Kematch admitted being a horrible mother. But she denied being a murderer. Her lawyers, Sarah Inness and Roberta Campbell, told jurors the Crown had failed to prove the case and urged them to convict her on the lesser charge of manslaughter. "She was an abusive, horrible mother. She could have prevented her daughter's death and she didn't," said Inness. "There are many things that she should have done and should not have done. She treated her daughter terribly. But she did not kill her. [Karl] McKay killed Phoenix."

She called McKay a "violent man who ruled the home with an iron fist" and clearly "despised" Phoenix because she wasn't his biological child. She noted McKay's violent history of abusing other women and children in his life. "There was an obvious power imbalance in the relationship," said Inness. She said it was McKay's idea to bury Phoenix's body after he delivered the final, fatal beating. "The fact she hid the truth and helped McKay cover it up doesn't mean she intended to kill her. She did nothing to encourage or assist McKay," said Inness.

Karl McKay says he took marching orders from his common-law wife and was mostly in the background as Phoenix's life was being taken away.

"That woman is a cold-hearted woman," defence lawyer Mike Cook said during his closing argument, pointing a finger directly towards the prisoner's box where Samantha Kematch sat. "She is most definitely the type who could kill, and would kill, her own child. A callous woman who cares nothing about her child."

Cook, along with fellow defence lawyer John Corona, said it was ridiculous for Kematch to suggest McKay had some kind of control over her. "This is not some wallflower type of woman who has been intimidated and dominated by Mr. McKay. Ms. Kematch was the dominant force in that house," said Cook, who believes Kematch began to turn on Phoenix after giving birth to another baby in 2004. "She rejected that child to the point it became easy to abuse her," said Cook.

He told jurors to remember how upfront McKay was with police following his arrest, even leading them to Phoenix's burial site. "Mr. McKay is a truthful man. You can accept and believe everything he said," said Cook. He also suggested the Crown had failed to prove confinement: the key element of the murder charge. "Phoenix was not forcibly confined. Mistreated, abused ... absolutely," said Cook.

FRIDAY DECEMBER 12, 2008

It had taken four long days of deliberations, a sure sign they were wrestling with the difficult task before them. But in the end, a Winnipeg jury came back with the only verdict that made sense to those who'd followed the case closely, Guilty.

Samantha Kematch, now faced with the opportunity to finally explain her actions, was defiant to the end. "I know the truth. I was there. I loved Phoenix and she loved me. Everyone can say what they wanna say, call me what they wanna call me. I never did this and I know this," an emotionless Kematch said, shortly after being convicted of first-degree murder and given an automatic life sentence with no chance of parole for 25 years. She told everyone in the packed courtroom they will likely "never know the truth" and took aim at her former lover, Karl McKay, by suggesting he acted alone and took her down with him. And she said "saying sorry won't change anything." So she didn't.

Kematch learned her fate first, staring blankly ahead as she pursed her lips. McKay was seen to take a series of deep breaths and close his eyes. He then clasped his hands together and held them to his mouth while bowing his head after hearing his verdict. McKay later told court he was "ashamed" at his role in Phoenix's killing and he shed several tears during the hearing. "I'm truly sorry from my heart. This should not have happened. This girl was full of life and happy when she entered my life," McKay wrote in a letter read aloud by his lawyer, Mike Cook. "I've let everyone down. I am shameful. Phoenix, I know you can hear me. I'm sorry. Please forgive me."

Kim Edwards, Phoenix's former foster mother, had the courtroom in tears while reading her victim impact statement. She described Phoenix's eyes, which she called "big brown mesmerizing saucers" and said the little girl would have been in Grade 2 today if not for the actions of her mother and stepfather. "I can see her now, all inquisitive and curious and showing other kids how to rock out and have fun," said Edwards. "It is beyond words to describe how I feel about that precious child. In all honesty I believe she was a gift sent to me from the heavens. Phoenix's heart belongs to me, and mine to hers."

Edwards said she feels rage toward Kematch and McKay and will never forgive them. "I've come to terms with what these people did to Phoenix. But I will never understand," she said.

Steve Sinclair, Phoenix's biological father, wrote that his daughter "never knew what pain was" until he gave her up. He said "the complete opposite was done to her" while in the care of Kematch and her common-law husband. "I always loved Phoenix. She was never a burden to me of any kind," he wrote. "She keeps my life going, and I'll always keep the memories of her going. I hope this never happens to another child again."

Many people close to Phoenix were in court as the verdict was read, including Edwards and Loretta Stevenson, mother of McKay's two teenage sons.

"I'm sad for Phoenix, but happy they're getting what they deserve," McKay's sister, Hilda, said shortly after hearing the verdict. "Justice is never going to be done for this little girl. Too much happened to her. It shouldn't have happened to her, we all know that. It shouldn't happen to any little child."

Tara Clelland-Hall, an RCMP officer who interviewed Kematch, was also in tears after the verdict. Top investigators in the case also attended court.

"This case reminds each of us what our fellow human beings are capable of," Crown attorney Rick Saull said outside court.

It was a rare sight—nearly every member of a jury returning to court to see justice meted out to the people they'd just convicted. All 10 women who served on the Phoenix Sinclair case sat through the sentencing of Karl McKay and Samantha Kematch. Only the two men on the panel weren't present.

"I've never seen anything like it," defence lawyer John Corona, who represented McKay, said outside court. He believed Phoenix's tragic story stuck an emotional chord with the jurors, who were stone-faced when they delivered their guilty verdicts. Most of the women were in tears and passing around a box of Kleenex as they listened to victim impact statements being read aloud in court. "I don't think they're ever going to forget this case," said Corona.

All members of the jury would now be offered counselling as a result of their five-week ordeal.

SUNDAY DECEMBER 14, 2008

"I failed her," Samantha Kematch said, her eyes cast downward and showing a hint of tears. Across the table sat a *Winnipeg Free Press* reporter. "She never deserved any of this to happen to her. She deserved better."

It was the first public show of remorse from Kematch, who displayed no tangible emotion during her month-long trial, and made no apologies in her brief and bitter final remarks before being sentenced. Kematch wanted the public to know she's not some heartless automaton. "You guys can sit there and say I have no feelings. Well, everyone shows their emotions in different ways. Not everyone cries. I'm one to hold their tears," Kematch said. "I'm not the type to freak out. I control my crying. But I hurt inside."

Saying sorry isn't the only reason Kematch was speaking out. She wanted to explain her courtroom comments, in which she told the judge that people will likely "never know the truth" and accused her former lover, McKay, of wrongly taking her down with him. "I didn't kill my daughter, I didn't do these things to her like everyone says I did," Kematch said. "What did I do to her? I loved her."

Admitting she's "not the best parent in the world or anything," Kematch insisted she was powerless to stop an abusive McKay from slowly taking Phoenix's life. And she painted herself as a victim as well, claiming McKay would often take out his anger on her. "I tried to stop it. That's where I failed. I failed her, I failed myself. But I tried to stop [McKay] from doing things to her. I would even take a beating so she wouldn't take it," she says. "I get so frustrated. He's only trying to make himself look good. I loved Phoenix and I cared for Phoenix. He's just sitting there, denying that he did anything." She admitted to having thoughts about attacking McKay in the witness box they shared during the trial. Those thoughts intensified after the guilty verdict and led to a sheriff's officer having to sit between them. "I was really angry, I was shaking," she said.

Under questioning, Kematch admitted she passed up many opportunities when she was alone with Phoenix and could have fled the home, call police, contact a friend or family member or take the injured girl to a hospital. "If I could go back and change all of this from happening, I'd do it in a second. A lot of people don't understand how these kinds of relationships work. The relationship was abuse, controlling, possessive. When you're in an abusive relationship it's not like you can just get up and leave. It's not easy to walk away," she said. Kematch admitted she was strict with Phoenix at times, but claimed McKay did all the physical damage.

One of the most damning pieces of evidence against Kematch was the fact she tried to hide Phoenix's death by pretending another little girl was her daughter during a meeting with child welfare officials. "I didn't want to go and pass off someone else's kid to hide the fact she was gone. It was [McKay's] idea to start doing shit like that," Kematch said. "I wanted to tell them about this but he said no." She said McKay was also behind her registering for child benefits in Phoenix's name, even after the girl had been killed.

Kematch says Phoenix would still be alive today if McKay, a longtime friend of her mother, hadn't entered their lives. He began asking her out after they met in December 2003.

"I didn't really want to go out with him. I was single and I wanted to enjoy it for a while. Plus he was so much older than me [20 years]," Kematch said. She eventually agreed. "[Before McKay], Phoenix and I were good. We laughed, had fun, we'd play. We'd say we loved each other, hug each other. That was life for me and Phoenix before he came into the picture," she said.

Being convicted of her daughter's killing was just the latest in a long line of tragedies for Kematch. When she was a child, her alcoholic father died after falling down a flight of stairs. Her oldest brother committed suicide in Swan River when she was 12. She and her two other brothers bounced around in foster care because their mother was unfit to care for them. She only finished her Grade 9 and had a spotty employment history. She had battled problems with drugs and alcohol for years.

Kematch said the reality of her conviction hadn't hit her yet. She wouldn't be eligible for parole until 2031, when she would be 50 years old. "I don't really feel like it's happened yet. I guess I'm feeling mixed emotions about it. I feel better in a way that this case is done so that [Phoenix] can rest," Kematch said.

THURSDAY DECEMBER 18, 2008

Karl McKay knew his words would likely ring hollow—but that wasn't stopping the convicted killer from speaking out about his role in the death of Phoenix Sinclair. "I know I'm the most hated person in this province and probably the whole country," McKay told the *Winnipeg Free Press* in an interview at the Winnipeg Remand Centre. "[Phoenix] didn't deserve this. It was a tragedy. I'm so very sorry. I can't turn back the clock. I just wish it never happened." McKay said he wanted to set the record straight about his feelings toward Phoenix and allegations made against him by his former lover and co-accused, Samantha Kematch. "That's bullshit," said McKay. "Samantha hated Phoenix. I know this because I was around. She's just trying to clear her name."

McKay, a long-distance trucker by trade, claimed Phoenix was always terrified when he'd hit the road and leave her alone with Kematch. McKay said his biggest mistake was staying in a relationship with Kematch, who he claimed was responsible for Phoenix's death. "I should have listened to my heart and not her," he said. "I can't imagine a mother would be that evil."

McKay denied Kematch's claims that he was physically abusive towards her, noting there were no records of police reports. McKay admitted he had abused other women in previous relationships but said he was a different person back then, largely because of excessive alcohol use. "People change, people can change overnight. I was a drinker back then, I had many binge blackouts. But that was then, this is now," he said.

McKay declined to talk about the testimony of his sons or why they'd say things he claimed were untrue. He said it was Kematch's idea to pass off a young relative as Phoenix once child-welfare officials began investigating the case. He said Kematch was "white as a ghost" when she realized the truth was about to emerge and was desperate not to have her other two children by McKay taken from her.

McKay said he was happy a provincial inquest would now be held into Phoenix's case. "People, in general, should love their children. This is a wake-up call to love your child," said McKay. "I just don't want this to happen to another child. It's just not right."

Phoenix Sinclair's legacy would be a massive overhaul of Manitoba's child-welfare system. A public inquiry was held into the tragic case, exposing how the little girl fell through a massive series of manmade cracks. I personally didn't cover the inquiry. To be honest, I couldn't stomach it. I'd covered the initial investigation, the trial and then conducted the jailhouse interviews with the two murderers. It was just too much.

But I did follow the inquiry closely, and was glad to see Commissioner Ted Hughes pull no punches when he released a 900-page report in January 2014. Hughes made 62 recommendations, warning that future tragedies would occur if changes weren't made. He specifically cited the failures of front-line social workers to protect Phoenix.

"I believe that the Child and Family Services workers who testified at this inquiry wanted to do their best for the children and families they served," Hughes wrote. "I believe that they wanted to protect children.

However, their actions and resulting failures so often did not reflect those good intentions."

One of the biggest recommendations was for the provincial government to abolish the office of the Children's Advocate and replace it with a more powerful independent office with the ability to keep close check on the child-welfare system. Hughes said frontline workers and supervisors knew from the moment Phoenix was born that she required close monitoring given the conditions she was being raised in. Yet he noted CFS got tips or information at least 13 times that Phoenix was in danger or neglected. And despite having more than 25 CFS workers involved with the family, none had any clue she was missing.

"Deficiencies in the delivery of services to Phoenix did not result from a lack of understanding of policies, procedures and provincial standards, or from confusion about which standards applied. Rather, they resulted from a lack of compliance with existing policies and best practice," Hughes wrote. "Even when the agency asked the right questions and did an appropriate assessment, it failed to follow through on providing the services that it had identified as necessary."

The provincial government issued an apology for Phoenix's death hours after the report was released. It was the first time they acknowledged wrongdoing. "We know now how a little girl became invisible, and we have already implemented changes to prevent other children from disappearing like she did," Family Services Minister Kerri Irvin-Ross said.

Hughes said the system was on the right track but had "more distance to cover." "To truly honour Phoenix, we need to provide all of Manitoba's children *with a good start to life and offer to the most vulnerable an escape from the cycle of poverty and vulnerability that trapped Phoenix and her family,"* wrote Hughes.

CHAPTER 6

THE LOBSTERMAN

There's an old saying in legal circles that a person who acts as their own lawyer has a fool for a client. I can vouch for this, having covered numerous cases over the years where self-represented accused turn the courtroom into a three-ring circus. But of all the bizarre situations I've seen play out, absolutely none come close to matching the antics of a former Winnipeg man named Ronald Hickey.

He pretty much held a jury hostage for two long months while pulling stunt after ludicrous stunt. Just when you thought you'd seen it all, something new would come along to top it. It was fascinating to cover, never knowing what was coming next. And it proved that sometimes, fact really is stranger than fiction.

MONDAY DECEMBER 13, 1999

The axe-murderer settled into his seat, staring down a jam-packed courtroom that had come to watch him testify. He felt like a star. Jack Bender, 49, said he was angry about missing a fried chicken dinner at the maximum-security prison in Ontario that had been his home for the last several years while he was serving a life sentence for brutally killing a man. He'd been flown to Winnipeg under RCMP guard for the most unusual purpose: He would be a "character" witness for his good friend, Ronald Hickey, who was on trial for drug trafficking.

"They just grabbed me and told me I was needed as a witness. I didn't even have a chance to change my clothes. I smell," said Bender.

After swearing on the Bible to tell the truth, Bender told court he didn't know what he could offer to Hickey's case but said he was willing to answer questions as a favour. "I know they're trying to screw you. I'm going to try and help out," Bender told Hickey. It was quite the spectacle. And perfectly fitting for a trial that had pretty much turned into a gong show. The case was only supposed to last a couple weeks, and the poor jurors selected to hear it had no clue what was in store.

Things got really wacky when Hickey's lawyer fell ill at the start of the trial, and Hickey, a city businessman, chose to act in his own defence. The result had been several confrontations with the Crown and Justice Albert Clearwater over techniques Hickey used to question witnesses. At one point, Hickey claimed to have a broken jaw that required emergency surgery, to which Clearwater responded by telling him to "give it a rest."

On another occasion, Hickey claimed he was having a heart attack and slumped to the floor of the court. The Crown believed he was faking to delay questioning of a key witness and called an ambulance. Paramedics found nothing wrong with him, and he was ordered to continue by Clearwater. During the trial, Hickey had also accused a sheriff's officer of staring at him with "an evil eye" and threatened to call former Prime Minister Pierre Trudeau to act as his lawyer for a constitutional argument. He never did. And now he had a notorious murderer in on the stand as his character witness.

Hickey, 45, was arrested along with 14 other people during an RCMP sting in 1997. He was accused of selling RCMP informant Margo Redsky—Bender's ex-wife—4.5 kilograms of marijuana at his Winnipeg home in December 1996. Hickey was also charged with pointing a gun at Redsky's head during the transaction. When Hickey's trial began an eternity ago, the Crown told jurors Redsky routinely came in contact with members of the drug underworld as she delivered drugs and collected debts for the Los Brovos motorcycle gang. She also smuggled drugs and other contraband to bikers inside Stony Mountain Institution, the Crown alleged.

Bender, wearing sunglasses and a bandanna, sat calmly in the witness box during nearly two hours of testimony. He began to detail his criminal record but told the jury "it would take a year" to finish. Bender did rattle off several incidents, including murder, cutting a nurse's throat, stabbing "a lot" of prisoners and assaulting prison guards. He referred to himself as one of the most dangerous killers in Canada.

Bender told court he met Hickey while both were serving time at Stony Mountain in the late 1980s. Hickey was being attacked by another inmate until Bender stepped in and saved him. Bender said he collected on the favour by asking Hickey to help Redsky financially. Under cross-examination from the Crown, however, Bender said he never instructed Hickey to sell drugs to Redsky. Bender was supposed to be Hickey's final piece of evidence. But he clearly had more tricks up his sleeve as he instructed jurors they would hear from one more witness—himself.

TUESDAY DECEMBER 14, 1999

His direct examination came in the form of a seemingly never-ending monologue. Ronald Hickey had full control of the courtroom and was clearly relishing his moment in the spotlight. On numerous occasions, Justice Albert Clearwater interrupted Hickey's testimony to scold him for veering off topic and making arguments about evidence heard during his trial.

"I'm going to make my closing argument at the same time now to save time so all these people can go home for Christmas," said Hickey.

"No you are not, Mr. Hickey," said Clearwater.

During his full-day of giving evidence, Hickey denied selling drugs or pointing a gun at anyone. Hickey did admit he felt pressured to come up with drugs for Margo Redsky because her husband, Jack Bender, had saved his life while both were in prison together. He said Redsky claimed she had terminal cancer and needed cash to go for treatment in Mexico. Hickey said Redsky wanted him to come up with marijuana so she could take it to Northern Manitoba and re-sell it for a huge profit.

"I didn't want to get involved with this person, but there's no hiding from Jack," he said. "I knew he was an axe-murderer. I know it was gruesome and over nothing. I knew he was psychotic."

Hickey said he eventually backed out of the deal but didn't deny a drug transaction may have gone down at his home between Redsky and someone else. However, he said he never provided Redsky with the marijuana and the only drugs he had in his home were about 10 marijuana plants for personal use in his basement.

FRIDAY DECEMBER 17, 1999

Ronald Hickey was in no hurry to finish. And so it was no surprise a closing argument that he promised would only last a couple hours actually couldn't be finished by the end of the day. Hickey spent much of his five hours speaking to jurors by reading directly from the 5,000 pages of transcripts of the trial. On repeated occasions, Queen's Bench Justice Albert Clearwater cautioned him to stop rambling and stay within the evidence. "Mr. Hickey, stop talking for a moment please," he said during one exchange.

When he began his argument at 9 a.m., Hickey apologized to the 12 jurors for occupying their time for so long, and for some of his courtroom antics, which have been openly criticized by the judge and Crown. He had repeatedly asked for mistrials, adjournments and presented statements to the jury that Clearwater had told them to disregard. "I wanted to keep you wondering what was next, like a good movie," said Hickey. When it became clear Hickey could not finish his arguments by the end of the day, Clearwater told him he would continue the following Monday at 10 a.m. and must be finished by noon. Clearwater then told the jurors he didn't want them to feel pressured into quickly reaching a verdict because of the upcoming Christmas holidays. He asked if they would like to adjourn the case until January following final arguments. But after a brief adjournment, the foreman said they want to begin as soon as possible.

In summing up his case, Hickey repeatedly made reference to his inability to conduct himself properly as a lawyer. "In my bumbling, I have tried to make the truth clear," he said.

WEDNESDAY DECEMBER 22, 1999

They weren't buying what Ronald Hickey was selling. And so it took jurors a few hours of deliberations to find Hickey guilty of trafficking marijuana and possessing the proceeds of crime. The weapons charge ended in an acquittal. The length and nature of the trial had taken a major toll on all involved. And that prompted the judge overseeing the case to try and play Santa Claus by granting them a cash bonus for the hardship they endured. In an unusual move, Justice Albert Clearwater ordered that the four-man, eight-woman jury receive $130 each per day for sitting patiently through the nearly three-month trial.

But it appears Scrooge, in the form of provincial legislation, would get in his way. Under provincial legislation, jurors are allowed only $30 per day once they have sat for 10 days. The law allows for a judge to order a $10-a-day increase when there has been unusually lengthy and undue hardship caused by the trial. In his closing remarks, Clearwater acknowledged the existing legislation but said he was making an order to give each juror $100 more per day anyway. "If there's one time I've seen a case that deserves extra compensation, this one is it. Your lives have been tied up for far longer than anyone could have reasonably anticipated," he told the jurors following the verdict.

Under his order, each juror would collect $3,120 for their efforts—for a total cost to the province of

$37,440. However, a provincial government spokesman said Clearwater's generous offer would not be approved because a change in legislation would be required to raise the pay. As a result, each juror would only be allowed to collect $10 more per day, or $40 total. That would amount to $960 per person—with a total cost to the province of $11,520. "He had no authority to grant that amount, and he acknowledged that in his remarks to the jury," assistant deputy minister Bob Giasson said. "To be honest, this was pretty unusual. But this trial was getting to be one of the lengthier ones we've seen. It was unreal."

The Hickey trial had attracted an eclectic mix of curious spectators. A constant parade of Hickey supporters and associates was often searching for seats in the public gallery next to off-duty judges, defence lawyers and Crown attorneys who wanted a first-hand look. "This was a travesty, an absolute abuse of the system," said one veteran lawyer.

Following his conviction, Hickey was taken into custody pending sentencing and a motion he had filed arguing he was the victim of police entrapment. Hickey wished his wife, daughters and several other spectators a Merry Christmas and said "let's rock and roll" as he was led away in handcuffs.

TUESDAY MARCH 14, 2000

He had boasted of being western Canada's greatest marijuana grower. But Ronald Hickey would have to put his green thumb on hold for a while after being sentenced to seven years in prison.

"In short, Mr. Hickey was a teacher," Justice Albert Clearwater said during a long-delayed sentencing hearing that came following a long-delayed trial. The Crown had sought a 10-year sentence. Hickey asked for three years.

Clearwater said a strong message must be sent given the large number of grow operations being unearthed in Manitoba. "Manitoba appears to be becoming one of the larger producers [among the provinces] of marijuana," said Clearwater. "It appears we're no longer an importer, we're an exporter."

As he'd done to the jury, Hickey once again apologized for taking up so much of the court's time. But he wasn't done from making headlines just yet.

WEDNESDAY SEPTEMBER 6, 2000

Ronald Hickey walked into Manitoba's highest court—and was promptly greeted with applause from a group of devoted supporters who had packed the public gallery. Just another day in his seemingly never-ending legal saga.

Hickey was taking one last shot at reducing his prison sentence, arguing it was harsh and excessive. He told the Court of Appeal he was being unfairly punished by Queen's Bench Justice Albert Clearwater because of his unusual antics during his jury trial. "I know I was an annoyance. But this is the kind of sentence given for manslaughters and rapes and all sorts of heinous crimes," said Hickey, whose movement in the Appeal Court was restricted by shackles around his legs and two sheriff's officers standing guard. "I think the jury would just feel terrible to hear I got seven years."

He told the Appeal Court that marijuana was a "soft drug," and his prison sentence didn't stack up against similar offences. Hickey argued the judge failed to consider the fact an undercover RCMP agent was used to gather evidence against him. "The police orchestrated these events. If that agent had not come to me and did what she did, that crime would not have happened," said Hickey.

Crown attorney Karen Molle said Hickey's sentence was proper considering his two previous drug-related convictions, which landed him a five-year prison sentence in 1990.

TUESDAY OCTOBER 10, 2000

Score one for the self-represented pot grower. Ronald Hickey had won a bid to reduce his sentence as the Manitoba Court of Appeal announced they had knocked two years off his punishment.

Justice Michael Monnin said the original penalty given by Queen's Bench Justice Albert Clearwater was outside the range of sentences given to similar offences around the country. However, the appeal court judges said they found no fault with Clearwater's reasons for sentencing and that Hickey's claim he was targeted because of his behaviour was "without merit."

WEDNESDAY MARCH 28, 2001

The justice system wasn't quite finished with Ronald Hickey. As usual, the circumstances were anything but routine. Hickey was convicted of his one outstanding criminal charge of causing a disturbance for a stunt he'd pulled during jury selection for his wife's trial. Gail Hickey had also faced drug charges from the same operation that netted Hickey. When lawyers were going through the process of narrowing down a large pool of potential jurors, Hickey had picked up a list containing their names, then tried to flee the courtroom with the document. When sheriff's officers tried to stop him, Hickey resisted.

Queen's Bench Justice Barbara Hamilton rejected Hickey's bid for an absolute discharge or suspended sentence, saying his actions flew in the face of justice and deserve to be punished. Hickey blamed his arrest and conviction on a "personal vendetta" that sheriff's officers had for him, given his history with Manitoba's justice system.

THURSDAY AUGUST 8, 2002
Ronald Hickey had moved from cannabis to crustaceans in his latest "you've got to be kidding me" charade that had Manitoba justice officials seeing red. Inmates at Rockwood Institution had been gorging on lobster in recent weeks, thanks to a certain inmate who'd opened up a fine dining pipeline into the minimum-security jail. Hickey was also being accused of smuggling in liquor and narcotics along with the contraband seafood. No items had been seized, as prison staff believed the evidence had been quickly consumed by inmates in their cabins at the jail. The jailhouse lobster fest was revealed in court documents filed by Rockwood officials, who cited numerous "reliable prison informants" in their allegations against Hickey. An internal investigation was continuing, but no criminal charges had been laid.

Hickey had now been moved out of Rockwood and into segregation while prison officials reviewed his security classification, which stood at "minimum." He was upgraded to medium-risk and transferred back to Stony Mountain Institution, based on the smuggling allegations and several confrontations with prison guards.

"Ronald Hickey... you are being placed in segregation as a result of inappropriate behaviour... including the importation of lobster into Rockwood Institution," read one prison document tendered in court.

Hickey filed an affidavit denying the allegations of importing lobster and other contraband. He claimed he should remain at Rockwood and that justice officials had breached his rights and freedoms. He appeared in court, acting as his own lawyer, wearing shorts, a muscle shirt and sporting a golden tan. Hickey said Stony Mountain was a dangerous place, citing several recent stabbings that had resulted in prison lockdowns. "Surely, in any reasonable person's opinion, taking a minimum-security inmate away from a peaceful farm environment [Rockwood] and transferring them to this cesspool of crime and lethal violence must be seen as a punishment to allegations not proved," Hickey wrote in his affidavit. He believed he was being unfairly targeted by prison staff and other inmates because of his role as chairman of the Rockwood Inmate Welfare Committee, which handles complaints and negotiates settlements. He also claimed in his affidavit that prison officials were trying to derail an upcoming parole hearing he had, in which he could be eligible for day parole.

FRIDAY AUGUST 9, 2002

Ronald Hickey said he had no reason to smuggle lobster into a Manitoba prison—he and his fellow inmates were already eating like kings. Ribeye steak, corn on the cob, freshly picked blueberries and even the occasional catered meal from a high-end Winnipeg restaurant have helped him stave off hunger pangs while serving his prison term at Rockwood Institution. "We eat very well in here. I usually have ribeye four times a week, and lots of times we do have seafood. But we've never had lobster," Hickey told a *Winnipeg Free Press* reporter. He referred to Rockwood as "Rockapulco", comparing it to a five-star resort.

Mona Lisa Ristorante Italiano in Winnipeg was a favourite among inmates, with orders from the prison coming in at least once a month, owner Joe Grande confirmed. Veal, pasta and the Italian desert tiramisu are among the most-requested items, which Grande would personally deliver to Rockwood's gates. "They're allowed to order whatever they want on the menu. They order good food—they're not exactly going for a greasy spoon here," said Grande. "It's good for us, and I suppose it's good for them."

Tania Morrow, the unit manager at Rockwood, confirmed that steak is supplied at the prison, and that Rockwood inmates were also allowed to order take-out on rare "special" occasions. However, the take-out meals were paid for by the inmates, not the taxpayers, she said. "The idea is to prepare them for entrance into the community, so we promote independence and responsibility," said Morrow. Convicts are allowed to choose from a list of groceries, but must ensure their allotment of food stretches out over a week for the six to eight inmates lodged in each cabin. Morrow said there were limits as to what an inmate could order, although she wouldn't go into specifics.

Hickey denied being the source of importing lobster and challenged jail officials and police to find the evidence to charge him. "It's totally ridiculous. I want to be charged, or moved back to Rockwood. These are serious allegations, and let me have my day in court and put up a defence," he said. "I believe you should be able to face your accusers."

Rockwood officials stood by their claims but admitted they hadn't recovered any lobster carcasses from within the jail. "Contraband of any kind is not sanctioned by administration, and we acted on the information we received," Morrow said. "I'm sure you can appreciate the nature of minimum security, and we're constantly gathering intelligence to try and put a stop to this sort of thing."

Hickey said he heard rumours in the jail that he was smuggling red wine into the facility. "Everyone knows you only drink white wine with seafood," he said. He also questioned why urine samples weren't taken to prove he hadn't consumed any alcohol or drugs. He suggested stool samples could be taken to prove the existence of lobster, which he admitted to eating regularly when he wasn't in prison. "I'm a seafood person. I love lobster and crab," he said.

There's a funny footnote to my coverage of the Ronald Hickey saga.

Charles Adler was the morning show host on top-rated CJOB in Winnipeg and invited me on the air to talk about "Lobster-gate" in 2002. He liked the story he read in print and wanted to bring it to his radio audience. It was the start of a great relationship, as

Charles began having me on the air as a regular guest. We also developed a strong friendship that remains to this day, and Charles played a key role in both inspiring me and assisting me in getting my own radio talk show in 2004.

Charles also decided to give me a nickname after that initial radio appearance—something he often did with guests he was fond of. Given the subject matter, it was a no-brainer. I was quickly dubbed Lobster Boy. The nickname has stuck to this very day, to the point I never know when I'll be hit with it.

Exhibit A: A few years back, while running in the Manitoba Marathon, I turned a corner down a residential street, aching and tired and wondering how I was going to make it to the finish line, when a complete stranger screamed "Go Lobster Boy!" It was all the motivation I needed to keep going.

So thanks, Charles. And thanks Ronald Hickey. I'm just glad it wasn't crab you were smuggling into Rockwood, as I don't think that nickname would have gone over quite as well.

CHAPTER 7

THE FINAL GOODBYE

It was one of the first big cases I ever covered for the Winnipeg Free Press. *It also remains, all these years later, one of the saddest.*

Bert Doerksen was the type of person you could spend an entire day just talking to, soaking in his wisdom and life experience, and still find yourself wanting to know so much more. Of course, I met Doerksen under the most tragic of circumstances. And there's no doubt he was plenty lonely and happy for the company. And so I listened intently during what would become several lengthy visits to his Winnipeg home. They were conversations I will never forget. And the fact he trusted me to share some of his most personal thoughts and feelings at an unbelievably trying time in his life is a responsibility I didn't take lightly.

Doerksen's case made national news and triggered debate on a controversial issue that still very much exists today. It was truly an honour to tell his story.

Bert Doerksen's handwriting is remarkably neat as he begins to describe the heart-wrenching end to his 59-year marriage inside a tidy Winnipeg bungalow. But the printing becomes sloppier, the ink less bold, as he tells exactly how the love of his life, Susan Doerksen, took her own life in November 1997 by sitting inside the couple's Oldsmobile that Bert helped fill with carbon monoxide. The eight-page diary was penned weeks later. At first, it would only be shared with immediate family members. Eventually, it would be released to the world. It tells a story of love, loyalty and deep loss.

A quick trip to Canadian Tire to buy some aluminum pipe. Fumbling around in the cold car to hook it to the exhaust pipe. Warming up the car so Susan would be comfortable. The short walk to the garage that seemed to last forever, arm in arm. A final plea to reconsider. A rejection. A last kiss and a hug. The sound of the ignition kicking in. And then the waiting.

Bert, sitting in his kitchen, staring at a clock, hoping to hear the sound of a honking horn signalling Susan had changed her mind. Nothing. Only silence.

"She never blew that horn, and I really did not expect her to. So I sat and watched the clock. After the longest 10 minutes of my life, I went to Susan," Bert wrote in his diary. "When I opened the door to the garage, she waved me back to go away. I blew a kiss to her. She tried to blow one back but could not quite raise her hand to her mouth," he continued. "I made no effort at this point to change her mind because I knew she was brain damaged. I waited ten more minutes and then opened the car door. There was no pulse. I kissed and hugged her for the last time."

Bert knew there was nothing he could do for Susan, who had long been plagued by chronic back pain and, in later years, by other serious health problems. Her ordeal was over. "I went inside and poured a straight whisky," Bert said of the moments immediately following his wife's death. Eventually, he called his daughter Jeny, who arrived followed by the ambulance, then the police. The paramedics wanted to work on Susan. Bert wouldn't let them, thrusting her living will in their faces.

Only hours earlier, Susan had been worried the pills she had swallowed weren't working. It was noon. "All this time I still wanted to call an ambulance. The answer was still no," Bert wrote. "Susan wanted to do something more drastic, such as slashing her wrists in the kitchen. I would not allow this, no way! No way!" he wrote. "She tried putting a plastic bag over her head but she could not do this either. By one o'clock she wanted to go into the garage and run the car. I would not let her do this either. Then, very suddenly, all her pain was gone. We hugged and cried and almost laughed." Their joy lasted only an hour.

"We were laying and holding hands, then the pain came back with a vengeance. Susan said to fix the exhaust, like we had once long ago talked about." With heavy heart, Bert reluctantly went to the cold, barren garage, using a rubber hose from their Shop-Vac. It melted in the exhaust pipe.

"I came back in and said every effort had been made and it had failed. Maybe there was a God after all and she should let me call an ambulance. But she would not hear of it. She wanted to know if I could not buy something at Canadian Tire. So after two hours of stalling, I went," Bert wrote. He bought aluminum dryer pipe, returned home, rigged it to the exhaust and ran it through the rear window of the car.

"I warmed the car up nice and warm, removed my key and shut it off. I went inside to Susan and begged once more not to go ahead. She asked me if it was ready. I said yes. She asked if anything would happen to me and I said no, she was going to do everything herself," Bert wrote. "We went arm in arm to the car. I was very careful walking down the three steps to the garage level as she had taken all these pills. Susan picked up her own car key, opened the car door, inserted the keys and started the car. We kissed and hugged once more."

They met in the Dirty Thirties—Bert tall and handsome, Susan elegant and charming. "By 1936 we were known as a couple," Bert wrote in the diary. Two years later they married. Bert was conscripted into the Royal Canadian Air Force in 1942, shortly after the birth of their second child. Being away from Susan and the kids was rough, but Bert had a lot of company to soothe his sorrow. But the toll of raising two children by herself was too much for Susan, who began experiencing terrible back pain stemming from an injury in her teens when she was kicked by a horse. By 1946, she was desperate to bring her husband home. Bert was given a compassionate discharge from the RCAF, returning home to Winnipeg to help with the daily grind. A third child soon followed—exactly the number Susan wanted. Bert had hoped for six, but gave up his dream as his wife's injury persisted. "It was very hard on her back, but she carried on," Bert wrote.

Life was fairly unremarkable, Bert working in construction while Susan stayed home with the kids. There were good days and bad days with Susan's back, but the bad began to outweigh the good in the 1970s after the couple was forced to evacuate an airplane in Denver by sliding down the emergency chute. "As time went by it reached the point that very often there were only partial good days," Bert wrote. "By the 1980s she often talked about wishing to die. Then Susan got breast cancer."

She began radiation treatments, becoming violently ill after her 13th. She stopped wanting to go, missing two further treatments. "It took all my begging and the cancer clinic personnel to continue. She did finish all her prescribed treatments, but by this time Susan made no bones about it that she wanted to die," wrote Bert. "By suicide if need be."

Susan began attending the Health Sciences Centre pain clinic, but the positive effects wore off after about four years. She would occasionally return for painkillers, but they would barely mask her agony, Bert said. "By 1997 she had taken painkillers for over 15 years," he wrote. Susan regularly asked her doctors about having back surgery, but was told there was a 50 per cent chance of becoming wheelchair-bound, according to Bert. She wanted to risk it, but the doctors did not.

In 1994, the couple stopped taking their regular winter trips to Phoenix, where the dry air helped ease some of her pain. "Susan still did her crafts and baking, etc., during this time and some cooking. But by three years ago [1995] I did more or less everything, such as all the housework—floors, washing, making beds and most of the cooking. Susan still looked after the flowers," wrote Bert.

On Christmas Eve 1996, she suffered a major heart attack and spent 16 days in hospital. "It was downhill on a fast track from here on in. She wanted to die so desperately, even if by suicide. She asked, and I promised, that I would not stand in her way if she ever made that final commitment. These were terrible times and these promises were made with tears flowing from both of us," wrote Bert, who took over his wife's gardening chores. Susan became bedridden by October 1997, then had one mild heart attack followed by a severe one while lying in bed one night.

"She would not let me call an ambulance, much as I begged. She became almost unconscious and I just held her in my arms. After about half an hour she sort of stabilized," Bert wrote. She remained in bed for days, but was adamant that she finish two baby blankets she had been working on for expectant friends. "There was a great deal of urgency in her activities. I sort of knew deep down that Susan was preparing to die," he wrote.

Susan never did finish the blankets, giving up her efforts and asking Bert to get her sisters to do them once she was gone. Discussions about death became frequent. "Susan requested that I do nothing rash and stay in our home for at least a year," he wrote. "It is lonely here but it would be elsewhere as well," he said. Rather than give them to his sisters-in-law, Bert finished Susan's baby blankets himself.

Bert railed at the Canadian medical system, saying people suffering chronic pain should have access to stronger painkillers such as morphine. Doctors refused to give Susan morphine because she wasn't terminally ill.

"On that day, Nov. 26, ended the longest day of my life. I am in a great deal of mental pain," Bert concludes his diary. "My great comfort is that my love, wife, the children's mother, is without pain for the first time in 53 years. Susan, Rest In Peace."

TUESDAY JANUARY 27, 1998

It was a day Bert Doerksen knew was likely coming. But seeing the front-page headline—SUICIDE CHARGE A FIRST—drove home the reality of the situation. Manitoba justice officials did, in fact, want their so-called "pound of flesh."

Allan Fineblit, assistant deputy attorney general, confirmed that his office had authorized police to lay a criminal charge against Doerksen. It marked Manitoba's first-ever assisted suicide case. And it was sure to spark intense debate.

Martin Glazer, a prominent Winnipeg defence lawyer hired by the Doerksen family, came out swinging. "Mr. Doerksen is a decent, law-abiding war veteran who has never been in trouble with the law in his life," he said. "He lost his wife of 59 years. He's not Paul Bernardo. He's living a nightmare." Glazer said comparisons to another infamous Canadian case out of Saskatchewan were unfair. In that instance, Robert Latimer killed his severely disabled daughter. Latimer was ultimately charged and convicted of second-degree murder. "This woman [Susan Doerksen] had her own free will and made her own choice to die," said Glazer. "Even the Crown isn't saying this is a murder."

There was quick public reaction on both sides of the issue. Theresa Ducharme, a disabled-rights advocate in Winnipeg, applauded the move. "We must have the same rules. Just because we're aging, is that supposed to mean you should be excused from any litigation?" Ducharme told the *Winnipeg Free Press*. "If I was a Crown attorney, I'd treat him like anyone else. They have to be charged to the maximum. I'm getting frustrated because increasingly we don't know if there is a law protecting people like myself."

Barney Sneiderman, a law professor at the University of Manitoba, disagreed. He felt the Crown ought to have used their judicial discretion in this unique and tragic case. "It seems to me if there is ever a case not to proceed with, it's this case," he said.

Fineblit said there was no question his office had plenty of sympathy for Doerksen. But he said they must follow the letter of the law—specifically section 241(b) of the Criminal Code. The assisted suicide charge carries a maximum penalty of 14 years in prison. Doerksen would be invited to attend a city police station the following day to voluntarily turn himself in. Police would then immediately release him on a promise to appear in court. There would be no handcuffs. No confrontations. No "perp walks."

"This is taking its toll on him. He's not happy, and it's causing a lot of stress," said Glazer. "We've already had one suicide here. We don't want another."

WEDNESDAY FEBRUARY 25, 1998

He wanted to grieve in private, to be left alone with his thoughts and memories. But Bert Doerksen couldn't escape the public spotlight these days, now a month after police had formally arrested him for helping his wife commit suicide. His lawyer, Martin Glazer, knew the court of public opinion seemed to be siding with his frail, elderly client. And so Glazer continued to push the envelope. Doerksen sent the *Winnipeg Free Press* a letter—with Glazer's blessing—in which he lashed out at justice officials.

In my mind, I did not assist Susan to commit suicide. She did have a right to die. Now in my agony after losing my wife, lover, companion and friend I also have to put up with the so-called law to prolong my healing like salt in a wound. We were married 59 years and were a couple 2 1/2 years prior to our marriage. After 62 years the Minister of Justice should leave me alone. It is my sincere belief that the Minister of Justice and possibly he alone is responsible for all or most of my problems.

He advocated as much on CBC radio, which was broadcast nationwide. I have at this time pleaded not guilty. I feel I am not guilty. It is possible that this plea could change and not because of guilt.

If I carry on it could very well bankrupt me as my means are modest. The state has endless tax dollars including mine to persecute me. I do not mean prosecute. The Minister of Justice is in charge of all this. I do not qualify for Legal Aid.

My children have already spent thousands of dollars since Susan's death and will spend many more if I go to trial. The family is very supportive but they have their own life to live and I do not wish to place any more burdens on them, which are already great.

Should I be convicted, what would the state do with an 80-year-old man who is partly crippled and has other medical problems as well? The Minister of Justice would then be victorious. It would seem that just to satisfy his beliefs and ego it would at best be only a hollow victory.

> After 53 years of pain and the last year of pain beyond belief, no one or state can deprive Susan of her freedom now.
>
> So I say, get your pound of flesh. You can not increase my agony. You can only prolong it. The police have been outstanding and have shown nothing but kindness and compassion, as well as our neighbours, friends, etc. I am hard of hearing so forgive me to all that call.

Doerksen then followed up on the letter by sitting down with the *Free Press* at his home for an exclusive interview. "I want them to leave me alone to grieve by myself, rather than have the whole world looking at me. I'm a good citizen. They've got no right to do this to me," Doerksen said through tears. "It's already a terrible thing to lose your wife. This just makes the agony worse."

Doerksen went into great detail about his wife's suffering and her desire to end her life. "She wanted to die a long time ago. She kept it in the family, but in the last year she told everyone. Of course it upset me. I didn't want her to give up. But I didn't hold that against her," he said.

Glazer sat at his client's side, admitting they hoped enough pressure might convince justice officials to ultimately drop the controversial case. "We're asking the justice department to back off and drop the charges," said Glazer.

WEDNESDAY AUGUST 26, 1998

Another six months had passed. Six long, stressful months for Bert Doerksen. The case had largely disappeared from the headlines. But it continued to hang over Doerksen like a dark cloud. And now there was another layer of tragedy in play. Doerksen had just been diagnosed with terminal cancer.

Lawyer Martin Glazer fired another volley by sending a letter to Manitoba Justice Minister Vic Toews. He said continuing to go after a dying man in these circumstances was cruel and unusual punishment.

"Based on the facts of the case and the lack of a likelihood of conviction, I'm asking him to step in and review and reconsider the case," Glazer told reporters. Of course, this was mostly a public relations move. Glazer knew the odds of a sitting justice minister actually using his "prosecutorial discretion" to quash a charge were slim. "There is obviously a renewed sense of urgency as a result of his illness," said Glazer. "I'm seeking his compassion as a result of the man's medical condition."

Not surprisingly, Toews wasn't willing to take the bait. Hours after delivering the letter, Glazer received a response. "It is a long-standing practice of attorney generals in Manitoba not to become involved in individual cases despite the legal and constitutional ability to do so," deputy attorney general Bruce MacFarlane wrote in the reply. MacFarlane added there was a "need to avoid even a perception that political considerations may be involved in the decision-making process." The charge remained. The fight would continue.

The Doerksen family had seen enough. Frustrated by what they viewed as a lack of compassion from senior government and justice officials, several members mounted a full-scale attack.

"He's being treated like a test case," Jim Doerksen told the *Winnipeg Free Press*. He said his father didn't deserve what he was being put through. "He's in a lot of stress. I don't know how long he will live. This shouldn't be happening."

Jim Doerksen took direct aim at justice minister Vic Toews, blasting him for sitting on the sidelines. "Vic Toews, as the minister of justice, is doing a terrible thing. You can't prosecute someone who is innocent. The Crown is starting to look pretty stupid now," he said. He revealed the Crown had made his dad an offer—plead guilty in exchange for receiving no jail time. As a matter of principle, it was immediately refused. "To me that's outright blackmail," he said. And he added this wasn't a matter of wanting special treatment for his father, who he described as "lonely" and in a constant state of grieving. "I don't think he should be getting any special treatment because of the cancer. There never should have been charges laid in the first place," he said.

The Crown's office responded the following day with their own public statement. For the first time, a slight window of opportunity appeared to open. "The Crown has maintained, and will continue to maintain, an open dialogue about [Doerksen's] medical condition," the statement said. Sources told the *Free Press* there was fear within the justice department of potential backlash from special interest groups should they drop the case against Doerksen. And so it continued to move forward.

In January 1999, a one-day preliminary hearing was held to determine if there was sufficient evidence for the case to proceed to trial. Provincial court Judge Arnold Conner ruled there was after hearing an abbreviated summary of the Crown's case. Prosecutor Brian Wilford told court his office had plenty of sympathy for Doerksen but he said they must follow the law as it was currently constructed. Outside court, defence lawyer Martin Glazer repeated the family's growing frustration. Barring a miracle, it seemed now like Doerksen was going to trial.

"I'm hopeful a jury will find him not guilty," said Glazer.

FRIDAY JUNE 16, 2000
Now 81, Bert Doerksen was ready to give up—in both his battle against the assisted suicide charge, and the battle against the disease slowly eating away at his body. "The end is inevitable. I'm just not anxious to prolong it, so why go through the agony of that?" Doerksen, his voice raspy and wavering, said in an interview from his home. And so he was going to let "nature take its course" and discontinue all medical treatment. He blamed the heavy burden the province had placed on him by branding him a criminal and bringing him to court. "This is just terrible. I have never, ever had a criminal charge against me in my life. I have done nothing that is criminal," he said.

Lawyer Martin Glazer renewed his call for the Justice Department to drop the case against his client. "Mr. Doerksen has suffered enough. This process is only exacerbating his suffering and I think enough is enough," said Glazer. Glazer had just received a letter from Doerksen's doctor that prompted him to make the renewed request for mercy. He faxed a copy of the letter to the Justice Department and requested an immediate stay of proceedings based on its content.

"Mentally, I believe Mr. Doerksen has deteriorated. On May 19, he indicated he had 'had the biscuit' and the communication which is enclosed on May 30 indicates that he is 'tired, old and lonesome,'" wrote Dr. Paul Galbraith. "I do not think that this 81-year-old man is capable of pursuing the rigours of a criminal trial."

Doerksen suffered a relapse of lymphoma in March. It was originally diagnosed in the summer of 1998 and appeared to be under control, according to the letter from his doctor. Doerksen was also experiencing night sweats, nausea and acute pain. Doctors were awaiting results of a CT scan to see if his cancer had spread further. Although he continued to take painkillers, Doerksen was adamant he no longer wanted to be treated with chemotherapy, radiotherapy, surgery or any other aggressive medical technique. "Sometimes the treatment can be worse than the disease," he said. "The state wants to make a criminal out of myself where no crime has occurred." Doerksen said it was "obvious" justice officials had no sympathy for him by insisting he stand trial. "Their ideology and zeal have not diminished," he said. "Physically, it would be out of the question for me to spend time there in court.

FRIDAY JULY 28, 2000

He was just days away from going to trial when the news he'd been praying for finally arrived. Manitoba justice officials had a change of heart. They were going to drop the assisted suicide charge. Bert Doerksen broke down in tears after hearing Crown attorney Brian Wilford had formally entered the stay of proceeding.

"This is an example of compassionate justice," defence lawyer Martin Glazer told court. "The stress level, the nightmares have been just awful. Now he can die in peace without this hanging over him."

Wilford explained how Doerksen's current medical condition, which included recent updates from his doctors and even a face-to-face meeting, led them to this decision. "Given his physical and mental deterioration since his wife died, it has been determined that it would not be appropriate in the public's interest to proceed with this prosecution," Wilford told Queen's Bench Justice Nathan Nurgitz. "Let me just say this decision has nothing to do with the merits of the case. It has everything to do with the status of Mr. Doerksen's health. He is incapable of attending for his trial or participating in it mentally."

Nurgitz agreed it was the right decision. "This has nothing to do with his guilt or innocence, and everything to do with the public's best interests," the veteran judge said.

Doerksen was unable to attend court in person to hear the news. And it took several telephone rings at his home before he picked up. His frail, shaken voice suggested it was not a good time to call. "I'm not feeling too much of anything right now," he said, noting the heavy dose of morphine he was currently taking.

Other family members proclaimed victory following the ruling. "We are so very relieved. His health has deteriorated so badly, and this has put so much stress on him," said Doerksen's son, Jim. The California resident came to Winnipeg to be with his father. "We don't know how much longer he will live, but this case was definitely going to shorten his life," he said. "My mother was in severe pain and couldn't stand it anymore. My father has had a tremendous amount of support and believes this has been a serious intrusion of his life."

Glazer said he believed the merits of assisted suicide should be debated by government, not lawyers. "Today is a victory, but this case is a tragedy. Hopefully we've learned a lot from this," he said.

Rob Finlayson, assistant deputy attorney general, said the Crown had no choice but to lay the assisted-suicide charge against Doerksen. "The province is not responsible for the laws of the land. That is up to our elected officials," he said outside court. Finlayson said the Crown had a solid case. He said the Crown had discretion to drop the case only when it became clear he would not be fit for trial. "I don't think this will be precedent-setting. This is an exceptional case because of the age of Mr. Doerksen and his deteriorating health," he said.

SATURDAY NOVEMBER 8, 2003

There was no trial. There would be no inquest. And now, more than three years after his high-profile case faded from the public spotlight, Bert Doerksen lost his battle with cancer. He was 85.

"Nobody knew when he was going to be terminal—he outdid the doctors' predictions by a mile," Doerksen's son, Jim, told the *Winnipeg Free Press*.

Defence lawyer Martin Glazer said he believed justice officials helped extend his former client's life by showing mercy. "I'm pleased to see he was able to live out the rest of his life in peace without the threat of a criminal prosecution hanging over his head," said Glazer. "Had the charge not been dropped, I think he would have died sooner."

Jim Doerksen said his dad had hoped the case would ultimately lead to changes within the medical system, so people like his mother could get relief from chronic pain to avoid such drastic measures. "He really felt the province should get their act together and come to terms with people suffering," he said. "I would hope nobody else has to go through what he went through. Hopefully someone will grab it by the horns and do something to change this. I still feel if she had been properly looked after by the medical system she would be alive today." Doerksen said his dad was lucid to the end and had a good quality of life in the time since the charge was dropped.

"Palliative care nurses took care of my father for the last two weeks of his life and did a marvelous job," said Jeny Forest, Doerksen's daughter. "It allowed him to die at home peacefully and without pain. With my mother they insisted she wasn't terminal, but she was. Any person contemplating suicide is terminal and at some point she will succeed. Most important, we were there when my father died, but with my mother, because she didn't want us there, she died alone."

It has been more than a decade now since Bert Doerksen passed away. But there's no doubt his case—and the important issues it raised—continue to generate debate within both the justice and medical community. And as the population continues to age, these types of tragic stories will continue to play out. I've even covered a few of them. Two in particular stand out.

In 2004, I wrote about an elderly Manitoba couple who formed a suicide pact, then killed themselves with a single bullet inside their Ashern-area home. The couple, who were both 75 and had been married 56 years, somehow managed to configure the weapon and themselves so they would die at the exact same time.

"They loved each other and did everything together. They were very attached. Even in death," a brother of the elderly woman told me from his Ashern home, located about two hours north of Winnipeg. "They were so much in love, so happy. Clearly they had put a lot of thought and planning into this."

"I've often thought that if one should go, what would happen to the other? Obviously they had thought about that as well," said a close friend of the deceased woman.

The elderly woman had undergone gall bladder surgery about six weeks before her death and had been struggling with pain and discomfort, according to the family. Her husband was also battling poor health, having recently undergone treatment for a prostate condition. The couple was survived by four daughters, one son, numerous grandchildren and siblings.

Later that year, 86-year-old Tony Jaworski stabbed his 83-year-old terminally ill wife, Sophie, to death as she lay in her bed at Seven Oaks Hospital in Winnipeg. Jaworski then turned the knife on himself, plunging it into his own stomach in a failed suicide bid. He ultimately pleaded guilty to a reduced charge of manslaughter—sparing him the automatic life prison sentence required for murder—and was given a sentence of 17 months time in custody and three years of probation. It was a compassionate resolution to a case which legal experts say made Jaworski Canada's oldest convicted killer.

"He took an action here which is illegal but understandable," provincial court Judge Fred Sandhu said in agreeing to the plea-bargain. "This is a situation many people have faced, and will continue to face, when a loved one is dying or withdrawn from a quality of life they had and living becomes a mere existence," he said.

Jaworski's lawyer, Greg Brodsky, told court his client acted out of love. "Mr. Jaworski had one love in his life, and that was his wife, Sophie," he said. "If anyone could have asked her if she wanted to live in the condition she was in, she would have said no. But she couldn't answer. She wasn't competent. She relied on her husband to take care of her."

The court heard that in the hours before he killed his wife, Jaworski sat at her hospital bedside, holding hands and quietly reflecting on 63 years of marriage. Several tubes protruded from Sophie's fragile body, which had been ravaged by colon cancer in recent months and resulted in a nearly 100-pound weight loss. A large, bulbous tumour was visible on her stomach. Doctors figured she had less than a year to live. Jaworski desperately wanted to take her home to spend her final days—but the restraints that kept the elderly woman secured to the bed wouldn't allow it. Nor would the doctors at Seven Oaks Hospital, who had just lifted a ban— at the family's urging— which had been preventing Jaworski from visiting his wife. Sophie couldn't express what she was feeling, as Alzheimer's disease was eating away at her brain. But Jaworski was positive she was suffering. "Thank God she's not suffering anymore," he told investigators after the killing.

Jaworski—who was legally blind and partially deaf—struggled to understand much of his court hearing.

"This was a man under extreme duress. It was no longer life as he knew it," said Crown attorney Melinda Murray.

Just before going to the hospital on the fateful morning, Jaworski stopped at his granddaughter's home and left his wallet, other personal identification and a chilling note on the front steps. "Please forgive me," it read.

CHAPTER 8

LIFE OR DEATH

Canada abolished the death penalty 1976, some 14 years after the country's 710th and final execution was carried out. And while public debate about bringing back capital punishment continues to this day—usually whenever a particularly heinous homicide makes headlines—it's extremely unlikely it will ever return. However, that didn't prevent me from being able to cover a notorious criminal case for the Winnipeg Free Press *in which the life of a suspected killer was literally on the line. And I didn't have to go far for it, either. A horrific crime had occurred just a couple hours south of Winnipeg, in the city of Grand Forks, North Dakota. The trial would be held one more hour down the highway, in Fargo. The case certainly hit home with Manitobans—and for me, personally.*

My family and I were actually in Grand Forks on the very weekend that Dru Sjodin went missing. We saw the posters going up around town the following morning, having no idea just how serious this would end up being. My wife even recognized her picture as belonging to friendly store clerk she had spoken to while shopping in Columbia Mall. That was just a few hours before this awful crime occurred.

In the early days of my trial coverage, dozens of readers phoned and emailed to weigh in on the case or pass along their sympathies to the victim's family.

Some of Manitoba's youth attend the University of North Dakota and knew the victim from campus. Dozens of people made the 150-minute drive south to volunteer in the search for the missing girl. Thousands visit the mall she was abducted from every year. To many, it felt like she was "one of our own."

It was a truly surreal and memorable experience. I may have just been a short distance from home, but the differences in the Canadian and American justice systems were on full display.

She was the blond, blue-eyed beauty, a homecoming queen and all-American girl with a million-dollar smile. The world appeared to be hers for the taking. Yet Dru Sjodin wouldn't see her 23rd birthday, graduate from the University of North Dakota, get married or accomplish her many goals and dreams. Her future was stolen, her life snuffed out, in the cruelest and most inhumane of ways.

Now the man accused of Sjodin's horrific November 2003 kidnapping, torture and killing was locked in his own battle to survive. Alfonso Rodriguez, 53, was about to begin his murder trial in Fargo in a case expected to attract the same kind of international attention and emotion as Sjodin's heartbreaking, five-month disappearance did. He had pleaded not guilty. Prosecutors were seeking the death penalty if Rodriguez was convicted, based on a previous criminal history that includes a 23-year kidnapping and rape sentence he'd just finished serving in May 2003. They also hinted at the "especially heinous, cruel and depraved manner" in which Sjodin's killing was carried out. What was already known was difficult enough to digest.

"Oh my God." Sjodin's last known words, screamed into a telephone while speaking with her boyfriend, Chris Lang, immediately hinted at something sinister. It was shortly after 5 p.m. on Saturday, November 22, 2003, when Sjodin was walking out of the popular Columbia Mall shopping centre in Grand Forks and heading to her car. The senior at UND had just finished her shift at Victoria's Secret.

Sjodin's cellphone went dead. Police later found her car sitting empty in the snow-swept mall parking lot. An immediate appeal for help was launched. Posters were plastered around Grand Forks and surrounding communities. Police went public looking for tips. The case quickly captured international media attention due to a combination of the random nature of the abduction, Sjodin's "girl-next-door" looks and her family's willingness to speak out. There were tearful family appearances on all the major network shows.

Rodriguez, who was living just across the border in nearby Crookston, Minnesota, was quickly identified as a suspect. He was arrested and charged with kidnapping. But there was still no sign of Sjodin. And Rodriguez wasn't talking. An unprecedented investigation and search continued. Numerous federal, state and municipal police agencies and more than 200 officers became involved. Nearly 2,000 volunteers turned up, including family, friends, fellow students and complete strangers from all over, to help search daily over a frozen plain that spanned two states and dozens of kilometres. It all ended in sorrow on April 17, 2004. Sjodin's body, wrapped in a blanket, was found in a ravine just outside Crookston. There would be no miracle happy ending.

North Dakota abolished capital punishment decades ago, but Rodriguez was now facing potential death because he allegedly kidnapped Sjodin in North Dakota, then disposed of her in Minnesota, making the act a federal crime, not a state crime. North Dakota hadn't executed someone since 1905. The case was expected to generate much regional debate about the merits of the death penalty. Even Sjodin's loved ones appeared divided, with some suggesting nothing but death for Rodriguez would satisfy them while others questioned whether it was what Sjodin would have wanted.

"This is a decision most of us wanted. If this case doesn't warrant the death penalty, then they might as well just do away with it," said Bob Heales, a Sjodin family friend and private investigator who led search efforts for months.

U.S. Attorney General John Ashcroft's decision to seek the ultimate punishment for Rodriguez upon conviction came despite strong opposition to the death penalty in North Dakota. "My overall sense is that people are very accepting of the decision in this case," said Heales, noting the extraordinary circumstances of Sjodin's case.

Sjodin's mother said she supported the decision to seek the death penalty. "We look forward to the case moving ahead," Linda Walker told the *Grand Forks Herald*. "We appreciate the continued support and prayers we have received from people who have brought Dru into their hearts."

Richard Ney, the expert death-penalty attorney who was helping defend Rodriguez, said he was disappointed but not surprised. "One thing that certainly disappointed us is that this decision was made despite the longstanding position of the people of North Dakota against capital punishment," Ney said. Ney predicted the wide opposition to the death penalty in North Dakota would pose a practical problem for the defence and for the trial in general. "The jury in a death-penalty case can only be made up of people who say they are not morally opposed to the death penalty, or they will be excluded from the jury," Ney said. "In a state where there is not widespread support for the death penalty, it may be more problematic to get a jury of one's peers."

The life-and-death battle was about to begin.

THURSDAY JULY 6, 2006

There was an angel in the courtroom. Dru Sjodin's family members said they felt her spirit when they walked in to face the man accused of kidnapping, torturing and murdering her.

"She sits on my shoulder. She's my strength," Allan Sjodin told a throng of nearly two dozen reporters outside the Quentin N. Burdick federal courthouse in Fargo. "She's always in our hearts. She will be forever," added Sjodin's mother, Linda Walker. The couple was expecting the death penalty trial against Alfonso Rodriguez to finally begin and walked into court with a mix of emotions. "We're tense. And very anxious, of course," said Walker.

Unfortunately, the case got off to bumpy start when a computer glitch forced an unexpected adjournment. Lawyers were supposed to begin selecting jurors to hear the case against Rodriguez. But the trial was delayed when justice officials noticed the first 15 prospective jurors who were supposedly randomly selected from a pool of nearly 600 all hailed from the same small town of Valley City, ND. The company behind the computer program originally claimed it was a statistical "anomaly" and not a sign of a problem with the random selection process. They later conceded there might be a glitch. US District Judge Ralph Erickson said it wasn't safe to proceed and decided to put off jury selection for a day so that a new list of 15 could be generated.

"We have one mission here. And that's for justice," Allan Sjodin said after learning of the adjournment.

FRIDAY JULY 7, 2006

It was a clear message sent from several prospective jurors: Finding an unbiased panel to hear the case was going to be a monumental task. The challenge only grew larger after an entire day of intense examination by prosecutors and defence lawyers yielded just one person that lawyers could agree was suitable for jury duty. Many others were sent packing based on their candid responses to questions about Sjodin case.

"The Bible states, 'he who kills shall be killed.' That's God's message," said one woman, who also admitted her husband and parents have made their views about capital punishment crystal clear in the wake of her jury subpoena. "Everyone close to me is very much for it and that [the accused] should get the death penalty," she said.

An elderly grandmother of six was also sent home when she admitted her mind was already made up about Rodriguez's guilt. "Given the evidence already provided through the media, I believe he committed the crime," she said. She also proclaimed she's in favour of executing people who commit "horrific" crimes.

Another woman expressed doubt at her ability to be fair, noting she has a daughter the same age as Sjodin who was attending UND at the time. "It will be hard for me to be impartial, knowing it could have been her," she said.

A married, middle-aged stay-at-home mother of three told court she would only consider death—not the alternative of life in prison with no parole—if Rodriguez was found to have committed an intentional murder. "Why should the life of a criminal be spared?" she asked.

MONDAY AUGUST 14, 2006

The jury was finally set. The answers would finally start coming. How exactly did Dru Sjodin die? Was the University of North Dakota student killed immediately? Did she suffer? What prompted the shocking daytime kidnapping outside a busy Grand Forks mall? How well planned was the attack? Did she know it was coming? Why was she targeted? And what exactly do prosecutors mean when they say she was murdered in an "especially heinous, cruel and depraved manner?"

Assistant U.S. Attorney Keith Reisenauer held nothing back in his opening statement. Jurors were told how Sjodin was kidnapped from the busy Columbia Mall parking lot in Grand Forks and how her body was found five months later in a ravine near Crookston, MN, after snow melted. Sjodin was nude from the waist down, her hands bound behind her back, a rope around her neck and the remnants of a plastic bag still around her face. She had also suffered a slashed throat and possible stab wound to the chest. "He left her in a ditch to die," said Reisenauer, who also alleged that Rodriguez sexually assaulted Sjodin before killing her.

Rodriguez's lawyers also made an opening statement and offered up an unusual defence—taking no issue with the allegation Rodriguez killed Sjodin but focusing almost entirely on where the murder took place. Defence lawyer Robert Hoy told jurors Rodriguez shouldn't face federal charges because Sjodin was likely already dead by the time she got to Minnesota. "This is simply the wrong charge in the wrong court. It's entirely possible Dru Sjodin died... in a matter of minutes while still in the Columbia Mall parking lot. The transportation of a deceased person across state lines is not a federal kidnapping," said Hoy. Hoy said prosecutors laid the federal charge "in their zeal to become involved in an already highly publicized case." He said Rodriguez should instead be facing a state charge of murder, which would not make him eligible for the death penalty if convicted.

An autopsy couldn't provide a conclusive cause of Sjodin's death but found asphyxiation, trauma and/or exposure to the winter elements could all be factors, Reisenauer said. Doctors were also unable to pinpoint a time of death.

Police found Sjodin's cellphone just a few feet away from her body—a discovery that could prove critical for the theory of the prosecution. Sjodin had called her boyfriend, Chris Lang, as she walked out of Columbia Mall around 5 p.m. following her shift at the Victoria's Secret. The line suddenly went dead. Police believe it was at that moment Rodriguez grabbed Sjodin and forced her into his car.

Lang was concerned and called back at least eight times but got no answer. His hopes were briefly raised when he got a call from Sjodin's number around 8 p.m. However, Lang could only hear static and muffled sounds. The connection was lost again, said Reisenauer. Police traced the call to a cellphone tower near Crookston, MN, and focused much of their search on the area but were initially unable to find anything. But prosecutors intended to argue that phone call proved she was still alive while in Minnesota.

Police began looking at known sex offenders in the area and interviewed Rodriguez two days after Sjodin went missing. He was living at the time about 6.5 kilometres from where Sjodin's body would eventually be found. He admitted he had been in Grand Forks on the day in question to do some shopping but claimed he was in a movie theatre at the time, said Reisenauer. When asked to name the movie, Rodriguez initially couldn't but later told police it was *Once Upon A Time* starring Antonio Bandares. However, his apparent alibi began to unravel when police checked around and learned the movie wasn't playing anywhere in Grand Forks at the time.

Police got a warrant to search Rodriguez's vehicle and home and made several key discoveries. A knife— matching an empty sheath found near Sjodin's car in the Grand Forks parking lot—was in the trunk. Rodriguez claimed he was using it to cut sheet rock, but his employer claimed that wasn't true. Police also found tiny droplets of blood in Rodriguez's car, which they eventually matched with Sjodin's DNA. Forensic experts were also able to find a strand of Rodriguez's hair on Sjodin's body and fibres from Sjodin's shirt and jacket on his boots, gloves and in his car. They had the proverbial smoking gun.

Canadian air force pilot Julian White would never forget the desperate search for his good friend, Dru Sjodin, or the void left in his life by her tragic death. White, who was currently living in Moose Jaw, Sask., was one of the first witnesses to testify. He was also one of the last people to speak with Sjodin and raced around Grand Forks the night she disappeared hoping to find a trace of her. "She was a bubbly, happy girl. Everybody loved her. She was an American sweetheart," White told reporters outside court after finishing his day on the witness stand.

White met Sjodin while both were attending the University of North Dakota. White—who returned to Canada after completing his aviation studies—was dating Sjodin's roommate, Margaret Flategraff, at the time. He was in Toronto on the day Sjodin went missing but spoke with her briefly around noon. Sjodin mentioned she was on her way to work. White told jurors he flew to Winnipeg and then drove back to Grand Forks later that evening. He arrived at his girlfriend's apartment to learn Sjodin hadn't been heard from since her phone went dead in a conversation hours earlier with her boyfriend.

"I went out to look for her and was driving the route between Dru's apartment and the mall. I drove all around but I found nothing," White told court. White said he even checked one of the parking lots at Columbia Mall but didn't see her car. Police found it hours later in another nearby lot.

Flategraff testified how she called 911 when Sjodin didn't come home that night. Several other concerned friends gathered at her apartment to worry and wait. Danielle Mark, a sorority sister of Sjodin's, told court how they'd gone out for dinner the previous night following a fun-filled "initiation" week. She tried to call Sjodin several times on the evening she went missing and couldn't understand why there was no answer.

WEDNESDAY AUGUST 16, 2006

They were begging him to take them to a body—but Alfonso Rodriguez refused to admit guilt despite a crumbling alibi and mounting evidence against him.

"You're in a position where you could end this investigation…I think you can take us to that girl," a clearly desperate Dan Ahlquist of the Minnesota Bureau of Criminal Apprehension told Rodriguez in one of three audiotaped interviews played for the jury. "There are lots of things that could make this not so bad. Showing you care for the outcome of the investigation would help. If this were to drag on, it would hurt your Mom. The family of the girl is hurting right now. They'd like to know where she is," he said. "It would better your position to be the helper, instead of just giving silence."

The pleas fell on deaf ears as Rodriguez refused to budge from his position that he wasn't involved in crime. "I didn't do nothing. What do you want me to admit to something I didn't do? I've never met that girl. I've never talked to her. I've never seen her until I saw her in the paper," Rodriguez said during one of his three Nov. 26, 2003 interviews.

Ahlquist described how investigators honed in on Rodriguez after compiling a list of seven known sex offenders living in the immediate vicinity through a national sex offender database. Rodriguez—who had just been released from prison in May 2003 after serving a 23-year sentence for kidnapping and rape—was the first to be interviewed because he had the worst history of all those on the list, said Ahlquist. The interviews began with Rodriguez admitting he was in Grand Forks on the day Sjodin went missing but claiming it was a non-eventful trip. "It was pretty quiet, not too much of anything," he said. He claimed he did some early afternoon shopping before going to a movie around 4:30 p.m. and being in the theatre until 7 p.m. Sjodin was grabbed at 5 p.m. It hadn't taken him long to strike.

TUESDAY SEPTEMBER 5, 2006
It took less than four hours for jurors to reach their verdict. Alfonso Rodriquez was guilty. But this was just the first legal hurdle. Now prosecutors would begin telling—and graphically showing— jurors why they believed Rodriguez should be sentenced to die. Close-up photos of a bound and battered Dru Sjodin,

references to God and accounts of Rodriguez's criminal past would all be presented as part of the prosecution's sentencing bid. Jurors would then have to begin deliberating whether Sjodin's killing meets the eligibility requirements for Rodriguez to be sentenced to death under federal law.

If they ruled it didn't—as Rodriguez's lawyers urged—the case would immediately end with Rodriguez being sentenced to life in prison with no chance of parole. If they ruled it did—as prosecutors strongly urged—jurors would continue sitting for a final phase of the case that would involve additional evidence and argument on the sole point of whether Rodriguez lived or died.

Defence lawyer Richard Ney told jurors they had already given Rodriguez a "death sentence" and said there was no need to inflict further punishment. "Alfonso Rodriguez will die in prison. You've already decided that. The thing to decide now is whether that will happen when God decides or when man decides," Ney said during his opening statement. Prosecutor Drew Wrigley immediately objected to the statement. Erickson told Ney "we've had enough" and ordered him to move on. Ney admitted Sjodin's death was "terrible" but said it didn't meet the legal definition of being "especially heinous, cruel or depraved."

Rodriguez had three prior sex-related convictions. Two of his three former victims were called to the witness stand to describe how their lives had suffered as a result of the attacks. The evidence could be used by jurors to weigh Rodriguez's fate.

One woman, who was 18 at the time she was raped in 1974, said she was still battling depression, anxiety and thoughts of suicide. She described having a breakdown only days earlier which involved barricading herself in a bedroom, pushing furniture up against the door and arming herself with a flute. She also admitted to being admitted to mental health facility last winter. "I was having suicidal thoughts. I was grieving. My brother had died. And Dru Sjodin had died," she said, fighting back tears. She also described several failed relationships, including two divorces.

The other victim, who was also sexually assaulted by Rodriguez in 1974, described dropping out of college following the attack and many years spent as a transient living in her car and doing odd jobs across the United States. "It seemed like nothing made any sense anymore, in terms of having any hope, faith for the future. All of that seemed broken," she said. "I was looking for a fresh start. But I found out it was something you couldn't really run from," she said. The woman had since turned her life around, got married and found full-time work but said she always remembered what Rodriguez did to her. "It just eats at you. You think about it every second," she said.

The most explicit evidence came when jurors were shown several close-up photos on large television monitors of Sjodin's decomposed body as it was found. There were also images of her bound wrists. Sjodin's friends and family, including both parents, were visibly upset and darted their eyes to avoid seeing the pictures, which prosecutors showed to enhance their argument that Rodriguez deserved to die.

In his final argument, Ney told jurors federal death penalty provisions require certain evidentiary tests must be met in terms of planning. Ney suggested there is no evidence of a cold-blooded killing and that while Rodriguez may have planned to kidnap Sjodin, the murder wasn't something he anticipated. "This was a crime of immediacy, of impulse. It was very disorganized," said Ney.

But Wrigley told jurors they should have little doubt about what Rodriguez planned to do. "Don't let anyone draw your attention away from Alfonso Rodriguez and how he terrorized Dru Sjodin in her final hours," he said. "The facts regarding his intentions are very clear and very troubling."

It didn't take long to reach their decision. Jurors concluded on their second day of deliberations that the case certainly met the requirements for a death penalty sentence. Now the only question left to answer was whether they would dish out the ultimate penalty. There were three final steps jurors would have to consider:

1. Had prosecutors proven beyond a reasonable doubt there were "non-statutory aggravating factors" present in this case? Those factors involved the emotional impact on Sjodin's family and friends.

2. Had Rodriguez proven there were any mitigating factors in his favour? Defence lawyers claim there were many, including remorse and exposure to toxic chemicals, sexual abuse and racism.

3. Did the aggravating factors outweigh the mitigating factors?

Judge Ralph Erickson told jurors it was not a contest to see whether there are more aggravating factors or mitigating factors, but rather a question of weight. And jurors had to be unanimous on the question of death, or else the sentence would automatically be one of life in prison with no chance of parole.

MONDAY SEPTEMBER 11, 2006

Prosecutors went straight for the heart of the jury, with several members reduced to tears as they listened to moving tributes to the young victim. Dru Sjodin's mother, father, stepfather, boyfriend, roommate and good friend all took the witness stand to offer painful glimpses into how Sjodin's death impacted them.

"My world exploded," Sjodin's mother, Linda Walker, told court. "She was a soft, tender, caring child. She was a wonderful contributor to society. A daughter, a sister, a friend. I was excited for her future."

Sjodin's stepfather, Sid Walker, described the raw emotion that followed her devastating death. "Linda would wake up at night, screaming. I felt helpless. All I could do was hold her," he said.

Allan Sjodin, Dru's father, said she left a lasting impression on all who knew her. "She was my baby. People would be drawn in by those beautiful blue eyes of hers. Once you met her you didn't forget her," he told jurors. "We've lost the love of our life. We struggle with every second of every day."

Sjodin recalled his final meeting with his daughter just days before her death. He had already said goodbye and driven away but was suddenly struck by a "panic attack" after going about eight kilometres. "I turned around, went back and told her I needed to give her another hug," said Sjodin.

Dru had been dating Chris Lang for several months before her death and the couple seemed destined for a bright future together, court was told. "Her smile was very captivating. She was a kind soul. It was real," Lang told jurors in his statement. "She treated me like I mattered. She made me feel wonderful about myself." Lang said he called Sjodin "my lovable goofball" and felt she could achieve anything she set her mind to. Sjodin was hoping for a future in the arts or photography and often dazzled loved ones with her sketches, paintings and pictures. "She really seized life, every minute. There was so much ahead of her. Everything was blooming," he said.

Danielle Mark, one of Sjodin's best friends, recalled how she took great pride in doing volunteer work with underprivileged kids and raising money for diabetes and victims of crime. And Sjodin's former roommate, Meg Flategraff, told jurors how Linda Walker was a bridesmaid at her recent wedding. "She stood in for Dru because she couldn't be there," she said.

Defence lawyers had objected to much of the heart-wrenching testimony being heard and even moved for a mistrial once the prosecution had called all its evidence. Judge Ralph Erickson refused, saying there was no prejudice to Rodriguez.

In his opening statement, prosecutor Drew Wrigley said the death penalty was the only fit punishment for an "intentional, heinous, cruel and tortuous crime." "The facts in this case cry for justice," he said.

TUESDAY SEPTEMBER 12, 2006

Alfonso Rodriguez's elderly mother made a tearful plea for her son's life by painting a glowing picture of a "kind, loving" man who struggled in life because of brain damage caused by exposure to toxic farm chemicals. Dolores Rodriguez showed jurors several pictures of Alfonso as a toddler as she described her fears that he will be sentenced to die. "I would suffer. I'm not in good health," wept Dolores, who had to use a walker to get to the witness box. "He's a wonderful son, kind, loving. I'm happy when I talk to him, when I visit him. That's the only time I feel happy."

Rodriguez—known as "Tito" to family members—was repeatedly exposed to dangerous pesticides while growing up with his migrant farm family in Minnesota, his mother told court. The family would come up from Mexico every spring to work with sugar beets and lived in a small home with no electricity or running water. Rodriguez was a very sick, undersized child who also faced ugly racial taunts while attending school with several siblings, she said. "The other children used to call them dirty Mexicans and other names. They weren't happy and used to cry when they had to go to school," said Dolores. Her son first got in trouble with the law in his early teens when he began making obscene phone calls to women living in the Crookston area, said Dolores. She spoke to police and detailed her son's troubles, which included severe headaches, a swollen head and tremors.

Dr. Karen Froeming, a clinical neuropsychologist from California who had met with Rodriguez three times in the past year, testified she believed he suffered brain damage as a result of "significant" exposure to farm chemicals as a child. She put Rodriguez through a series of clinical tests and found he suffered from a very low IQ and that his reading, writing and math skills were at an elementary school level. "These impairments have a lot to do with impulse control," said Froeming, who was retained by defence lawyers as an expert. Froeming told jurors she believed Rodriguez was being truthful. But she admitted being in the dark about additional background information, including how he'd lied to police about being involved in Sjodin's death while a desperate search for her body was underway. "That would certainly have raised my index of suspicion," she said in cross-examination.

Defence lawyers called another expert to detail the dangerous side effects of the types of chemicals being used on farms in the 1950s and 1960s, most of which are now banned. Dr. Donald Ecobichon—a Canadian who had taught at several universities and authored three books on toxic chemicals—said young children like Rodriguez would have been most vulnerable. "The toxicity of these chemicals weren't appreciated in their early use," he testified. He described several possible impairments from exposure, including poor judgment, anger management and aggressive behaviour. "People can recover somewhat over time. But they're never back to normal," said Ecobichon.

Rodriguez turned to drugs and alcohol in his mid-teens and eventually more serious crime landed him in prison for much of his adult life. After being released from prison in May 2003, he returned to Crookston to live with his mother until his arrest later that year for Sjodin's slaying.

"There were no problems at all [when he came home]. I was happy. I had someone to help me with chores around the house. I was glad he was with me," Dolores said.

WEDNESDAY SEPTEMBER 13, 2006

The seeds were planted early for Alfonso Rodriguez to grow into a serial sex predator and killer. Sylvia D'Angelo repeatedly wiped away tears as she described the horror of watching her little brother get molested inside a church when he was only four years old. They had been staying together in Minnesota at a summer camp for migrant children when Rodriguez had his innocence stolen by a woman who was working with the kids, she said. "I remember there was light coming through [the church] and reflecting off the Virgin Mary as he was [receiving oral sex]," said D'Angelo, who was only six years old at the time.

D'Angelo described another incident later that summer where Rodriguez sacrificed himself in order to stop a young adult man from sexually assaulting her in an outhouse on their rural farm property. "Tito would say 'leave her alone, I will do it,'" said D'Angelo, adding the sex assaults occurred against her brother on several occasions. He also protected her when they were a bit older from a drunken caretaker who would try to attack her. "He'd try to fondle me but Alfonso wouldn't let him. He would always hide me under a pile of clothes and say I wasn't home," she said.

Dr. Marilyn Hutchinson, a psychologist who had met extensively with Rodriguez over the past year, told jurors this sort of horrific abuse left Rodriguez confused and angry. Those emotions began to manifest themselves in various disturbing ways. Rodriguez was smoking cigarettes and drinking alcohol by age nine; was one of several boys to have group sex with a 19-year-old when he was just 11; began using drugs like LSD, along with sniffing lighter fluid, paint and glue by his early teens; and started making obscene phone calls to girls when he was 14. Rodriguez was suffering from "very confused sexuality" and began having fantasies about having sex with strangers, said Hutchinson.

"He became very angry that women had the power to make him aroused. When he gets angry, he either has sexual thoughts or he explodes," she said. "Remember, he had people who wanted sex from him when he was just a little kid."

Hutchinson said Rodriguez continued to suffer from post-traumatic stress disorder caused by his childhood experiences, which also included racial taunting from other children at school. Rodriguez recalled an incident where kids threatened to pour white paint on him because his skin colour was dark. He danced with a young white girl in the fourth grade at a school event, only to watch as the girl's mother grabbed her away and said "wash your hands because you touched him," said Hutchinson.

THURSDAY SEPTEMBER 14, 2006

A prison official admitted Alfonso Rodriguez's unusual request to be kept in supervised care beyond his mandatory prison release date was ignored—opening the door for him to kill.

Ted Mickelson, Rodriguez's former caseworker, told jurors he had serious concerns Rodriguez posed a threat to the public in light of his three prior sex-related convictions, lack of sexual-offender counselling and the fact Rodriguez himself feared being let out into the community. "I really didn't think he would reoffend, but his history was so severe he shouldn't be released," Mickelson testified. Rodriguez had approached him in early 2003 and asked to be sent to a treatment centre through a civil process in which he could be further detained following the expiration of his 23-year sentence in May 2003. "He was experiencing some anxiety, some concerns about being released," said Mickelson.

Mickelson told Rodriguez that senior Minnesota justice officials had already ruled in late 2001 he wasn't a candidate to be "civilly committed"—the designation some high-risk US sex offenders receive through the courts if they are still deemed a risk to public safety. Mickelson admitted he thought Rodriguez should be detained beyond May 2003 but never voiced his concerns—or said Rodriguez was asking not to be freed—to prison officials in the hope they would take another look at his status. He also didn't make officials aware of the fact Rodriguez had also gone back on a promise he'd made to seek sex-offender programming as his release date approached.

"He wasn't interested in treatment and he refused to meet with the psychologist," said Mickelson. Instead, Mickelson referred Rodriguez to a prison psychologist to deal with his concerns. "I couldn't argue with what they had already decided. I didn't think anything had changed to the point they'd take another look at it," said Mickelson.

"But they didn't have this new information. Weren't there alarm bells going off in your head at this point?" asked defence lawyer Richard Ney.

Mickelson said he would have taken stronger action if Rodriguez had voiced specific thoughts about reoffending. "He never indicated to me or anyone else he had any intention to go out and hurt anybody," he said. "If he had, I would have been on the phone right away."

Rodriguez was granted his mandatory release that spring. And Sjodin would quickly become his next victim.

Ruth Johnson, the program director of an inmate community integration program based out of Minneapolis, testified about phone conversations she had with Rodriguez's concerned sister just months before his release.

"It was the first phone call I'd ever received from a family member saying we don't want him released from prison," said Johnson. Sylvia D'Angelo had asked Johnson about potential halfway houses her brother could go to as opposed to being simply cut loose in the community with no conditions. "She said he really felt like he needed to be in a structured environment," said Johnson. She told D'Angelo she wasn't aware of any such programs in the Crookston area and took no further action.

Mickelson said Rodriguez also asked him about a halfway house. "I told him he wasn't eligible," he said.

Rosa Rodriguez also testified she was concerned—and confused—about her brother's future pending his release from prison. "I couldn't understand why someone would want to stay locked up forever," she said.

WEDNESDAY SEPTEMBER 20, 2006

Clutching a grainy black-and-white photo of Alfonso Rodriguez as a toddler, defence lawyer Richard Ney made a passionate final plea to jurors to show the convicted killer some mercy and spare him a death sentence.

Rodriguez was once a sweet, innocent child who wasn't given a fair shake at life because of several factors beyond his control, said Ney. "We're dealing with an individual here who wasn't starting out at an even level. This is not someone who's functioning as well as you or I. We as a society don't execute people who are striving to be good," Ney said in his closing arguments. "You have the capacity to say 'I can be merciful here.' Mercy is just something we would give a fellow human being who tried to be good but failed."

Ney also echoed emotional pleadings to jurors from Rodriguez's family members. "Sure, you will be killing the man who murdered Dru Sjodin. But you'll also be putting to death that little boy who was exposed to neurotoxins, who couldn't keep up in school, who was exposed to racism and poverty, who was hungry, who was sexually abused," said Ney. "Death here would just break one more mother's heart, just devastate one more family."

Several Rodriguez family members burst into tears when Ney talked about the specifics of execution. "The government is asking you to put a living, breathing human being to death. And if that's what you decide today, make no mistake. That is exactly what will happen. He will be taken from his cell and strapped to a gurney," said Ney. Ney also took aim at federal justice officials for failing to stop a killer. "The better angels in Alfonso Rodriguez cried out to the people who could stop his release and said 'Stop.' But nothing was done. There was a system failure here," said Ney.

FRIDAY SEPTEMBER 22, 2006

The verdict was in. Alfonso Rodriguez would lose his right to live. On the third day of deliberations, jurors sentenced Rodriguez to die by lethal injection. The stunning decision was the first of its kind in North Dakota in more than a century.

"Justice has been served," proclaimed Allan Sjodin in a tearful news conference following the long-awaited end. "For Dru's sake, this needed to happen."

Linda Walker thanked everyone who followed the difficult case and she hopes her daughter's legacy lives on. "I know it wasn't easy for the jurors. But Dru's voice was heard today and will hopefully be resounding around the world. We won't tolerate violence against women, much less our children," she said.

Prosecutor Drew Wrigley said Rodriguez was getting what he deserves. He also acknowledged the rarity of such a penalty. "And we hope the need doesn't arise for another 100 [years]," Wrigley said. "But as I told the jury, ours is a gentle area. The people of this region are loving people," Wrigley said. "It is the defendant's acts of the last three decades that have brought us to this place, at this time. In the end, we believe this is justice."

Rodriguez showed no visible reaction to the decision when it was read aloud by the court clerk shortly after 11 a.m. His mother and two sisters burst into tears. One juror was also crying, while the rest had stoic looks on their faces. Sjodin's family and friends embraced outside court. In the end, it appeared Wrigley's passionate argument that such a chilling crime cried out for the ultimate punishment was accepted.

"The jury decided this case with the care, dignity and integrity that Dru deserved," Chris Lang said outside court. "These matters have been decided today. But don't forget Dru. Celebrate her life as long as yours. She was beautiful, she was wonderful. Keep her in your thoughts forever."

Alfonso Rodriguez is still alive as of the writing of this book. Like pretty every inmate condemned to death, Rodriguez is exhausting every single avenue of appeal in hopes of finding a court that might overturn his fate. His lawyers have repeatedly pushed the theory that Rodriguez is "mentally retarded" and therefore should be exempt from execution. They have lined up several medical experts to bolster their argument. They are also relying on a decision released by the US Supreme Court in the spring of 2014 that strikes down rigid intelligence tests used to determine if a prisoner has a mental disability.

Prosecutors, of course, take a much different view of Rodriguez's brain. And they have their own experts who support their position. The legal fight may drag out for a few more years, at various of levels of federal court.

Meanwhile, Dru Sjodin's legacy lives on. "Dru's law" came into effect in 2007, requiring convicted child molesters and those convicted of violent sexual offences to be listed on a national online database and face a felony charge if they don't update their current whereabouts. A memorial website, which includes additional background on the case, the legislation and detailed updates on Rodriguez, can be found at www.drusvoice.com.

CHAPTER 9

JUSTICE WASN'T SERVED

It was an eight-year legal odyssey unlike few others in Manitoba history. A botched police investigation. A controversial plea bargain. A damning public inquiry. An explosive criminal trial. And so much more. But it all began with a situation that is all-too-familiar— a senseless, completely preventable tragedy where alcohol is involved.

I've lost track of how many of these cases I've covered over the years, of how many tears I've watched be shed in courtrooms from grieving family members, of how many sputtering apologies I've heard from the guilty party that was behind the wheel. And yet drinking-and-driving remains an epidemic. In many ways, this case represents a perfect storm of everything that could possibly go wrong, on so many levels.

WEDNESDAY MARCH 2, 2005

The cross of yellow and purple flowers was laid gently on the median. A small group of people huddled at the intersection while police blocked off traffic. Someone began reciting the Lord's Prayer. A *Winnipeg Free Press* reporter stood to the side, observing the solemn ceremony.

Robert Taman stood stone-faced, his three adult children by his side. Several other family members and close friends were also present. Many were choking back tears. All of them wore the same pin on their coats, bearing the name of Mothers Against Drunk Drivers. Taman had just buried his wife, Crystal, at a service attended by more than 700 people. Crystal had been killed just a few days earlier at this very intersection, where Lagimodiere Boulevard meets the north Perimeter Highway.

"How do we go on living knowing that this could happen to any of us?" Rev. Don McIntyre had asked the congregation. "Life is not always fair."

The pain was still raw. There were so many unanswered questions about what had occurred. Crystal had been on her way into work as a dental assistant, taking the same route she travelled all of the time. She had done nothing wrong. She was stopped at a red light in her convertible. Then along came another vehicle—a Dodge Dakota pick-up truck—with catastrophic results. It slammed into her from behind, crushing her vehicle and killing her. Crystal's two daughters drove by the scene moments later and witnessed the horrific aftermath.

Police had made an arrest. And the Taman family was stunned to learn who was behind the wheel of the vehicle which had killed Crystal. Derek Harvey-Zenk, 31, was a constable with the Winnipeg Police Service. He was off-duty at the time of the tragedy. And he was now facing several criminal charges: refusing a breathalyzer test, dangerous operation of a motor vehicle causing death and criminal negligence causing death.

"Sometimes a person is forced to step up," Robert Taman said at the roadside service. "We want to get through this day. We will have more to say."

WEDNESDAY AUGUST 22, 2007

The wheels of justice had been moving very slowly. And now, two-and-a-half years after a high-profile deadly crash, Manitoba justice officials had struck a plea bargain with the killer driver. It was only serving to inflame an already irate public.

Alcohol-related charges had been dropped against Derek Harvey-Zenk. In exchange, he pleaded guilty to a lesser offence of dangerous driving causing death. It was a deal that was likely going to keep him out of prison, thanks to a joint-recommendation Crown and defence lawyers made to the judge calling for a conditional sentence to be served by Harvey-Zenk in the community.

"This is so messed up. The system has let us down in a way that is so bizarre," said Robert Taman. Justice officials—including a special Crown prosecutor hired by the province—hadn't told the family what went wrong. "We're being kept in the dark here, but we know this is as a result of the East St. Paul police. I don't know what happened here, but you start to wonder about the brotherhood that exists among police officers," Taman said.

He said the drunk driving charges should have stuck against Harvey-Zenk unless police "put a gun to his head" in making a demand for a breathalyzer—which he refused. "They made that law so that people can't just refuse and get away with it," Taman said. He recalled the words of the former East St. Paul police chief, Harry Bakema, who assured him: "He refused a breathalyzer, he's guilty," following the arrest. "Had all of the evidence been shown in this case, we wouldn't be dealing with a joint-recommendation here," Taman said. "I'm very disappointed. I believe this is a slap in the face to Crystal."

Details of the tragedy were revealed in court for the first time. Harvey-Zenk and other officers had gone to a lounge in northwest Winnipeg following the completion of their shift the night before the crash. After the bar closed, Harvey-Zenk and his colleagues went to a fellow officer's house in East St. Paul to continue partying. Harvey-Zenk admitted to having some drinks but he denied being drunk. Harvey-Zenk was coming back to the city alone on Highway 59 about 7:10 a.m. when he failed to brake and smashed into Taman's vehicle. Taman died of massive head injuries. The crash also injured the wife of a Winnipeg police inspector who was in another vehicle.

Special prosecutor Marty Minuk, along with defence lawyer Richard Wolson, made a joint recommendation for a two-year conditional sentence. But chief provincial court Judge Ray Wyant expressed concern about the deal and reserved his verdict. He said there should be a "higher standard of conduct" from those involved in the justice system and also questioned the fact Harvey-Zenk refused a breathalyzer. Both Wolson and Minuk told the judge he must disregard that because the Crown dropped the charge, along with charges of impaired driving causing death and criminal negligence causing death.

Minuk didn't give an explanation as to why the charges were dropped. However, he said there were problems with the case that had forced it to drag out so long. Minuk admitted he also recommended an "independent investigation" be done on the East St. Paul police probe. Outside court, Wolson said he believed

East St. Paul police made the breathalyzer demand on his client without evidentiary basis for it. Wolson said Harvey-Zenk may have fallen asleep just prior to the crash and added that alcohol wasn't a factor. East St. Paul police Chief Norm Carter—whom the Taman family said was the lead investigator—wouldn't comment.

Harvey-Zenk, who joined the Winnipeg Police Service in 2000, had been suspended without pay shortly after the crash. He had since resigned and moved to Brandon with his wife and son. "I've taken someone away who was so loved and cherished and for this I'm profoundly sorry," Harvey-Zenk said in a brief statement in court.

FRIDAY AUGUST 24, 2007

They had been called incompetent, unethical and incapable of handling even the simplest of assignments. One local radio commentator compared them to the gun-toting buffoons portrayed in the popular Police Academy movies. Others had suggested they should hang up their handcuffs for good and make way for a "real" police service such as the RCMP. So it was safe to say the East St. Paul police and administration had seen better days.

"It's been a rough week," admitted Michael Wasylin, the deputy reeve of the municipality that oversees the operations of its police service. "It seems like everyone who's ever got a parking ticket from us is now coming out of the woodwork with a complaint."

The 10-officer East St. Paul detachment—with a history dating back to 1916—now found itself the subject of intense public scrutiny and a pending judicial review that would likely put its future on trial.

Manitoba Justice Minister Dave Chomiak—citing a series of recent controversies and scandals—said the only way to "restore public confidence" was with a thorough review of the force's operations. The icing on the cake was the handling of the Derek Harvey-Zenk investigation.

"We want our residents to have the respect they should for their police department. We've implemented a number of recommendations, policy changes, all for the better," Wasylin said. "But we want to know that our policies make sense, that the people we have in place are the right people and that our officers can be counted on." He said the old-boy's-club mentality that dominated for years was gone, giving way to a fresh perspective.

Police Chief Norm Carter, Reeve Lawrence Morris, Chief Administrative Officer Jerome Mauws and citizen's protection committee member Gerry Jennings, a retired Mountie, were also speaking publicly.

"It's important to know that council has full confidence in Norm and his department," Wasylin said. Wasylin, who works as a defence lawyer, said senior East St. Paul officials were confident in their message: Their police detachment had changed from two years ago. One of the biggest changes, said Wasylin, was the screening process used to hire new members. This became a major issue following an embarrassing revelation in June 2006 that one of their former members, Michael Sandham, had been arrested and charged with murdering eight Bandidos bikers in southern Ontario in April 2006.

Wasylin said what many members of the public forget was that Sandham was fired from the force in

2002 after it was learned he'd been secretly providing security for local biker events. "As soon as we found that out he was gone within a day," Wasylin said. Still, the stench of employing a man who would eventually become a high-ranking biker and get involved in one of the worst mass killings in Canadian history lingered.

Wasylin said another troubling issue for East St. Paul was a sudden rise in Law Enforcement Review Agency complaints against its officers. "We had probably gone about 10 years with maybe one or two complaints, but all of a sudden, in a short period of time, we had like eight or nine," he said. "That indicated to us we had a significant problem." The complaints from members of the community largely involved excessive use of force. Several were settled out of court, a few were dropped and a couple were pending.

Wasylin and his fellow administrators were now pointing the finger of blame squarely at Harry Bakema, a former Winnipeg police officer who took over the East St. Paul detachment in 2004. Bakema was fired in February 2006 following an in-camera meeting of the municipal council. Wasylin said Bakema's actions during his short tenure as chief left them no choice. "He no longer had the confidence of his officers. He certainly didn't have the confidence of the administration," Wasylin said.

The Harvey-Zenk controversy had been quietly brewing behind-the-scenes for nearly 30 months before it bubbled over when reaching court. Wasylin and other community members, including the present police chief, wouldn't disclose what went wrong. But they said Bakema, who was the lead investigator, failed "to follow proper investigative techniques."

"What happened here is inexcusable. For our part in that we feel sorry," Wasylin said.

Bakema fired back later in the day through his lawyer, Hymie Weinstein. He denied any wrongdoing in the Harvey-Zenk case. Weinstein said his client spoke briefly with Harvey-Zenk at the scene of the fatal crash, observed him to be in a "state of shock" but didn't smell any alcohol. He turned Harvey-Zenk over to another East St. Paul officer and remained at the scene for the rest of the day, Weinstein said.

Bakema said he recognized Harvey-Zenk, having worked with him in the North End district of the Winnipeg Police Service prior to working in East St. Paul. However, Weinstein said his client never worked directly or socialized with Harvey-Zenk. He said suggestions from East St. Paul police and administration that Bakema was fired based on his actions in the Harvey-Zenk case were false. "That was a whole different issue," said Weinstein, who didn't want to provide any further details. Bakema was now selling real estate.

Wasylin said it was Carter—then a sergeant in East St. Paul—who first voiced concerns about Bakema's conduct and other problems within the service. He said that alone should give the public confidence that serious changes had been made.

East St. Paul had launched a review of its police department a year ago, with retired RCMP officer Robert Tramley finding evidence of "unprofessional behaviour by officers, poor police practices and use of excessive force." He also discovered examples of some officers downloading pornography onto police computers.

Wasylin also revealed that RCMP were called in to investigate East St. Paul police and their handling of Harvey-Zenk's case the previous year. The Mounties forwarded their finding to an independent lawyer, who ruled that no criminal charges should be laid.

MONDAY AUGUST 27, 2007

The truth was slowly beginning to emerge. And the scandal was starting to grow. Former East St. Paul Police Chief Harry Bakema was now being accused by fellow officers of ordering them in advance not to refer in their notes about Winnipeg police officer Derek Harvey-Zenk's alcohol consumption.

A justice official—speaking to the *Winnipeg Free Press* on the condition of anonymity—shed new light on the increasingly alarming situation. "[The officers] said they were told not to put anything in about the alcohol, to go light on what they saw at the scene. Harry [Bakema] told them what to put in their notes," said the source. "It was because he [Harvey-Zenk] was a city cop." The source said the revelation about Bakema influencing the police notes came on the eve of Harvey-Zenk's preliminary hearing in 2006 from Norm Carter, who took over as East St. Paul chief after Bakema was fired.

The retired RCMP officer who spearheaded a review of the municipal detachment following Bakema's firing was also joining the chorus, calling the controversial plea-bargain with Harvey-Zenk a "travesty." "If there's going to be an inquiry here, [the province] should look at their own department and how they handled this case," said Robert Tramley. He believed the case should have gone straight to trial where the truth about what happened would have come out.

The source said the revelation about Bakema influencing the police notes came on the eve of Harvey-Zenk's preliminary hearing in 2006 from Norm Carter, who took over as East St. Paul chief after Bakema was fired.

Tramley's operational review—which had not been made public—looked at many cases including Harvey-Zenk's and noted that a paramedic at the scene of that crash believed alcohol was involved. "The paramedic noted a strong odour of alcohol from Harvey-Zenk," according to the source.

The source said the case against Harvey-Zenk was in trouble because of the fact Bakema—the lead investigator at the crash scene—didn't make a breathalyzer demand. Harvey-Zenk wasn't brought back to the East St. Paul detachment until at least 45 minutes after the crash. It was there that Carter—then a sergeant—made a breathalyzer demand which Harvey-Zenk refused.

"He observed what he felt were signs of impairment," said the source. "I don't know why [Harvey-Zenk] wouldn't have been exhibiting any signs to Bakema. He certainly was to Norm Carter."

Tramley said he didn't understand why Carter's demand, along with the observations from the paramedic, couldn't have still resulted in a strong impaired case against Harvey-Zenk. It was believed Harvey-Zenk's lawyer was going to fight the case on the grounds Carter had no right to ask for something which Bakema, a superior officer, clearly felt wasn't necessary. Tramley's review had also cited two incidents where Bakema ripped up traffic tickets given out by his members to a Winnipeg police officer and the son of a city cop, the justice source said.

Tramley also took aim at Manitoba justice officials for turning to Minuk as special prosecutor, given his previous history of defending police officers and working closely with Harvey-Zenk's lawyer. "That doesn't smell very good to me," he said.

It didn't smell good to a lot of people.

WEDNESDAY SEPTEMBER 12, 2007

It was music to the ears of the Taman family—and members of the public who thought justice wasn't being served. The judge tasked with sentencing Winnipeg cop Derek Harvey-Zenk was now expressing serious concerns about a controversial plea-bargain. Chief Judge Ray Wyant said he was being left in the dark about important details of the deadly driving case and was seriously considering rejecting a joint-recommendation that would spare Harvey-Zenk a jail term.

Wyant even took the rare step of suggesting the case be reopened to allow evidence to be called. He said there were too many questions—especially as it related to alcohol consumption—which he hoped to have answered as he struggled with a proper punishment for Harvey-Zenk. "The court is being left with a gap as to what occurred at the end of [Harvey-Zenk's] shift until the accident occurred," said Wyant. "There really isn't much information being presented to me." But special prosecutor Marty Minuk quickly turned down the offer without explanation.

Taman's family said they were stunned at the latest developments and blasted Minuk for his handling of the case. Victoria Sveinson, Taman's mother, said they had previously been told the Crown had 33 potential witnesses lined up for trial. "This is a complete cover-up," she said. "It's like there were two defence lawyers on Harvey-Zenk's side," added her husband, Sveinn.

Taman's husband, Robert, said he couldn't believe how hard Wyant had to work to get any information from either lawyer about the facts of the case or the circumstances surrounding the plea bargain. He said Minuk should have jumped at the chance to call evidence when there was nothing to lose and everything to gain.

"I don't understand why he didn't," said Robert, adding the family was not consulted about the decision. "This is all very confusing. If you weren't shaking your head in that courtroom you weren't awake."

Minuk had stated during the sentencing hearing weeks earlier that Wyant could consider the fact Harvey-Zenk consumed an unknown quantity of alcohol in the hours preceding the crash as an aggravating factor. But Harvey-Zenk's lawyer, Richard Wolson, took exception with that fact and said he should have made his objections clear at the initial hearing. He told Wyant he couldn't consider alcohol a factor in any way.

"I'm not meaning to be rude but you have the position of my client and should sentence him accordingly," said Wolson. "If the Crown wants to advance that [alcohol consumption], then prove it." Wolson suggested his client "failed to keep a proper look-out" in causing an "unexplained accident"—a statement that drew audible gasps and groans from Taman's family. Wolson sat down in disgust, saying "I can't make submissions in these conditions." Wyant warned the public gallery to refrain from any more outbursts or they'd have to leave.

After repeated questioning from Wyant, Minuk shed new light on the deal with Harvey-Zenk and admitted there were major problems with the way the East St. Paul police conducted their investigation at the crash site. No specific details were given. Minuk said the botched probe forced him to cut a true "plea bargain" with Harvey-Zenk—a fact Wyant said hadn't been made clear during the initial sentencing hearing. "I'm confused. I've never heard that before. And it is very, very, very, very important," said Wyant, noting judges must give greater emphasis on deals in those types of scenarios.

Minuk said he never meant to imply the Crown had a strong dangerous-driving case against Harvey-Zenk but Wyant, citing passages from the transcript of the previous hearing, said that's exactly what was done. Wyant said his main source of concern with the proposed sentence was the fact Harvey-Zenk was a police officer at the time and should be held to a higher standard because of it. Both Wolson and Minuk claimed a conditional sentence was within the appropriate range for such a crime and filed a casebook with 20 precedents from across Canada in support of their position. Wyant adjourned his verdict, needing more time to think about it.

MONDAY OCTOBER 29, 2007

There was no getting around just how bad this looked. A former Winnipeg police officer spends the night drinking and partying and gets behind the wheel of his car "loaded." Fellow off-duty officers who are with him at the time apply the "thin blue line" in refusing to tell the truth about what they saw. An innocent mother of three is then killed in a crash and the cover-up begins, ending in a watered-down case being presented to the court "wrapped in a tight package." In the words of Chief provincial court Judge Ray Wyant, that was the troubling chain of events to explain what the vast majority of the public believed had occurred in the controversial Derek Harvey-Zenk case.

Moments later, a clearly frustrated Wyant held his nose and grudgingly went along with a plea bargain that spared Harvey-Zenk jail and allowed him to remain free in the community under a two-year conditional sentence. Wyant said the differences between "what we all know happened" and the limited facts presented in court for him to consider "are worlds apart" and made this such a difficult case.

"It's a perfect storm of cynicism and why many feel you are, in the proverbial sense, getting away with murder," he told Harvey-Zenk.

The city's largest courtroom was packed with family and friends of Harvey-Zenk and Taman, along with a large contingent of reporters and other lawyers.

"I've spent countless hours thinking about this case," said Wyant, who told the Taman family he was deeply sorry for their loss. "I wish I could wave a magic wand and turn back time. Instead of a lifetime of hope and happiness, you have a life of pain and anguish."

Wyant said the consumption of alcohol would be a "significant factor" and questioned where the evidence of Harvey-Zenk's colleagues was. "Why did trained police have no relevant information to give? Is it because they weren't paying attention to the actions of [Harvey-Zenk]? Well, that's what we're asked to suspect," he said. "If there were police officers who witnessed Mr. Zenk consuming alcohol, why weren't they called?"

Wyant said judges were under clear instructions from higher courts to give serious consideration to true plea bargains such as the one that apparently existed in this case. But his comments would only increase the public's belief that justice hadn't been served here. Not by a long shot.

The sentencing was finished. But the controversy was far from over. A public inquiry had now been called into the circumstances of the investigation and plea-bargain. Crystal Taman's family said they hoped the true story would finally emerge. "We did want the evidence to come out, so if this is how it's going to happen, we're happy," said Robert Taman.

Tory Leader Hugh McFadyen said the case had eroded public confidence in the justice system. "When situations like this arise, it shakes people's confidence and that confidence can only be restored through an open and transparent process," McFadyen told reporters.

Lawyer Hymie Weinstein, who was representing former East St. Paul police chief Harry Bakema, said he felt the decision to have an inquiry was driven by the media and "some of the comments in the media." "The government responded to that. Sometimes that's a good thing. Sometimes it's not," he said.

DECEMBER 2007

He was a couple hundred kilometres away from the scene of the crime. But Derek Harvey-Zenk remained under a microscope as he served his conditional sentence in his new western Manitoba hometown. Harvey-Zenk had already been subjected to at least 12 curfew checks from police and probation officials in Brandon in the four weeks since he began serving his sentence. Sgt. Rick Semler of the Brandon Police Service said the public should have confidence Harvey-Zenk would be closely monitored to ensure compliance with all terms of his sentence. Harvey-Zenk must be in his home at all times between 8 p.m. and 6 a.m. but was allowed to go to work at a local auto shop.

Winnipeg police had long complained that a lack of resources made it difficult for them to enforce conditional sentences and execute existing warrants in the city. Violators were usually only arrested if found to be committing another crime. "That's one of the advantages we have out here [in Brandon], being a bit smaller, is that we can do these kinds of checks. And we do them," Semler said.

A justice source said the high-profile nature of Harvey-Zenk's case would likely result in plenty of attention, at least initially. Harvey-Zenk appeared to be taking his sentence seriously. Semler said there had been no alleged breaches. Brandon police said there would be no special favours for Harvey-Zenk. "He won't be treated any differently than anyone else," Semler said.

MONDAY OCTOBER 6, 2008

It was a damning indictment of the East St. Paul police—and a long-awaited measure of justice for members of the Taman family. Inquiry commissioner Roger Salhany pulled no punches in issuing his report following several weeks of public hearings. His findings included 14 recommendations aimed at several guilty parties.

"There are a lot of changes that are going to be made in the name of Crystal," Robert Taman said upon reviewing the findings.

Special prosecutor Marty Minuk came under attack, with Salhany questioning both his ability and willingness to accept the controversial plea-bargain that dropped all alcohol-related charges against Derek Harvey-Zenk. "Minuk gave up much on behalf of the people of Manitoba, without receiving anything of value in return," said Salhany. "Moreover, he failed to prepare adequately before resigning himself to the deal he made." He directed Manitoba Justice to reconsider all contracts with independent prosecutors, and use a larger pool of private bar lawyers to act when a case cannot be handled by line prosecutors.

Meanwhile, the inquiry was now going to lead to a new criminal investigation into the actions of former ESP Chief Harry Bakema. "It is clear that Bakema's conduct, indeed his misconduct, had a devastating effect on the ability of a prosecutor to proceed with alcohol-related charges against Zenk," said Salhany. "I am satisfied that Bakema not only falsified his own notes and reports to create a false impression of his own actions, he also prompted a fellow officer to falsify his notes… I am also satisfied that Bakema told [the other officer] not to record what he said about Zenk's condition (that he was 'pissed' or impaired or possibly impaired) or what… the ambulance attendant said."

In another major development, Salhany's findings would officially spell the end of the much-maligned ESP police detachment. Justice Minister Dave Chomiak announced he was disbanding the local force in favour of the RCMP. "It is clear that the investigation of the accident, conducted by the East St. Paul Police Department, was flawed to such an extent that a successful prosecution of was rendered fatal from the time that Bakema...arrived at the scene," said Salhany.

Winnipeg police also came under intense scrutiny. Salhany recommended the province set up a special investigative unit to handle all cases of alleged police wrongdoing, to avoid the perception of conflict that clearly existed in this case. "Police officers who are witnesses to criminal activity are not entitled to be treated with kid gloves simply because they are police officers, as the WPS members were treated in this case," said Salhany. He also took aim at the nearly two dozen police officers who had socialized with Harvey-Zenk in the hours before the crash, first at a Winnipeg restaurant and then later at the home of an officer. He questioned the fact they all claimed to have little recollection of important details from that night.

"I find it difficult to accept that 10 officers in close proximity to one another in [the officer's] kitchen for a couple of hours would be unable to say whether Harvey-Zenk had too much to drink or were unable to comment on Harvey-Zenk's condition to drive home after leaving [the officer's] residence," said Salhany. "If they were unable to do so, the reason probably lies in the fact the officers had a great deal more to drink at [the officer's] residence than they were prepared to admit."

MONDAY APRIL 30, 2012

The finger of blame had been pointed in his direction. Now Harry Bakema would finally have his day in court. An Alberta Crown attorney had been brought in to prosecute Bakema. The former East St. Paul police chief began his trial by pleading not guilty to six criminal charges, including perjury, breach of trust and obstruction of justice.

RCMP Cpl. Chris Blandford, a collision-reconstruction expert, told court he met with Bakema at the scene to discuss what had happened. Blandford said Bakema revealed a police officer had been responsible—and that drunk driving appeared to be the cause.

"He told me [Harvey-Zenk] was impaired; it was an attitude like 'My God, what was he thinking?' He was very disappointed that this had occurred and a member of the Winnipeg Police Service was the offender," said Blandford. Paramedics on the scene of the fatal crash reported smelling alcohol on Harvey-Zenk's breath, according to testimony at the Taman inquiry. But Bakema later testified he didn't believe Harvey-Zenk had been drinking.

Blandford said he shared his disappointment with Bakema as they chatted at the scene. He also credited the East St. Paul police for doing a good job in securing the crash site upon his arrival.

TUESDAY MAY 1, 2012

Was it an innocent conversation—or the sign of something nefarious? Details of a face-to-face chat between Harry Bakema and Derek Harvey-Zenk at the scene of a deadly crash were raising new questions. A pair of witnesses to the tragedy told court how they observed

Bakema and Harvey-Zenk speaking around the same time firefighters were frantically working on the wreckage of Crystal Taman's crumpled car.

"They were having words back and forth. That interaction seemed to go on for a while. I wouldn't say it was a heated conversation," said Garth Shaw. He was driving into Winnipeg for work that morning when Harvey-Zenk flew by him at high speed and smashed into Taman's vehicle. "I would say he was doing at least 80 km/h," said Shaw. He rushed to check on Taman after the crash and realized there was nothing he could do. So he returned to his vehicle to call 911, then watched later as Harvey-Zenk and Bakema walked together to go speak on the side of the road. Shaw said Harvey-Zenk appeared to be walking "slow and deliberate."

Another witness to the crash told a similar story of seeing the two men chatting as she was being checked out for possible injuries in the back of an ambulance. The woman had been driving a car that was hit by Taman's after the initial collision.

TUESDAY MAY 8, 2012

His former police colleague had just been involved in a high-speed crash that left an innocent motorist dead. Nevertheless, Harry Bakema seemed to quickly reject suspicion the off-duty officer may have been impaired despite conflicting reports at the scene.

Ken Graham, a former East St. Paul officer, told court he smelled a strong aroma of booze inside Harvey-Zenk's empty vehicle following the deadly crash, but Bakema didn't agree. "He stuck his head in and said he couldn't smell anything," Graham said.

Bakema had personal contact with Harvey-Zenk at the scene and told Graham "he could not smell any alcohol on him." Graham never dealt with Harvey-Zenk to make his own observations, court was told.

Rolland Fontaine, a paramedic who responded to the crash, previously testified about a "very noticeable" smell of alcohol on Harvey-Zenk. Bakema also told Graham he had worked in the same Winnipeg police district as Harvey-Zenk before Bakema moved to East St. Paul. "He said this is a mess. We have a mother, a wife, who's been killed. He felt bad for the family and bad for the kids. And he said we have a Winnipeg police member who just screwed up his career," Graham said. Bakema told Graham he was going to assign another veteran East St. Paul officer to take over the investigation because he didn't want to create any perception of bias based on his personal history with Harvey-Zenk.

Under cross-examination, Graham said Bakema would not have deliberately sabotaged an investigation. "Harry is not the type of guy to ask someone to change their notes," Graham said. But he described Bakema as having a very poor memory, which seemed to be getting worse around the time of the fatality.

WEDNESDAY MAY 9, 2012

It was perhaps the most explosive piece of evidence yet. Jason Woychuk, a former constable with the East St. Paul police service, told court he was ordered by his boss, Harry Bakema, to exclude details of suspected impairment in his notes about Derek Harvey-Zenk.

Woychuk said a paramedic at the scene indicated that Harvey-Zenk may have been intoxicated at the time of the tragedy. But Bakema ordered him to keep those details out of his report. "I was told not to put that in my notes. I don't recall him giving me a reason why," Woychuk testified. He said Bakema himself indicated that Harvey-Zenk was "impaired, or possibly impaired" as he brought the accused over to his cruiser car and placed him in the backseat.

Woychuk said he was also told by Bakema to write that he was transporting Harvey-Zenk to the ESP police station for the purpose of making a traffic accident report. In reality, he took him back there to be arrested. Woychuk claimed Bakema gave him these instructions in response to Woychuk's concerns they may have breached Harvey-Zenk's Charter rights at the scene by detaining him in a cruiser car without any formal charge or caution. "I felt there was probably a Charter breach," said Woychuk. Woychuk told court how he signed an immunity agreement with RCMP in 2010—only to be arrested months later and threatened with charges including obstruction of justice and perjury. However, no formal charges were ever laid.

Under cross-examination, Woychuk admitted he never observed any signs of impairment on Harvey-Zenk. But he rejected suggestions from defence lawyer Hymie Weinstein that Bakema never commented about possible intoxication or that the paramedic didn't express an opinion about Harvey-Zenk's state of sobriety. "[The paramedic] made one of those motions with his hand tipped to the mouth, like he'd been drinking," said Woychuk. He told court he doesn't believe the investigation was deliberately botched and agreed with a previous statement given to police in which he said there was "maybe a screw-up, but not a cover-up."

THURSDAY MAY 10, 2012

An innocent woman had just died, and yet Harry Bakema was allegedly more concerned about the fate of the off-duty Winnipeg officer responsible for her death. Corrine Scott, a retired superintendent of the Winnipeg Police Service, told court about a puzzling call she received from Bakema immediately after the crash. "Harry was really focused on Derek Harvey-Zenk and not on the lady who lost her life. He was very concerned for Derek Harvey-Zenk's well-being," Scott told court. "I was honestly a bit disappointed in Harry."

Bakema called Scott directly from the crash scene, less than an hour after the deadly incident, to warn her about Harvey-Zenk's involvement in the tragedy. "Harry told me Derek had been drinking, he was at a party and smelled of liquor," said Scott. She began the process of notifying other senior members of Winnipeg police. "I've never experienced an incident before where a member was impaired to the extent of causing this type of accident," she said.

Harvey-Zenk testified earlier in the day and told court he had no memory of the events surrounding the deadly crash. He was asked numerous questions about the specific details of the case—including socializing at a lounge with fellow off-duty officers, partying at one of their homes overnight and then driving his vehicle directly into Taman's. But he claimed to only recall vague flashbacks, such as an arm-wrestling contest at the house party and feeling the brunt of the impact. The rest is a foggy blur, he said.

As for his consumption of alcohol prior to the tragedy?

"I don't have any recollection of that," he said repeatedly. Harvey-Zenk said he also didn't recall ever dealing with Bakema, either at the scene of the crash or at the East St. Paul police station. "I don't really recall being at the police station," he said. "I don't recall ever seeing Harry Bakema at the station."

Harvey-Zenk admitted he previously worked with Bakema in the same Winnipeg police station before Bakema left to pursue the top job in East St. Paul. But he said there was never any personal friendship between them, although he did play in hockey games organized by Bakema.

Winnipeg police patrol Sgt. Cecil Sveinson added to the growing amount of alcohol-related evidence when he repeated testimony he previously gave at the Taman inquiry—that Bakema told him at the scene of the crash Harvey-Zenk was "pissed."

Sveinson, who was cousin of Taman's, went to the crash scene to perform a ceremonial smoke ceremony for the victim. He said Bakema added they had to get Harvey-Zenk "out of there right away."

FRIDAY MAY 11, 2012

He was the police officer left holding the proverbial bag when a high-profile prosecution fell apart. Yet the most senior former member of the East St. Paul police pointed the finger of blame at former chief Harry Bakema for the botched investigation of a deadly car crash. Norm Carter testified as the final Crown witness against Bakema. Carter was a sergeant at the time of the February 2005 incident.

Among Carter's discoveries were a set of "rough notes" from Bakema that hadn't been included in disclosure to special prosecutor Marty Minuk. Carter said he also noted Bakema continued to take witness statements despite the fact he wasn't the lead investigator. "He was chief of police. I didn't question that," said Carter, who was later appointed East St. Paul police chief after Bakema was removed.

Bakema's lawyers tried to pin the blame on Carter, accusing him of making numerous mistakes with the investigation, including failing to get a warrant for a sample of Harvey-Zenk's blood at the request of the prosecutor. "I maintain to this day I did not feel I had the grounds," Carter explained. As well, Carter admitted to an "oversight" in not forwarding a traffic reconstruction report to the Crown upon request. He also admitted to inadvertently writing that Harvey-Zenk refused a "blood demand" in his report, when really it was a "breath demand."

THURSDAY MAY 17, 2012

It had been a compelling legal odyssey that had already cost a woman her life, a Winnipeg police officer his job and a municipal police service its status. Now the only question left to answer was whether the scandal surrounding a fatal car crash would also claim one final victim: the former East St. Paul police chief who headed up the controversial investigation. Harry Bakema sat stone-faced in court as Crown and defence lawyers vigorously debated whether he should be convicted of perjury, obstruction of justice and breach of trust. Provincial court Judge Kelly Moar reserved his decision following a full day of closing arguments.

Both sides presented dramatically different views of Bakema's role in the case. Crown attorney Ashley

Finlayson told court there was no doubt Bakema deliberately overlooked compelling evidence that suggested his former police colleague, Derek Harvey-Zenk, was drunk at the time of the deadly crash. "Harry Bakema took no further meaningful steps to investigate Derek Harvey-Zenk. One can only speculate what might have happened after that," said Finlayson.

Bakema's lawyer, Hymie Weinstein, argued the Crown had failed to prove there was any criminal intent on behalf of his client. He suggested several former police officers who testified at the trial were either mistaken or misleading the truth about what happened. At worst, Bakema was guilty of making unintentional errors, he said. "What was done was not done for any criminal intent," said Weinstein. He argued other East St. Paul officers were also negligent in how they handled the case. Weinstein also pointed to the words of Bakema in a 2010 interview with the RCMP while urging Moar to find him not guilty.

"This was not an intentional cover-up to protect a Winnipeg member. I was not covering up impaired symptoms of Zenk. I did my job. I tried to make sure everyone does their job. I did not botch the investigation intentionally. I wouldn't throw my name away for nobody," Bakema had said.

Weinstein took issue with the testimony of several witnesses, who had painted an ugly picture of Bakema's role in the investigation. The decision was now in the judge's hands.

FRIDAY NOVEMBER 1, 2013

A memorial still sits at the intersection of Lagimodiere Boulevard and the Perimeter Highway, serving as a constant reminder of a horror that unfolded more than eight years ago. Now, the family at the centre of the ongoing legal saga admitted they'd grown tired of fighting for justice after what may be the final chapter played out in a Winnipeg courtroom.

"It's time to move on," a clearly frustrated Robert Taman said outside the downtown courthouse. "We're done." Moments earlier, he had watched Harry Bakema walk free of any criminal wrongdoing for his role in the botched investigation surrounding the death of Taman's wife, Crystal. It was a decision Taman expected. But it didn't make it any easier to stomach. "Let's just say justice takes two steps backwards today," said Taman. "I think when we all look at everything that took place over the last 8 1/2 years, it's pretty clear."

Bakema, now 62, was found not guilty of perjury, obstruction of justice and criminal breach of trust. Provincial court Judge Kelly Moar said there was no doubt Bakema made several terrible decisions that fateful day "which he will have to live with the rest of his life." But he ruled the Crown failed to prove beyond a reasonable doubt Bakema intentionally sabotaged the case.

Taman's said it was "ridiculous" it took Moar 18 months to come up with the verdict. "Everyone should be embarrassed by that amount of time," he said. Now the family planned to focus on the future and hoped nobody else would endure what they had. "When it comes to matters like this, we've learned that what's clear to the general public is sometimes foggy to the people that make the decisions and create our laws," said Taman.

I am a firm believer that every would-be driver should have to sit in at least one sentencing hearing for an impaired driver before they obtain their licence. The raw emotion that is present in every courtroom would impact them in a way that advertising campaigns simply cannot. Because let's face it: The current model is simply not working. Not enough drivers are getting the message. Increased sentences don't seem to be changing behaviour. And there's certainly no shortage of public awareness on the issue.

Yet the tragedies continue to mount. And the roadside memorials—like the one that still exists to this day for Crystal Taman—continue to pile up.

CHAPTER 10

A HEARTLESS ACT

I have covered well over 500 homicides in my career. Sadly, many of the same root causes are often involved. Excessive alcohol abuse. Drugs. Domestic conflict. Gang warfare. All of them are deeply troubling, tragic and senseless. It's so hard to fathom the sudden, violent ending of a human life. But every now and then, a case comes along that chills you to the core. One where it seems the only way to explain what happened is with these two words: Pure evil. This is one of those cases.

TUESDAY FEBRUARY 27, 2007

It was the worst-case scenario that everyone had feared. Roxanne Fernando was dead. The 24-year-old Winnipeg woman—known affectionately known to loved ones as "Apple"—had last been seen nearly two weeks ago. Her mysterious disappearance had triggered plenty of panic among her friends and family members. This was so unusual, so out of character, that something just had to be wrong. And so they had been peppering the Internet with her photo and police contact information by sending out e-mail alerts to hundreds of people asking for assistance. They also contacted local media outlets, linking them to a YouTube video they had created which showed Roxanne's photo over the music of Coldplay's "Fix You."

Winnipeg police had also put out a call for help, hoping to generate some leads, shortly after hearing from the family on February 18th. But nobody could have anticipated where their investigation would take them. A body, quickly identified as Roxanne, had just been found buried in a snowy ditch in the northwest part of the city. Foul play was obvious. She had been brutally beaten, almost beyond recognition.

"Oh no, I can't believe it. That's so cruel," said a stunned Carrie Barroga upon learning of the killing. Barroga worked in the Philippine Canadian Centre of Manitoba and recently met Fernando's sister when she came in to distribute posters seeking information about the missing woman. Fernando and her family had come to Canada from the Philippines in 2003.

"She said she wanted our help and asked to put it up on our bulletin board, which she did," said Barroga. "This is just terrible."

"It's just horrible," Fernando's co-worker at the Radisson Hotel told the *Winnipeg Free Press* following the discovery. "None of us can believe it. She was just one of the nicest, sweetest girls."

Now the focus turned to bringing whoever was responsible for this heinous crime to justice. Police quickly made a series of arrests, charging three young men with first-degree murder. That indicated they believed the killing was a planned, pre-meditated act. Nathanael Mark Plourde, 19, Jose Manuel Toruno, 19, and a 17-year-old youth who couldn't be named were all in custody. For now, police were saying little publicly. They confirmed it wasn't a gang or drug-related killing. They also stated their belief that Roxanne was likely killed within hours of when she was last seen.

The rest of the story would be kept from the public. For now.

TUESDAY OCTOBER 23, 2007
"Guilty." The 17-year-old stood in the prisoner's box and answered directly after the first-degree murder charge was read aloud. It was a surprisingly quick resolution, just a few months following his arrest. And now details of one of Winnipeg's most chilling homicides would be revealed publicly for the first time.

"The circumstances of this crime are extremely aggravating. [The teen killer's] conduct is completely inexplicable," provincial court Judge Marvin Garfinkel said. Roxanne Fernando had been lured to her death as part of an elaborate plan. All because she had refused to have an abortion. The Crown called it a "callous, well-planned execution."

The teen killer—who couldn't be named under the Youth Criminal Justice Act—was given the maximum youth sentence of six years prison and four years of probation. Justice officials had agreed not to seek to have him raised to adult court in exchange for his guilty plea to the most serious charge in the Criminal Code. It was hoped the plea bargain would also give the Crown plenty of leverage in the remaining case against two adult co-accused. Nathanael Mark Plourde, 19, and Jose Manuel Toruno, 19, remained before the courts.

The youth made a quick apology in court to Fernando's family, who sat weeping as Crown attorney Brent Davidson read the facts of the case. "I'm so sorry, even if this apology seems hollow. She deserved much better and this ordeal has been unfair to her. I hope God blesses Roxanne's family," the youth said. Davidson said the man wasn't remorseful when he was overheard in jail following his arrest talking about how he should have "raped" Fernando after her killing. "His moral compass is so out of whack," Davidson said.

Fernando had learned she was pregnant weeks before her death. The father was her boyfriend, Nathanial Plourde. The two met when they worked together at a McDonald's restaurant on Main Street. "She thought this was the man of her dreams," Davidson told court. Fernando was pressured to terminate her pregnancy and initially agreed. She later had a "change of heart" and that set in motion a chilling chain of events, he said. "It would be the fetus that would drive the planned and deliberate killing of Ms. Fernando," Davidson said.

The youth was offered $500 and a 32-inch television to carry out the act. He initially refused, but began participating in the plot, Davidson said. A meeting was set up on February 15—the day after Valentine's Day—in which Fernando had expected to exchange gifts with her boyfriend. She wrapped a box of chocolates and got into a waiting car—unaware that the youth was hiding under a blanket in the back seat, Davidson said. He had also participated in an earlier trip to the store to buy supplies, including leather gloves and rolls of tape. Fernando was driven to Little Mountain Park on the northwestern edge of the city on the guise there was a "surprise" waiting there for her.

While en route, Fernando revealed details of a recent dream. "It was of seeing her own obituary," Davidson told court. "There's a belief she may have unconsciously been aware of the fate that awaited her."

The youth sprung out from under the blanket and began attacking Fernando at the isolated park, along with a second man. Fernando was hit with a wrench up to 20 times, bound with tape and wrapped in a blanket before being stuffed in the trunk of the car. It was thought she was dead. But as the car began driving away, sounds could be heard coming from the rear.

"There was a realization Roxanne Fernando was still alive. They could hear moaning," Davidson said. Panic set in and a third accused was picked up and paid $120 to assist in Fernando's killing. The youth had taken the money out of Fernando's purse as she lay dying in the trunk, Davidson said. Fernando was taken to a remote area near Mollard Road and Ritchie Street in northwest Winnipeg and repeatedly beaten with a broken hockey stick until she was obviously dead.

"The beating was long lasting and extreme," Davidson said. Her body was then buried in a snow ditch. Fernando's killers went to McDonald's for a bite to eat, stopped at Safeway for some cleaning supplies for the vehicle and then text-messaged at least one of Fernando's friends—using her cellphone—indicating all was well. "This was sheer callousness," Davidson said.

Her body was discovered several days later.

Perhaps anticipating some public blowback, Davidson went to great pains why his office agreed not to seek an adult sentence against the teen killer. "This [deal] is not the result of any deficiencies in the Crown's case," he said. Instead, Davidson took aim at the much-maligned Youth Criminal Justice Act that he said made it nearly impossible to force killers—such as Fernando's—to be raised to adult court. "Only the imposition of the Youth Criminal Justice Act, with all its deficiencies, is saving this youth from a life sentence with no chance of parole for a very long time," Davidson said. As an adult, he would have been given an automatic life sentence with no chance of parole for 25 years. As a youth, he would be released from custody before he turned 24.

A court-ordered pre-sentence report found the teen a "low-risk" to re-offend despite committing one of the most chilling murders in recent Winnipeg history. That's because he had no prior record, had strong family and community supports and the fact he'd finished high school and has been employed. Davidson said that meant this case just wasn't "exceptional enough to take it out of the youth range" despite aggravating factors surrounding Fernando's slaying.

Federal Conservative Justice Minister Rob Nicholson had recently announced plans to strengthen the YCJA by putting greater focus on "deterrence and denunciation" as sentencing principles. Since the act became law in April 2003, rehabilitation had been the main focus. That had resulted in numerous controversial sentences—including one day in jail for a Winnipeg teen who killed a man with a pool ball wrapped in a sock. Changes were on the way. But they were too late to have any impact on this heartless killer.

They had struggled to get to Canada to start a new life for themselves. Now one of them was dead, the victim of a sadistic plot. Elisa Fernando conveyed her feelings in an emotional victim impact statement presented in court:

"My life will never be the same again. I feel as if I have died with her, too. One will never know until it happens to them. I have gone through a tough life, being poor, and raised five children on my own. I didn't have a good life until my daughter sponsored me and "Apple" to live with her here in Canada. I thought it would be the beginning of a new and good life, and not the end of it.

I didn't have the chance to say goodbye. She looked so happy when she left the house that night, all dolled up and carrying a Valentine present that we wrapped together. I jokingly asked if I can have one of the presents she had.

I thought that was going to be one of the happiest days of my daughter's life. She even asked me to look out the window to see if I could see the car that was waiting for her outside. I said I could only see the headlights. I didn't know that would be the last time I was going to see and talk to my daughter.

I feel so betrayed by this and regret that I let her go out that night. She had no idea she was in danger. I have so much regret and always the question of "What if?" My feelings of hurting are beyond imagination. I could write and speak about being hurt, but it will never end."

Roxanne's sister, Ana Maria Deluz, also shared her grief publicly:

"I remember when she was born. It was a very special date because I was celebrating my birthday. I was with my aunt, cousins and brothers celebrating when I found out my mom had given birth to a healthy baby girl.

It made by birthday extra special because I found out I had a baby sister. I will never, ever forget that day because that's how my life of being a big sister began.

I became a second mother to her. I took her under my wing, took care of her from the very beginning, since our mother had to work a lot. I have so many loving memories of her, from registering her first grade of school until graduating from elementary. I watched her grow up and that became part of my life and now that she's gone, it's like losing a part of myself.

I miss her so much that I'm still hoping one day she'll walk through the door with a big beautiful smile on her face. She was the kind of person that would brighten up the house, always dancing and singing.

She was a very caring person, too, always ready to lend a helping hand to those she loved, especially her family back home who she supported financially.

There are absolutely no words to describe how it feels when someone you truly love is unjustly taken away in an instant. I am not who I used to be and probably never will be. There is a big hole in my heart, and my family's heart.

I am now left with only memories of my sister and no words to adequately describe the depths of my sorrow. I not only lost a sister, but an irreplaceable friend. We knew each other like no one else does, and had an understanding that only sisters can provide each other.

I have this feeling of regret because I brought her to Canada. I remember crying in front of a judge for permission for her to be able to live here so that she could have a better life. Now I am crying in front of a judge because her life was taken."

To many people, there were actually two homicide victims that night. But the death of Fernando's unborn baby didn't result in an additional murder charge because Canadian law, unlike the United States and other countries, doesn't recognize a fetus as a living being. This triggered plenty of public outrage. From local radio talk-shows to Letters to the Editor, it was clearly many were upset.

"The brutal murder of Roxanne Fernando and her unborn child continues the violence directed toward pregnant women who refuse to abort their babies" said Maria Slykerman, president of Campaign Life Coalition Manitoba. "Statistics show that many women are coerced into having abortions by boyfriends or husbands. These same women, who have submitted to the threats and bullying of their baby's father, subsequently seek the help of grief counsellors to comfort them in the guilt and sadness that overcomes them."

Slykerman called for legislative changes. "The Canadian Criminal Code must be revised to recognize the obvious fact that in cases where the mother is murdered, charges must also be laid in the death of the child who is equally worthy of recognition as a human being," she said.

FRIDAY OCTOBER 9, 2009
They had stalled and delayed as long as possible, knowing full well justice officials had a rock-solid case against them. And just as their long-awaited jury trial was set to begin, Roxanne Fernando's two adult killers finally accepted their fate.

Nathanael Mark Plourde took the unusual step of pleading guilty to first-degree murder, earning himself a mandatory life sentence with no chance of parole for at least 25 years. Few ever plead guilty to this charge because the penalty was automatic, with no room for judicial discretion. "He didn't want to put the victim's family through any more of an ordeal," defence lawyer Roberta Campbell said outside court.

Jose Manuel Toruno did manage to get the Crown to back down, as he pleaded guilty to a reduced charge of second-degree murder. He was given a mandatory life sentence with no chance of parole for at least 15 years.

"This murder was coldly conceived and deliberately executed," said Queen's Bench Justice Glenn Joyal upon hearing the facts. That included Crown attorney Mark Kantor saying how the men "buried her alive." "She was subjected to a prolonged, horrific suffering. [The killers] had a callous disregard for human life," Kantor said.

A copy of the men's police interview was tendered as evidence at the sentencing hearing. In it, Plourde claims he was driven to kill Roxanne because she ignored his repeated attempts to sever their relationship. "I didn't want to be part of her life, but she didn't take no for an answer," Plourde told Winnipeg police homicide detectives in the February 2007 videotaped confession. "She was crazy about me. She had an obsession with me. I just couldn't take it. Like, I'm 19. I can't handle a 24-year-old."

Plourde said he was facing additional pressure after learning Fernando was pregnant, a claim he initially thought was a ruse to keep them together following a brief romance that began while working together at McDonald's. "In my fears, she'll come back in nine months with a kid or something," he said. "I don't understand why she liked me because I didn't like her. I'm just a young punk. I showed no interest in her."

Police repeatedly pressured Plourde to tell them what happened to Fernando and lead them to her body. He initially denied involvement, even volunteering to take a polygraph test, but broke down following hours of questioning. "I've been living a lie," he said. "I thought she was crazy. But in the end, I ended up being crazy."

Elisa Fernando had confronted her daughter's youngest killer two years earlier in court. Now she had more words to share with the other two responsible for Roxanne's death. "When a husband loses his wife or when a wife loses her husband we call them widows. When a child loses his parents we say they are orphans. But when a mother loses a child there is nothing because no word in this life can possibly define such loss and pain. I feel so betrayed by this and regret that I let her go out that night. She had no idea she was in danger. I have so much regret and always the question of 'what if'?'. My feelings of hurting are beyond imagination. I could write and speak about being hurt but it will never end."

Plourde was in tears as he spoke to Fernando's family. "I'm sorry to you, Roxanne's mother and father, who lost a daughter. I'm sorry to you, Roxanne's siblings, who lost a sister. I regret everything I did and take full responsibility for my actions," he said.

Toruno's father was a local minister who wrote a letter read aloud by defence lawyer Greg Brodsky. The man said he was praying for his son, Fernando and her family. "I always teach my children to respect others, as the Bible instructs. Jose is not a bad kid. He made a mistake. Everybody does," he said. "I've been waiting a long time for this day to come so I can apologize to you," Toruno said. "I can't imagine how you feel. I hope that one day you take the time to forgive me. These words are coming from my heart. God bless you."

Joyal questioned the sincerity of the two killers given the way they acted after the slaying. He noted Toruno even took the chocolates and stuffed animal that Fernando had brought for Plourde and gave them to his girlfriend.

"You knew when you left her that she was still alive. You knew these were the gifts of a woman you had just helped murder," Joyal said.

Rod Bruinooge, MP for Winnipeg South, eventually took up the cause and proposed private member's Bill C-510, which was nicknamed "Roxanne's Law." He wanted to amend the Criminal Code to make it a separate offence to coerce a woman into an abortion. The hope, Bruinooge said, would be to stop men from the type of pressure that was applied to Roxanne in the days before she was killed. Bruinooge was adamant the proposed legislation had nothing to do with trying to outlaw abortion. "No pregnant woman should ever have to choose between protecting herself and protecting her baby," he said.

Parliament voted down the bill in December 2010 by a count of 178 to 87. Among the more notable "No" votes were Prime Minister Stephen Harper and many prominent cabinet ministers. In fact, many Conservatives voted against it, as did all NDP and Bloc members. "The prime minister has always said he wouldn't support a bill that reopens the abortion debate," Harper spokesman Andrew MacDougall told reporters.

"The focus of this bill was always pregnant women facing domestic abuse," Bruinooge said at the time. He vowed to continue working on the issue, although no similar legislation has since been tabled.

Meanwhile, Roxanne's youth killer—now an adult—is back in the community after serving his full prison term. He still can't be named under provisions of the YCJA. Plourde and Toruno, of course, are still years away from even having a shot at release.

CHAPTER 11

LEGAL LOTTO

It's often said that money is the root of all evil. I definitely saw the ugly side of wealth while covering a scandal over a winning lottery ticket. This case had it all: Compelling characters, allegations of fraud and deceit, surprise witnesses, conflicting stories, betrayal, backstabbing and plenty of riveting courtroom theatre. Many folks were quick to pick sides, triggering intense debate over who was in the right. It's one of the few civil court trials I've ever covered. But it remains one of the most memorable cases in local legal history.

MONDAY MARCH 20, 2000

They were Manitoba's newest multi-millionaires. And they were, somewhat reluctantly, emerging from a self-imposed bubble to face the public. After sitting on their winning ticket for the past week, Larry and Helen Tessier were now ready to come forward to claim their $11.4 million jackpot—the largest ever handed out in provincial history.

The Winnipeg couple was still in shock as they were introduced by provincial lottery officials at a news conference. Larry, a maintenance worker at Winnipeg Transit, explained how he didn't initially believe his wife of nearly 25 years when she checked their Lotto 6/49 numbers in the paper at work and called to say they'd won. Helen, who was employed with Manitoba Public Insurance, admitted she had to look a few times to ensure her eyes weren't playing tricks on her.

"The last few days we haven't ate or slept," Larry told a throng of media. He explained how he had purchased the Quick Pick ticket when he stopped to gas up at a Shell Select service station on Notre Dame Avenue. After verifying the numbers were the right ones and that they were the only winners, the couple gathered their thoughts and some clothes and left town to consider their future.

It was overwhelming, the realization that they suddenly had more money than they could have ever imagined. "It's a state of unbelief that you can only experience if you go through this," said Larry, 50. He was asked how it might impact their lives and their relationship. He cracked a joke about sleeping with one eye on each other before they finally cashed in the ticket. One decision had already been made: Neither wanted to move from their Transcona home. There were just too many memories. A few purchases were already spoken for, namely some much needed appliances for their kitchen. The rest would be sorted out later. For now, they were basking in the glory, trying to maintain a sense of normalcy in a situation that was anything but.

MONDAY NOVEMBER 6, 2000

It was a legal bombshell the likes of which had never been seen before. Court documents filed in Manitoba Court of Queen's Bench had the downtown courthouse buzzing. And it wasn't long before they made their way to the front page of the *Winnipeg Free Press*. Corazon Macatula, a Filipino home-care worker who lived in the city's north end, was claiming to be the rightful owner of half the $11.4 million Lotto 6/49 prize handed out eight months earlier.

In her affidavit, Macatula said Larry and Helen Tessier had lied to lottery officials—and the general public—about the nature of their high-profile win. She claimed she was the one who actually bought the winning ticket from a Notre Dame Avenue gas station, as part of an ongoing deal she had with an elderly client, Jean Tessier.

The family's lawyer immediately fired back, denying the allegations and vowing to file a statement of defence. "From their perspective this is just sad. But they have no choice but to defend it," said John Scurfield.

According to Macatula, she and Jean Tessier had been buying 6/49 tickets together since 1998 and had a standing, oral agreement to split any winnings. They even shared a handful of $10 winning tickets only weeks before the big one, and had joked that their luck appeared to be changing for the better, the lawsuit claimed. However, Macatula said she had been completely shut out of the winning prize, as the Tessier family promptly claimed it as their own. According to the lawsuit, Larry and Helen had split the winnings with their three sons, his two brothers and his mother, Jean. All family members were named in the lawsuit.

"Obviously, we have two very different stories here. Somebody is not telling the truth," said lawyer Bill Olson, who was acting on behalf of Macatula. He said his client was not seeking publicity and simply wanted "what she believes is hers"—exactly $5,700,951.85.

Olson said Macatula did not have any written agreement with her elderly client but relied on trust. Macatula would buy $5 worth of tickets every Wednesday and Friday, and Tessier would pay her $2.50 every time she would deliver the tickets to her, he said. Olson said he tried to quietly resolve the case with the Tessiers' lawyer over the last few months with no success. Now the stage was set for what promised to be a juicy legal showdown.

SPRING 2001

It appeared there was no resolution in sight. Six months after the lawsuit was filed, both sides remained in legal limbo. And it was clear there were two vastly different stories being presented.

In the family's statement of defence, they admitted to deceiving lottery officials about the true nature of the win. And they confessed it was Macatula who delivered the winning ticket to Jean Tessier. The couple claimed Jean Tessier, who had a heart condition and was in poor health, wanted to avoid the publicity of a major lotto win and agreed to have her son and daughter-in-law in the limelight. "In order to avoid the stress of the media attention which would accompany such a sizable purse and to protect the health of Jean Tessier, it was agreed between Jean and Helen and Larry that they would represent to Manitoba Lotteries Corporation and the media that they were the sole holders on the ticket," their documents stated.

However, the family said Jean Tessier paid for the ticket in full and had no existing lottery arrangement with Macatula. Larry Tessier claimed it was he who had an ongoing lotto partnership with his mother for more than a decade, and all winnings should stay in the family. The couple said they had "no direct knowledge who originally bought the ticket or where it was purchased."

Both sides had now agreed to an "expedited" trial to deal with the key issue of whether an agreement was in place for Macatula and Jean Tessier to split any lottery winnings. Lawyers cited the elderly woman's poor health and age as factors for having a trial as soon as possible.

THURSDAY AUGUST 16, 2001

It had mystery. It had intrigue. And now it had a surprise witness coming forward with a potentially explosive piece of evidence. Mark Singh, an employee at the Avenue Meat Market on Selkirk Avenue, had just provided lawyers involved in the battle over an $11.4-million lottery ticket with key information. He first contacted the *Winnipeg Free Press*, then repeated his claims to lawyers during an audiotaped interview.

Singh was then expected to testify at trial that, until he emerged, was shaping up as one family's word against another's, with no independent witnesses to corroborate either version. "At first, I was a little hesitant to get involved. But I think [Macatula] is getting a raw deal, and it's not right," Singh said.

Singh said he got to know Jean Tessier while delivering groceries to her home, located across the street from the Selkirk Avenue store, between 1996 and 1999. On several occasions, the senior would talk about the wonderful care she was receiving from Macatula, according to Singh. "She would say how she was so good to her, and how they even bought lottery tickets together. She said if they ever won they would split the money in half," Singh said.

He said he was shocked to learn the elderly woman had hit the jackpot, with her family claiming the ticket was theirs alone. "A promise is a promise, and if they make an agreement, they should have to stick to it," Singh said. Singh said he was an independent witness and had nothing to gain by coming forward. He said he only knew Macatula from meeting her once or twice in Jean Tessier's apartment but felt bad for her and her family.

MONDAY NOVEMBER 26, 2001

It was one of the largest civil cases involving individuals ever heard in Manitoba. Not surprisingly, the first day resulted in a standing-room-only crowd of friends and families of both parties, along with other lawyers and courtroom observers. "This is a fascinating case. Maybe we can get a larger courtroom and invite the law school down," cracked Court of Queen's Bench Justice Sid Schwartz.

The first witness was no surprise. Corazon Macatula took the stand to plead her case and told of a special relationship she developed with Jean Tessier while tending to the elderly woman's numerous physical needs since 1997. "We were very close, like mother and daughter. Sometimes she called me daughter, good friend, partner, honey," said Macatula, 49. Macatula said she and her family even visited Tessier in hospital after the senior suffered a heart attack in 1999, and the elderly woman requested she be reassigned to her care following her return home.

She also documented a history of financial struggles that forced her to continue holding down two jobs while the Tessier family enjoyed $5.7 million in lottery winnings she claimed they stole from her. She described being "shocked and upset" when Jean Tessier cut her out of a 50-per-cent share.

Macatula claimed she'd never bought a lottery ticket in her life until Jean Tessier asked her to become partners for the twice-per-week draws, with each paying for half the Quick Pick selections. Macatula said she purchased the tickets every week, then delivered them to Tessier to check the numbers. When her own mother became seriously ill in the Philippines in early 2000, Tessier told her to keep their fingers crossed, she said. "She told me we had to continue buying the lotto, because who knows, we might be lucky and I could go home," said Macatula.

Only weeks later, Macatula said Tessier phoned her to claim they had struck it rich. The elderly woman claimed her son, Larry, had told her to keep quiet but promised to call her back within a day with more details, she said. "I was really so excited," said Macatula.

The phone call never came, and Macatula said the next thing she saw was Larry and his wife, Helen, on television newscasts speaking to a throng of media about their lucky win. "She is simply being opportunistic and taking advantage of the fact she can demonstrate she was [Jean Tessier's] legs, to coin the vernacular," the Tessier's lawyer, John Scurfield, said in his opening statement.

Macatula was given a written reprimand by her employers after her lawsuit revealed she had purchased lottery tickets for one of her elderly clients, which is a breach of conflict-of-interest guidelines she claimed to be ignorant of, the court heard.

Macatula, who was born and raised in the Philippines, came to Canada in 1990 along with her four-year-old son to join up with her husband, Nilo, who had immigrated four years earlier. With a reasonable grasp of the English language—courtesy of her elementary school training—Macatula immediately sought to upgrade her education. She had completed high school and a midwifery course back home, and worked a variety of jobs, including secretarial and garment factory work. At Red River College, she completed a six-month home-care course. She also took some computer training, followed by a six month geriatric nursing assistant's course at Convalescent Home. She landed casual employment with Manitoba Health in 1991. A daughter was born in 1995, and her husband took a night job as an auditor at a local hotel to help the family make ends meet.

Macatula also took on a second job, working every weekend at Convalescent Home. Now, with a husband and two children, aged 14 and 6, Macatula was still working 55 hours a week to make ends meet. Lawyer John Scurfield suggested she needed money fast so she could afford a trip to the Philippines to visit her ailing mother, but Macatula said she was only seeking what was rightfully hers. Scurfield asked why she didn't pursue the family more vigorously on her own or call local media outlets who were reporting on the Tessier's win.

"For over $5 million, why wouldn't you call her?" he asked.

"I trusted her. But I'm still waiting," said Macatula.

TUESDAY NOVEMBER 27, 2001

They were strong words coming from a former friend of lottery winner Jean Tessier. But Lidia Shewchuk was adamant that the elderly woman had "lied to everybody" by claiming the lucky ticket belonged exclusively to her family and shutting her home-care worker out of the winnings. Shewchuk told a packed court she believed Corazon Macatula had a right to half of the Lotto 6/49 jackpot. Her claims were backed by several other witnesses who testified about their knowledge of a deal between Macatula and her elderly client to purchase lottery tickets and divide the winnings.

Shewchuk cleaned Jean Tessier's apartment between 1997 and 1999 while working as her home support worker. She said Tessier tried to get her involved in a lottery partnership. "She said 'Lidia, come play with me, 6/49.' She said 'you give a dollar, I'll give a dollar, we'll play and split winnings.' I said 'I don't want to play Jean, I'm not a lucky woman,'" said Shewchuk.

She said she was initially thrilled when she saw Tessier's son Larry and his wife Helen claim the big prize. "I love these people, and I was so happy, like my own son had won the ticket. I said maybe this was a gift from God," Shewchuk told court, adding the Tessiers became like a second family to her during her years of employment.

Shewchuk said Jean Tessier was stunned after learning Macatula was taking legal action against her family on the grounds she owned half the ticket under an oral agreement between the two.

"She told me 'honest to God, this ticket was bought by my son,'" said Shewchuk.

Shewchuk believed the family and thought poorly of Macatula until reading a newspaper story earlier this year in which they admitted, in court documents, that they didn't purchase the winning ticket, but deliberately misled the public and Manitoba Lotteries.

"I like when people respect each other, not when they cheat and lie. She lied to me. She lied to everybody," said Shewchuk. "I wish I could be here as a witness for Mrs. Tessier today, because she was my friend. But there's something fishy to this situation."

Shewchuk rejected claims from Tessier's lawyer, John Scurfield, that she was holding a grudge against her former friend because Tessier stopped taking her phone calls after her lottery win and never offered her money.

Jean Tessier's former grocery delivery man—who had first come forward to the *Free Press* earlier in the year—also testified how the elderly woman told him about her lottery ticket arrangement with Macatula. Mark Singh said Tessier told him she and Macatula "were such good friends, if we ever win we'll split it half."

Scurfield questioned his motives for staying silent so long and even had a private investigator dig into his past, which included allegations of theft from a Main Street grocery store he once worked at.

"You're on Cora's side, aren't you?" asked Scurfield.

"I just want the truth to come out," Singh said.

A former co-worker of Larry Tessier at Winnipeg Transit also took the stand, claiming he once spoke of his mother's deal with Macatula to purchase lottery tickets. "One time we were talking and he wondered if the home-care worker was going to buy the ticket [for an upcoming draw]," said Brian Brouillette, who worked as a mechanic but was on sick leave after recently suffering a heart attack. "He mentioned they would share if they ever got any winning."

Brouillette said he congratulated Larry Tessier after his mother learned she'd won the jackpot— but said his co-worker never mentioned having any stake in the ticket.

WEDNESDAY NOVEMBER 28, 2001

Jean Tessier was on the proverbial hot seat. The elderly woman took the witness stand, repeatedly denying a deal with Corazon Macatula to buy lottery tickets together and split winnings, despite accusations to the contrary and intense cross-examination from Macatula's lawyer. The senior also rejected earlier testimony from several witnesses who claimed she wasn't being truthful. "I am not too happy over this. It's not true," said Tessier, who was in poor health and confined to a wheelchair.

With one of her sons, a paramedic, at her side in court to monitor her high blood pressure, Tessier said she no longer liked Macatula, a woman she once considered a "good friend." "I am still mad at her for what she has done to me," she said. In fact, Tessier said Macatula immediately asked for a handout when she told her she and her son Larry had won the lottery three days after their numbers came up. "I said 'Cora, Larry and I won the big pot'. She said 'mother, do I get a million?' I said 'I don't think so, I have lots of children,'" said Tessier.

At one point, Tessier was asked by Macatula's lawyer why she didn't tell Macatula about her lottery win the first time she saw her, which was only hours after she checked her numbers in the newspaper and found a match. "We didn't know at the time who won, Cora or us," she replied.

Following a brief pause, Tessier explained she wasn't sure if the winner was a ticket bought by Macatula or another ticket bought by her son, Larry. She admitted her son was occasionally unable to buy the ticket for an upcoming draw so she would ask Macatula to pick it up for her. "I told her I didn't want to her to go out of her way, but she used to tell me 'Jean, don't worry, I'll get you the ticket, my husband and I play Lotto 6/49,'" said Tessier.

Another former Winnipeg Transit employee, Allan Lescoe, told court he overheard Larry Tessier tell his mother "don't tell Cora" when she informed him at work they'd won the lottery. But Jean Tessier insisted she had no such conversation with her son.

Macatula's lawyer, Bill Olson, took Tessier to task for several inconsistencies in her testimony in comparison with statements she provided lawyers months earlier during a pre-trial examination. Tessier previously told lawyers she didn't know Macatula very well. But while on the stand, she claimed they were once very close. She previously told lawyers that Macatula never referred to her as "mother." On the stand, she admitted she did. Tessier said the erroneous testimony in the past was caused by her intense anger at the time for Macatula.

THURSDAY NOVEMBER 29, 2001

Larry and Helen Tessier were about to face the music. And the pair started with explaining their web of lies—admitting they deceived the public and lottery officials, but insisting there were no sinister motives. "I had no reason to hide anything. I said things just to protect my mother," Larry Tessier told court.

He repeatedly faltered under intense cross-examination, often contradicting previous testimony. He responded with "I don't recall" and "it's possible" to many questions, prompting Queen's Bench Justice Sid Schwartz to level a warning at the new multimillionaire: "If he asks you a question, you are bound to give an answer. Sliding off the question is not appropriate. It makes me think you don't want to answer the question."

Larry Tessier also changed his testimony on when he realized the winning ticket wasn't one he'd purchased, how he planned to split his winnings, how he learned from his mother they'd won and what was said in the conversation. Later in the day, lawyer Bill Olson asked Helen Tessier if the couple ever considered telling the truth at their news conference and simply asking the media to leave Jean Tessier out of the spotlight.

"No," she said flatly, adding they didn't believe the media would have listened. "It was an awful circus. We were terrified. There's no way Larry's mom could have come forward as part owner of that ticket," she said. Helen Tessier admitted she invented several things, including references to finding the winning ticket lying around their home. Larry Tessier earlier told the public he bought the ticket from a Notre Dame

Avenue gas station, but he now admitted he learned the ticket was purchased at the gas station only when a lotteries official mentioned it to him minutes before the news conference began.

Larry Tessier said he'd played Lotto 6/49 with his mother since his father died in 1990. They tried to buy two $5 tickets for every Wednesday and Saturday draw, with Larry usually picking up the tickets and giving them to his mother to check, he told court. "It gives her something to do in the morning, I tried to keep her occupied and she enjoys checking the numbers," he said. "We had a long-standing agreement that if we ever won, we'd share with our families." Helen Tessier said she saw her husband and mother-in-law playing the lottery together "many, many, many times."

Larry Tessier said he knew Macatula was asked by his mother to pick up tickets on "five or six" occasions when he couldn't, but said Macatula had no joint financial interest in the tickets. He denied ever telling his former co-workers at Winnipeg Transit that Macatula and his mother played the lottery together, as some of them testified earlier in the week

"Why would I say, 'Never tell Cora?'" he asked Olson.

"It's a good question," the lawyer replied.

MONDAY DECEMBER 10, 2001

The hotly contested Lotto 6/49 trial ended with stinging accusations as lawyers on both sides of the dispute took turns pleading their case. Nearly seven hours of intense closing arguments left Queen's Bench Justice Sid Schwartz offering his own two cents on the testimony he'd heard throughout the week-long case. "Both parties have given evidence which isn't substantiated, and I don't believe both parties have been totally candid with me," said Schwarz. He reserved his verdict, saying he hoped to have it ready in a few months. He said the complex case boiled down to a simple issue that he must decide—who was telling the $11.4-million lie? "One of these two have to be correct. I'm inclined to the view that neither of them is, but that doesn't help solve the case," Schwartz said at the conclusion of closing arguments.

Macatula's lawyer, Bill Olson, said the evidence was clear the Tessiers had robbed his client of her share of the winnings. "Oh what a tangled web we weave, when first we practice to deceive," said Olson, quoting Sir Walter Scott in describing the actions of the Tessier family. "In many ways this is a troubling case, in that it shows what effect money may have on people. The [Tessier family] commenced weaving, and eventually got so tangled in their web," he said. "It is discomforting to see how comfortable Larry and Helen Tessier were in telling these lies."

He described the entire Tessier clan as "unreliable and untruthful" and said their testimony should be disregarded. "There is powerful evidence of convenient vagueness or denial. The Tessiers are all over the map. There is no internal harmony. That's what happens when one weaves a web," said Olson. He cited testimony from several witnesses who supported Macatula's claim to have regularly bought lottery tickets with Jean Tessier. "These are people with a sense of justice and morality, who are prepared to come forward and indicated what they know, even though there's nothing in it for them other than having their integrity or motives questioned," said Olson.

The Tessier's lawyer, John Scurfield, wasn't as kind. He called the witnesses who supported Macatula as a "team" and said they had more sinister motives for coming forward with false stories, such as jealousy and spite. He described Macatula as a "calculating type of person who's capable of tailoring her evidence" for her own personal gain and noted she waited eight months after the Tessiers claimed the lottery prize before filing a lawsuit. "There was a struggle in the conscious, ultimately forming a plan and then giving in to greed," said Scurfield. "Her actions are not consistent with someone who believes they were cheated out of $5.7-million, but more consistent with someone planning how to exploit that money. It is a tangled web, but her tangles are the material ones."

He said Macatula made no concerted efforts to contact the Tessier family in the days following the lottery win and simply went about her normal routine, which included working seven days a week at two jobs. He described as "corrupt and dishonest" the grocery store deliveryman, Mark Singh, who said he'd overheard Tessier mentioning her partnership with Macatula. And he said several of Larry Tessier's former co-workers who came forward had an axe to grind with him.

So many alleged agendas. So many questions. And one excruciating wait for everyone involved.

THURSDAY MARCH 28, 2002

The verdict was in. There would be no glass slipper for Corazon Macatula. A sombre-looking Macatula sat with her head bowed as Queen's Bench Justice Sid Schwartz ruled against her claim to have a verbal lottery agreement with the Tessier family.

Just metres to her left, an ecstatic Helen Tessier jumped out of her seat and embraced her husband, Larry, and the rest of their family. "They can't bash us anymore," she said, tears streaming down her face. The family refused to comment on the decision, which allowed them to keep the entire prize.

Macatula's lawyer, Bill Olson, said they would likely appeal the decision. "Cora is very unhappy. They're just devastated. It's our view this is an unfair judgment," Olson said.

Macatula left court without speaking publicly, returning to the small inner-city home she shared with her husband and two children. For her, the decision meant it was back to her old life: Two jobs as a home-care worker and nurse's aide, which took on even greater importance because her husband, Nilo, was recently laid off as a night auditor with a local hotel. To make matters worse, Schwartz ordered Macatula to pay the Tessiers' legal fees. The amount, which had yet to be worked out, would likely be several thousand dollars, said Olson.

When reached at home later in the day, Nilo Macatula said he and his wife were very upset about the ruling. "It's been very hard," said Macatula. "But we've had a lot of support from our family and from the community."

The Tessiers' lawyer, John Scurfield, said the family's joy of winning had been tempered by the damage done to their reputation and their portrayal by the public as the villains in this so-called fairy tale. "There have been all sorts of spins put on this story by the media and the public. This seemed to be their Cinderella story," he said outside court. "But anyone who looked at all the inconsistencies in this case was bound to conclude the same way as Justice Schwartz."

He said the ruling was sweet vindication for the family, despite not-so-flattering remarks from Schwartz about the way they've handled their newfound riches. "This is the end of a nightmare. It is finally a satisfying moment. They stood up for what they believed was right," said Scurfield. "When you win $11.4-million, you're subjected to all sorts of claims. This was motivated by [Macatula's] attempts to get her five minutes of fame."

The case came down to an issue of credibility and believability, with the onus on Macatula to show proof of a verbal lottery agreement between herself and Jean Tessier. Schwartz said she failed to meet that test. "I prefer the evidence of Jean Tessier in this claim. I reject the evidence of Corazon Macatula and find she had no interest in this winning ticket," he said.

Schwartz said he sympathized with Macatula but couldn't base his ruling on emotion. "Cora's circumstances likely raised for many people a lot of sympathy, but there's no power in the court to distribute the prize according to sympathy, need or human impulse," said Schwartz. "There is no second prize in this trial."

In his decision, Schwartz told the Tessier family there was "no excuse" for lying to the public, and to lottery officials, about their win. Schwartz called Larry Tessier's conduct "dishonest and disreputable." He admitted the popular decision would have been to cut Macatula into the winnings, but said there was no basis in law to do so. "It's not my duty to punish a person who has lied under oath by denying him or his family what is rightfully theirs," he said. "For those who would like to see the court punish Larry and his family and give Cora part of the winnings, that would not be an appropriate thing to do."

He cited a series of inconsistencies in Macatula's evidence, including a sworn deposition she made after filing the lawsuit in which she claimed no knowledge of what a Quick Pick ticket was. She changed her answer months later, but Schwartz said the damage was already done. He also agreed with Scurfield that she had financial motive for making the lottery claim, and questioned why she took so long to file a lawsuit against the Tessiers—about eight months—after allegedly being shut out. Schwartz also dismissed evidence from several so-called independent witnesses who came forward to testify on Macatula's behalf.

Schwartz agreed the Tessiers' evidence also raised questions and concerns. Despite claiming he lied to the public about who bought the ticket to protect his mother, Larry Tessier was also likely trying to protect against a possible claim from Macatula, Schwartz said. Larry Tessier knew she had bought the ticket and might ask for a piece of the winnings, and concocted the bogus story as a result. "Larry likely, at the time, didn't appreciate the purchase of the ticket could be traced back to Cora's husband [who bought it on her behalf]," said Schwartz.

Al Lesko felt like he'd gone from hero to zero. Three years ago, he was given a commendation by the city of Winnipeg for playing a key role in helping police nab three armed bank robbers, who later pleaded guilty to their crime. In October 1999, Al Lesko was driving a city van when he spotted a trio of suspects fleeing a bank robbery in downtown Winnipeg. He followed the getaway vehicle and called police, who arrested two men and a woman within minutes. Police also recovered stolen money and a handgun used in the holdup.

But now Lesko was deemed an unreliable witness filled with "jealousy and resentment" as his testimony was dismissed in the high-profile Lotto 6/49 trial. The stinging words from Court of Queen's Bench Justice Sid Schwartz had left a bad taste in the mouths of Lesko and his family, who believed his credibility had been tarnished unfairly in a "smear" campaign.

Al Lesko was a longtime co-worker of Larry Tessier who testified that he overheard Larry telling his mother "Don't tell Cora" during a phone conversation at work the morning after she'd won the lottery. Lesko's motives came under attack during cross-examination from the Tessiers' lawyer. John Scurfield accused Lesko of feeling slighted by his friend, and cited comments from some other co-workers who said all Larry brought them after winning the lottery was "a box of doughnuts." The judge also cited Lesko's apparent unwillingness to speak with the Tessiers' lawyers.

Dianne Lesko said they gave statements to a private investigator hired by the family, and refused on one occasion to speak by telephone with a woman claiming to be one of their lawyers. "If someone would have had the decency to come to the door with identification, we would have been happy to speak to anyone."

She said her husband never wanted to get involved in the lottery case to begin with because of his long-time friendship with Larry Tessier. "It was I who went behind my husband's back to advise a lawyer what Al had heard. Al was furious with me and was not going to co-operate. After what has happened, I can see why. It does no good to tell the truth, and if you don't know how to play the game you might just as well crawl in a hole and remain ignorant to everything around you," she said. Lesko said the judgment had damaged her husband's good name and reputation. "My husband has gone through hell for this, and I feel like we've been victimized here."

SATURDAY APRIL 6, 2002

Life had gone on. Nilo Macatula spent much of the day cleaning the house. His wife, Cora, completed yet another 60-hour work week by tending to the needs of residents at the convalescent home. The couple's two children, Mac and Nikki, juggled homework, sports practice and music lessons, with frequent stops to the baskets of Easter chocolates still piled up in the family's modest Arlington Street bungalow. The following morning, they planned to make their weekly trek down the street for Sunday services at St. Edward's Church. It appeared the Macatulas weren't wasting any time wondering what could have been or feeling sorry for themselves.

Nilo seemed to have adjusted nicely to his role as homemaker since being laid off last fall from his night auditor's job at the Lombard Hotel. It's a duty he accepted with pride, while Cora was working hard during her full-time weekday job as a home-care worker, and her part-time weekend work at the convalescent home. "I love to work, ever since I was young. It's in my system. I don't feel tired, and I enjoy my time with my clients," said Cora, who doubted even becoming a millionaire would have stopped her from clocking in. "I have to balance my time between my clients and my family, but they come first, especially my children," she said.

The Macatulas, who had no other close family members in Canada but a tight-knit group of friends in the city, didn't like pondering if life would be any different had there been a different verdict. "Definitely [winning the case] would have changed our lives. It would have changed things financially, but not socially. Presents can't buy friends," said Nilo.

They insisted they never planned how they would spend their newfound riches, had Schwartz ruled in their favour. There were no thoughts of replacing the home they'd spent the last 10 years in since coming to Canada from the Philippines, and no big trips on the horizon. "It's nice to have dreams, everybody has dreams. But to say, 'I want this, I want that' ... it's like the saying goes, until you cross the bridge, you can't say you're safe," said Nilo. "Like we told the kids, just wait and see, you never know what happens."

The money likely would have been used to ensure a bright future for the couple's children. Mac, 15, was in Grade 10 at St. Boniface Diocesan High School. Already taller than his dad at 5-10, he was a talented basketball player with dreams of being a professional athlete. Nikki, 7, was in Grade 1 at Holy Cross School and a budding performer. She was taking vocal lessons and was involved in theatre and dance. The Macatulas said putting their children in private school was a top priority, despite the added expense and burden on themselves. "We want them to have the best education they can have. That's the foundation of their life," said Nilo. "We have to maintain to keep things better for the kids."

The family took offence to the characterization by the Tessiers' lawyer that financial woes provided a motive for making a false claim on the ticket. "I cannot say we have the good life, but we're getting by," said Nilo. "Everyone has mortgages and loans and payments. We're no different."

The family members said they'd been overwhelmed by the support they'd received, both from the local Filipino community and from complete strangers who had phoned their home since their lawsuit became public. The calls had intensified since the verdict, said Nilo, with many people expressing their condolences. "People were calling us before, saying, 'We're praying for you and good luck.' It seems the whole community is supporting us," he said.

One thing the disappointing decision hadn't stopped was their love of the lottery. The Macatulas continued to play Lotto 6/49 and Super 7 every week, believing lightning could strike twice. "We always play, because you never know. It doesn't hurt to try. And if you don't buy, you have no chance," said Nilo.

MONDAY APRIL 15, 2002

It was a very interesting document that had never seen the legal light of day. The Queen's Bench judge who presided over the high-profile case and ruled against Corazon Macatula was neither aware of, nor allowed to consider, a May 2000 polygraph examination. Canadian courts had deemed polygraph tests to be scientifically unreliable and would not recognize the results as evidence in any case. And so test results that indicated Macatula was truthful when she said she and Jean Tessier jointly purchased the winning ticket were not presented at the trial.

Polygraph tests are often used by police and lawyers as investigative tools and bargaining chips, as was the case with Macatula, her lawyer, Bill Olson, confirmed. He said polygraph tests had been found scientifically reliable about 75 to 80 per cent of the time, which was not sufficient for the courts. John Scurfield, the lawyer representing the Tessier family, called polygraph tests "bogus science." "They have never been ruled as being scientifically valid," he said.

Details of the polygraph test were contained in a voluminous Queen's Bench file and formed the basis for a pretrial motion. Lorne Huff, who operated Huff Investigative and Polygraph Services in Winnipeg examined Macatula two months after the Tessiers announced their lottery win. He asked her a series of questions, but highlighted three he deemed relevant to the case in his report.

Huff's questions, and Macatula's answers, were:
- Are you truthful when you say you had an agreement with Jean Tessier to share in Lotto 6/49 winnings? Yes.

- Are you truthful when you say you contributed to the purchase of Lotto 6/49 tickets with Jean Tessier? Yes.
- Are you truthful when you say Jean Tessier paid you $2.50 for her share of the Lotto 6/49 ticket for the March 15 draw? Yes.

In his report, Huff found the test to be inconclusive on the first question, but it suggested she was truthful on the final two. He said Macatula explained the inconclusive result, saying "she feels the agreement was not discussed too much and should have been in writing."

MONDAY MARCH 3, 2003

The Tessier family would get to keep their riches by the absolute slimmest of margins. In a 2-1 verdict, the Manitoba Court of Appeal refused to order a new trial in the civil court battle over $11.4 million.

"My clients are tremendously relieved and extremely excited," lawyer Robert Tapper said after informing the Tessier family the cash was still theirs to keep. He had taken over the case after his colleague, John Scurfield, was appointed as a judge with the Court of Queen's Bench.

The Macatula's took the news in stride. "This is very disappointing. We have hoped that with three judges they might be more open-minded. I'm just not sure what to say. This is somewhat draining," Nilo Macatula said after learning of the decision. "We thought our chances were always 50-50. For some reason, it just didn't happen." Macatula said the appeal court ruled the case came down to a credibility issue and they couldn't interfere with the finding of the trial judge.

Tapper said the appeal court judges only disagreed on the application of the credibility test to the evidence, and not on a major point of law. "There is no way the Supreme Court of Canada is likely to hear this case," he said.

TUESDAY MARCH 4, 2003

There was one final bombshell to drop. Corazon and Nilo Macatula had turned their backs on a $2-million offer by the Tessier family to halt their high-profile case and settle out of court. The proposed settlement, which was outlined in a letter sent to their lawyer, came just one week before their civil court trial began in November 2001. It was only becoming a matter of public record now, splashed across the front page of the *Winnipeg Free Press*.

"If we were fighting for the money, people would say how could you refuse? But we were fighting for principle, for what was rightfully ours," Nilo Macatula said from the family's Arlington Street home. "Do you offer that kind of money if you're not guilty?" asked Cora Macatula.

The Macatulas said they submitted a counter-offer of 75 per cent of their alleged $5.7-million stake in the winning ticket, but it was refused. The settlement proposal followed an earlier offer of $100,000 in June 2000, before a lawsuit was even filed. The Macatulas promptly turned it down. A third offer of $100,000 was made last April by the Tessiers, after the Macatulas filed an appeal of Schwartz's decision. Again, they turned it down.

Lawyer Robert Tapper questioned the Macatulas' motives for releasing information about the settlement proposals. "This is a stunning development. This is a pitiful and spiteful thing. And my goodness, they should have taken the offer," he said. Tapper said he would research the law to determine if the Tessiers had any legal recourse against the Macatulas for releasing "private and confidential" information. He said the public would be wrong to view the offers as an admission of guilt by the Tessiers. He believed the Macatulas were simply trying to "embarrass" them after losing their case. "When you walk into a courtroom, anything can happen. Emotions aside, sometimes you have to make a business decision to deal with a lawsuit and you make an offer," said Tapper. "You can believe in the righteousness of your position, but it's a crapshoot when you go into court."

The Macatulas said the justice system had clearly failed them. Although Justice Charles Huband ruled a new trial should be ordered, two other judges overruled him in the split decision.

"He was the senior judge. Why couldn't they have seen things his way?" asked Nilo Macatula.

Many people naturally asked me which side I believed while covering this dispute. My answer was always the same: The Macatulas.

This feeling was cemented by the revelation that they walked away from the $2 million offer. From my perspective, if they knew they were in the wrong and simply after the Tessier's money, why wouldn't they have gladly accepted the proposed settlement? After all, that kind of cash would be life-changing for *anyone, especially the Macatula family. But the fact they turned it down told me one thing. This was a matter of principle to them. They firmly believed they had been wronged. And they were going to fight for what they believed was rightfully theirs. In hindsight, it probably wasn't a wise strategy. They lost the legal battle and ended up with nothing. The Supreme Court ultimately rejected hearing the case.*

Nilo Macatula ended up filing for bankruptcy in 2004. As for the Tessier family, they never did agree to any post-verdict interviews, despite countless attempts by myself and other reporters over the years. Jean Tessier passed away in 2007. Several other bigger lottery prizes have been awarded in Manitoba since. But none have attracted the kind of controversy that this one did.

CHAPTER 12

THE MASTER MANIPULATOR

It's a stunning number: More than 1,000 indigenous women were killed in Canada between 1980 and 2012. More than 100 of those cases remain unsolved. The reality is that there are countless killers who are currently walking the streets, no doubt feeling like they are untouchable. Shawn Lamb certainly fell into that category. He absolutely thought he would get away with his crimes. But a combination of factors—some luck, good timing, a controversial police tactic and Lamb's own big mouth—proved to be his undoing.

I followed this case as close as any I've covered in my career, due largely to the fact Lamb began calling me frequently from jail following his release. For whatever reason, I became his personal sounding board. Those lengthy conversations would reveal his true colours.

MAY 2010

"It's come true, one of my worst nightmares. I'm old and in jail."

Shawn Lamb stood before the judge in a scene that was all-too-familiar. The 50-year-old drifter and career criminal had just pleaded guilty to 15 more charges, increasing his total to more than 100 in a

30-year span. Like always, Lamb jumped at the opportunity all criminals were given to speak. He had plenty to say.

Lamb described how he was in the process of writing a revealing tell-all book about his troubled past, claiming he wanted to help steer vulnerable individuals away from making the same mistakes he'd made. "The elements-for-life concept is something I've embraced," Lamb said, in explaining the working title of his inspirational book. His lawyer then handed a sample of his writings to the court clerk, who passed them on to provincial court Judge Linda Giesbrecht and marked them as an exhibit.

"I'm just a coward pretending not to be afraid, sounding confident, powerful looking bold and fearsome as if I could rip off the heads of my opponents," Lamb wrote. "But in my belly, the wee bottom of my little belly, is a boy still afraid, feeling alone, unknown if what he has will be enough to win, to survive."

Lamb said he'd been working closely with native elders and a chaplain behind bars to come up with a blueprint for success that he, and others, would follow. "I am now in control of what I do, because I now know what it is that made me do the things I did do," Lamb said. "I don't want to do it anymore. I don't want to hurt anybody anymore. I want to take responsibility for what I've done, to use my writing skills in a positive way to help myself and others in the future."

Lamb was sentenced to 19 months in jail, in addition to nearly 14 months of time already served, plus three years of supervised probation. His crimes included mugging a young mother of her purse, threatening to stab another man for his beer, stealing a car and passing numerous bad cheques. He was on a conditional sentence at the time for a similar robbery in which he attacked a young mother for her bank card, flipping over a stroller carrying the victim's baby.

Lamb described how all his previous offences had been committed to help feed a drug and alcohol addiction he'd been fighting since the age of nine—when his adoptive parents first started forcing him to play the role of a "bartender" while they entertained other drunken guests in their home.

Giesbrecht told Lamb she was impressed by his honesty—and hopeful he had finally turned a corner following many previous attempts that ended with him back in jail. "You're clearly an intelligent, well-spoken person. You have a gift in your writing and your speaking. It's really too bad you've wasted so many years of the potential that you had. I really hope you're sincere. You appear to be sincere, you appear to be genuine," said Giesbrecht. "You seem to have very good insight into your past behaviour. If you don't achieve what you hope to achieve when you get out next time, I think you've burned your bridges. Ultimately it is your choice."

Giesbrecht also expressed sympathy after hearing of Lamb's upbringing, which would be the focus of much of his writing. "I appreciate you had a bad childhood and didn't have the benefits a child should have," said Giesbrecht.

He was born as Darryl Dokis on a First Nation near Sarnia, Ontario, to a 17-year-old single mother. He told court he was "ripped" away by social services at the age of 2 1/2 as part of the "60s scoop," taken from his First Nation community and put in foster care for a year before being sent to live with an adoptive white family near Sarnia.

"Once upon a time there was born a baby boy, a little Indian boy as sweet and fat-cheeked and gifted by the Creator as any baby anywhere. He was born innocent, as innocent as a puppy. An innocent baby deserves not to be torn apart from its mother," Lamb wrote. "Now take a puppy, when he comes up to you, wanting you to pick him up and love him. If you kick that innocent puppy instead, and when he's hungry you throw him out into the cold without food, and when he wants to be warm and safe you let the vicious neighbourhood dogs rip and tear at him. Well, what about that puppy? How will that innocent puppy grow up?"

Lamb admitted to harbouring years of pent-up anger over what he says were years of neglect and abuse at the hands of several important women in his life. Lamb claimed his now-deceased foster mother sexually and physically abused him while also introducing him to alcohol when he was just nine. He made similar claims against his now-estranged stepsister, saying she would play "doctor" with him as a young child and molest him.

"Why did they stomp out the last tiny vestiges of self-worth from this child? What wrong had he committed? Why was he kicked and beaten, raped and abused in both mind and body? Why?" Lamb wrote. "The baby is the wrong nationality, expendable. Send the child away, damn the damage this may cause."

His lawyer, Aaron Seib, told court this was a deeply damaged soul. "It's clear his upbringing was fraught with physical abuse, mental abuse and sexual abuse. At a very young age he was abusing alcohol, drugs, whatever he can get his hands on. It's something he still struggles with," Seib told court.

Lamb began running away from home at the age of 12, often spending long periods of time living on the streets of Toronto. He also began experimenting with mushrooms, acid, cocaine and heroin in his early teens and became hooked. Lamb told court there were many times he wanted to end his own life, especially after he began committing crimes to support his habit. He also had stints in psychiatric care in Toronto. "I felt really bad about what I'd done. I wanted to kill myself," he said. Lamb said he was diagnosed in 2001 as being bipolar and took solace in expressing his deepest, darkest feelings through the written word.

Lamb also had several sexual relationships and became the father of three children, none of which he maintained any relationship with, court was told. They include two sons, aged 26 and 20 and an 18-year-old daughter. Lamb said both his adoptive and biological parents were deceased, but he wanted to try to rebuild the non-existent relationship with his children plus other biological family members. He also expressed a desire to begin connecting with his aboriginal heritage.

"Throughout all a dim light, glimmer of hope, a feeling of worth. Ask for help, unload the shame. I'm wanting and worthy of a better life," he concluded in the excerpt presented to court.

Crown attorney Susan Helenchilde was skeptical about his chance of success. "It remains to be seen how committed he really is. Hopefully he'll get the message this time around," she said.

MONDAY JUNE 25, 2012

It was the break a police task force had been hoping for—and the announcement many had feared. Winnipeg police had caught a suspected serial killer. Shawn Lamb had been linked to three unsolved slayings of young aboriginal women—Tanya Nepinak, Carolyn Sinclair and Lorna Blacksmith. He was back in custody, a familiar place for him, facing three counts of second-degree murder.

Winnipeg police Chief Keith McCaskill told reporters how a 36-year-old woman had come forward just days earlier, saying she had been the victim of a serious sexual assault at the hands of Lamb. That triggered an interview with Lamb and sufficient evidence for members of the Project Devote task force to link him to the three cases. Police were being tight-lipped about the specifics of their investigation, knowing anything they say in this high-profile case could be used against them in court. "Sometimes you get a break in the case, and that's what happened here," McCaskill said during a news conference.

McCaskill said this was the very first sign that a serial killer might be at work. "We never said there was no serial killer, we said we had no evidence to suggest there is one. Now we have that evidence. I don't think we dropped the ball on this," he said. "The most important thing at the end of the day is that we do the best we possibly can and get that evidence before the courts."

There was another twist in the case: The body of Nepinak had yet to be found. Sinclair, 25, had been found in March 2012 in a dumpster in a back lane near Notre Dame Avenue and Toronto Street. She had been missing for three months at the time. Blacksmith,

18, had last been seen January 2012 in the West End. Her body was discovered just last week, on the same day as Lamb's sexual assault arrest, near a dumpster on Simcoe Street. Nepinak, a 31-year-old mother of two, was last seen around Sherbrook Street and Ellice Avenue in September 2011. Police admitted all three victims were living what would be considered a "high-risk lifestyle" but said that never impacted their resolve to solve the cases. "They are victims and they should never have been," said McCaskill.

A team of 24 "Project Devote" investigators—10 from the Winnipeg Police Service and 14 from the RCMP – were continuing their task-force investigation and wouldn't rule out the possibility of linking Lamb to other unsolved cases. There were still 20 slain women, and eight missing women, on the Devote list. Not to mention dozens of other potential victims across the country. Their work was really only just beginning.

THURSDAY JUNE 28, 2012

He had spent the past week stewing in a prison cell as his name dominated newspaper headlines and television newscasts. Shawn Lamb could stay silent no more. And despite the advice of his lawyer to keep his mouth shut, Lamb picked up the telephone and contacted a reporter with the *Winnipeg Free Press*.

It would be the first of numerous conversations over many months in which Lamb appeared to be reveling in the spotlight and doing everything possible to ensure it continued to shine brightly on him. On this day, Lamb noted how Winnipeg police were in the middle of conducting an extensive sweep of downtown and West End yards, buildings and dumpsters.

"I imagine they're out there looking for one thing. They're looking for bodies," Lamb said in a 20-minute telephone interview from the downtown Remand Centre. "They have a list with so many names on it." But Lamb denied suggestions he could be linked to any other unsolved homicides in Winnipeg or across Canada. "I've given them voluntary DNA, not to include myself but to exclude myself," he said. "The police are going to say what they're going to say."

Lamb described how he was arrested on the sex assault charge, then spent more than 48 hours in custody while going through a grilling marathon interrogation with homicide investigators, before the three charges of second-degree murder were laid. "The main thing for me is the victims. There are many people who are suffering out there," Lamb claimed. He said police wanted to show "their goodwill" to the community by making such a public display of their search.

Lamb said police confronted him with the names of dozens of other young Manitoba women who had been killed or gone missing. There were also ongoing investigations in other provinces to determine whether Lamb could be connected to any cold cases.

"I hope everyone who's responsible will be caught," said Lamb. He was asked to clarify if that meant there were many killers still walking the streets.

"Exactly," he replied. "It's a sad thing for the victims and their loved ones. There are so many questions."

Lamb was specifically asked if he planned to fight the allegations he killed Blacksmith, Sinclair and Nepinak. He refused to give a direct answer.

"I'm definitely going to fight to make sure this is done properly," said Lamb. He said that meant his "charter rights" must be upheld, but he offered no further details.

Lamb decried the conditions in jail, where he was confined to a maximum-security segregated cell 23 1/2 hours per day. "I know I'm not getting out of here any time soon," said Lamb. "I don't have a radio, I'm last on the list to get a newspaper. I get out for half an hour a day to shower and use the phone, that's it."

Still, Lamb expressed concern about some of the news coverage he'd been able to catch, wondering why media outlets were focusing so much on his tragic background. Lamb said he was able to visit the grave of his birth mother for the first time during a visit to Ontario last month. It was on the day he returned to Winnipeg that he was arrested.

"I found the closure I was looking for," he said.

MONDAY FEBRUARY 25, 2013

Shawn Lamb was playing games again. Frustrated that his case was dragging—and his name had largely disappeared from the public eye—Lamb was back on the phone. He claimed he had specific information that could help police solve at least five more cases of missing and slain women. And he expressed growing frustration that homicide investigators and a joint task force involving the RCMP, dubbed Project Devote, hadn't acted on his claims quickly.

Lamb said he was willing to co-operate and police were denying closure and justice for several grieving families. "Homicide doesn't seem interested in finding some more bodies," he said. Lamb threatened to go public to local aboriginal leaders and even begin calling families personally from the Remand Centre if immediate action wasn't taken. "I'm sure the cops don't want that to happen," Lamb said. "I told them I want to clear this up, for myself and to give closure to these people. Today would be ideal."

Lamb had also dismissed his lawyer, Evan Roitenberg, and was planning to represent himself. Lamb and Roitenberg had repeatedly clashed in recent months because of Lamb's continued desire to speak to a reporter.

Police and justice officials declined to comment publicly, citing the sensitive nature of the probe. But several sources said there remained much work to be done to verify much of the detailed information that had come their way. However, officials were proceeding cautiously because Lamb was a highly intelligent manipulator.

Homicide investigators had spoken with Lamb several times in recent weeks and planned to continue doing so. But those meetings provided more frustration than results. "He's very much… a chronic BSer. However he does come through when the timing is right," said a veteran police officer. "And sifting through the BS is what it's all about with these types, I guess."

Lamb repeatedly accused homicide investigators of having "serious tunnel vision" as it pertained to some of the cases of missing and slain women. "They're not interested in veering off the path they think… even if it means closure," he said. "I'm not saying I had anything to do with these five. I'm saying I have information. I'm denying any involvement with anything."

Lamb denied he was trying to "bargain" with police, saying he expected nothing in return. And he said he didn't want the public to think of him as a "media whore" who craved the spotlight. He then went on to conduct a series of interviews with local TV reporters later in the day.

Not everyone agreed with the way police were conducting the investigation. A recently retired Winnipeg homicide investigator said officers had dropped the ball in their investigation. James Jewell said it was a "travesty" police hadn't acted with more urgency since their initial arrest and interrogation of Lamb last summer. "Inexperience, lack of direction, lack of courage or combinations of all the above created significant delays for investigators who so desperately wanted to cut the red tape and get down to the business of a second interrogation," Jewell said in a public blog post. "It seems to me, incompetence of this magnitude should come with some sort of consequence(s)."

Jewell said police owed it to the public and victims' families to quickly get to the truth. "Sins of the past aside, the time has come for the police service to realize that a thorough debrief of alleged serial killer Shawn Lamb is in order. It's time to cut the red tape and end the debate regarding process and protocol. Sometimes, you just have to dance with the devil," he said.

WEDNESDAY FEBRUARY 27, 2013

"JUST ADDING TO THE PAIN"
Column by Lindor Reynolds in The Winnipeg Free Press

> Accused serial killer Shawn Lamb is tormenting the families of Manitoba's slain and missing women by claiming to have information that

would help solve at least five of their cases. He says police aren't taking him seriously and he's threatening to call the families personally.

Winnipeg police are taking Lamb seriously enough to have him locked up for the slayings of Tanya Nepinak, Carolyn Sinclair and Lorna Blacksmith. And, despite what a man with a three-decade-long rap sheet says, they're closely examining his latest set of allegations.

Bernadette Smith, the sister of missing woman Claudette Osborne, says officers from the Project Devote task force called her Monday to give her a head's up Lamb was claiming to have valuable information. She says her family isn't holding its breath he's telling the truth.

"We're just kind of waiting it out. We know he's kind of an attention-seeker," Smith says. "He says he wants to give these families closure. Why grow a conscience now? I just think he's talking out his ass."

She says police assured her they were taking Lamb's claims seriously and looking into them.

Kyle Kematch, brother of missing woman Amber Guiboche, is frustrated with Lamb's apparent confessions and retractions to the media.

"It's honestly f -- up," says Kematch. "Is he saying this to cause more pain? It's getting me angry. I don't understand what we've done to deserve this."

Joyce Nepinak, the mother of Tanya Nepinak, says her family is shocked by the twist.

"We don't know what to think. Whether he's lying or not, you have to get to the bottom of it.

If it happens to be true, moms can get some closure. We need that. I don't even know where my daughter is."

Gail Nepinak, Tanya's sister, says Lamb is "playing mind games."

"He's heartless. He's torturing us," she says. "He just wants publicity. He just wants the attention."

Community activist Chickadee Richard says it's possible Lamb does have more information to offer.

She believes he didn't act alone in the killings of Nepinak, Sinclair and Blacksmith. She thinks others in the community are preying on aboriginal people and there may be more than one serial killer.

"The families know that Shawn Lamb, he has no moral conscience. He says he wants to connect with the families. Why's he doing this? What's he after?"

Richard says the large number of missing and slain women speak to how aboriginal women are viewed.

"There's racism here. It's like these women don't matter."

Shawn Lamb seems a little short in the attributes column. He's been convicted of assaulting police officers, uttering threats, robbery, carrying weapons, forgery, possessing stolen property, break-and-enter and breaching numerous court orders.

He got 19 months in jail, in addition to nearly 14 months of time already served, plus three years of supervised probation. His crimes, according to a story by *Free Press* reporter Mike McIntyre, included mugging a young mother of her purse, threatening to stab another man for his beer, stealing a car and passing numerous bad cheques.

He was arrested for the murders of the three women in June 2012.

Winnipeg police believe Lamb is a highly intelligent manipulator. He's cunning and he's likely bored silly sitting in jail. He says he has film and keepsakes to back up his latest claims. He's got the police hopping and shattered families hoping for resolution.

Our police aren't ignoring him. They can't. After the debacle in the case of B.C. serial killer Robert Pickton, no law-enforcement team would risk slacking off and miss the chance to solve these killings.

Project Devote has to take every tip seriously, even if the source is an accused serial killer who may be acting out of spite or tedium.

THURSDAY NOVEMBER 14, 2013

He was a master manipulator, a sociopath who craved attention and took pleasure in the pain of others. So you can imagine the disgust among senior Manitoba justice officials who took a long, hard look at the case against accused serial killer Shawn Lamb and realized one alarming fact. Lamb held all the cards. They would be forced to play the game by his rules. The end result was a so-called deal with the devil.

Lamb appeared in court, where he pleaded guilty to two counts of manslaughter for the deaths of Carolyn Sinclair, 25, and Lorna Blacksmith, 18. Second-degree murder charges were dropped. He was given a 20-year sentence, with a requirement that he serve at least half before being eligible for parole. A "light at the end of the tunnel" is how defence lawyer Martin Glazer described it.

Extensive details of the investigation emerged publicly for the first time. The Crown revealed how Lamb, arrested for a sexual assault back in June 2012, stunned police by telling them he knew where to find a body. Police were led to Blacksmith's remains at the rear of a vacant home at 797 Simcoe St., partially covered by pallets and a metal cot. Her body was wrapped in plastic and in an advanced state of decomposition. Medical officials could not determine a cause of death.

He eventually implicated himself in Sinclair's death, which police had already been investigating since her remains were found March 31, 2012, wrapped in plastic inside a duffle bag near a garbage can on Notre Dame Avenue. Lamb admitted to both homicides, describing exactly how they went down.

He met Sinclair on Dec. 18, 2011, said they purchased crack cocaine and then went back to his apartment at 822 Notre Dame Ave. But the night took a violent turn when Sinclair grabbed the remaining drugs and locked herself in the bathroom. Lamb began smashing the door with an axe handle until she opened it. "What the fuck are you doing... why are you stealing this?" he asked. Lamb then struck Sinclair in the head several times with the handle, and then strangled her until she was lifeless. Lamb smoked some more crack, bought beer and eventually passed out. He finally disposed of Sinclair's body a few days later.

Blacksmith was killed in a similar drug-related dispute, just three weeks after Sinclair's slaying. Lamb claimed she grabbed his phone to call a drug dealer, prompting him to violently attack. Blacksmith was knocked to the ground and choked with an electrical cord. Lamb claimed he tried to revive her but she was already dead. So he wrapped her body in plastic stolen from a nearby construction site, and then left her behind the home on Simcoe.

Lawyers told court how there was no solid forensic evidence against Lamb. The only real case against him came from his own statement. "There were no eyewitnesses to the killings and despite the best efforts of police, only limited forensic evidence is available to be put before the court," Crown attorney Sheila Leinburd told Court of Queen's Bench Justice Rick Saull. "Consequently, the description of the killing of both women is taken solely from... Lamb's statement," said Leinburd. However, there were serious concerns it would hold up to a legal challenge. That's because of a controversial exchange of cash between police and Lamb. This marked the first time a payment had been mentioned. But no other details were presented in court, raising even more questions.

Defence lawyer Martin Glazer negotiated for months with justice officials, saying Lamb would only plead guilty to manslaughter. Keep the murder charge and they would see them in court, where convictions were anything but a guarantee. "This is, in fact, the quintessential instance of a true quid pro quo [meaning 'this for that']," Leinburd told court.

Glazer said it was obvious Lamb's statement would have been tossed out at trial. "Police were faced with a windfall because they had no clue he was involved. He provided the answers they needed... today he stands up in court and stands by his confession," said Glazer. "In effect, it is a life sentence. He will be in his 70s when he does get released—if he lives that long."

Naturally, news of the plea deal was not received well by the public. Social media lit up with outrage. Families of the victims erupted in anger. Even those involved in the prosecution held their noses.

"We're not happy at all. But you have to look at the big picture," mumbled one veteran cop.

No doubt their uneasiness was magnified on this day, when Lamb tried to hijack his own sentencing hearing. It was a pathetic, but not entirely surprising, performance by a man who did the "woe-is-me" act better than anyone. When given his chance to speak, Lamb stood up and claimed he wanted to withdraw his guilty pleas after the word "sociopath" was used to describe him in a report he said he never saw or read. "That is enough to make me want to rescind my pleas," Lamb said.

Glazer ultimately talked some sense into his client. Lamb then continued with his speech. "I wanted to take responsibility. Apologizing isn't going to do any good. An apology is nothing. It doesn't change what happened. I am sorry, and I mean that. I have empathy and I have remorse, for sure. I've taken responsibility," he said. "I left the door open for my addiction to take control. I grew up damaged and lost. Under the influence of drugs and alcohol... I turn into a monster at times."

It was the type of insight you rarely see from offenders, and typically not expressed as eloquently as Lamb did. And on the surface you may have wished to applaud him for his candour. Problem is, Lamb had pulled out this same spiel countless times. His comments on this day were eerily similar to ones he'd impressed many other judges with, convincing them this poor, lost soul was worthy of yet another chance at redemption and freedom. It was apparent to anyone in the courtroom that Lamb loved being in the position of power.

"You're a fucking monster, take some responsibility," screamed one of the victims' family members in court. He was promptly ushered out by sheriffs, clearly at his wit's end being forced to watch Lamb relish the spotlight.

FRIDAY NOVEMBER 15, 2013

It was the day after the deal went down. And now Winnipeg police were forced to explain their role in what many saw as a botched investigation and prosecution. At a hastily called news conference, police said desperation to bring closure to grieving families drove them to pay off Lamb—a move that was now under legal scrutiny and could have sunk the case against him. Full details emerged of a $1,500 deal, one day after Lamb's defence lawyer first raised eyebrows by accusing police of crossing a line and essentially buying a confession from his client, which likely would have been ruled inadmissible at trial.

Supt. Danny Smyth of the criminal investigations unit defended the decision, saying officers had the tough job of trying to break open a high-profile and sensitive investigation. "This is an extraordinary measure we considered," said Smyth. "The Winnipeg

Police Service is sensitive to the fact there are many missing and murdered women in Manitoba and in Canada. These investigations are a priority for us. In this case, the investigators explored all available options in the interest of justice and public safety."

Police outlined in detail how their contact and payment to Lamb came about. "I would say this is very unusual. In my time, this is the first time I can recall us going to that kind of a measure," said Smyth. Lamb was initially arrested on a sexual assault unrelated to any homicide. While being processed, "Mr. Lamb indicated he knew where a body was. This statement triggered a homicide investigation," said Smyth. In fact, court documents spelled out the scenario in greater detail.

"There is a human body, and it is in the city," Lamb said, according to police affidavits. He declined an offer to consult with a lawyer at this point.

"Mr. Lamb said he was going to do another crime and that he touched the body," police said. He provided directions to a back lane in the West End, where the body could be found among pallets and wooden crates behind a garage with an antique car inside. "Mr. Lamb indicated he had touched the body three months ago," police stated. Lamb went on to draw a map and lead police to the body of Lorna Blacksmith. Lamb then suggested he could offer a lot more to police – for a price. "He indicated he had more information to relate about the homicide and other crimes he committed," said Smyth.

Police consulted the Crown about how to proceed and set up a special "canteen fund" at the Winnipeg Remand Centre for Lamb. An initial $600 was deposited, which Lamb could use to buy personal items such as snacks and magazines. Smyth said it was important to note police were still treating Lamb as a potential informant at that time, not as a suspect.

Investigators then sat down with Lamb, who had plenty to say. He not only confessed to killing Blacksmith, but also slaying Carolyn Sinclair. Lamb was charged with the murders, but told police he would keep talking in exchange for money. "He continued to contact investigators, indicating he would provide more information about other homicides he was involved in," Smyth said. Police met with Lamb on two further occasions, depositing another $600 and then $300 into his account." Neither provided investigators with any additional evidence," said Smyth.

The issue hit the legislature when Progressive Conservative justice critic Reg Helwer said the government needed to review whether it's appropriate to pay criminals to solve crimes they commit. "The other real issue is, did the justice minister approve this beforehand?" Helwer said. "It's a very distressing way to go about prosecuting a crime if the only way that we can prove guilt is by paying the criminal himself or herself. Is that the direction that our justice system is supposed to operate?"

A spokeswoman for Justice Minister Andrew Swan confirmed the Crown attorney's office advised police after they made a request. Smyth said police were put in a difficult position, knowing there would be no case without Lamb's co-operation. "This brought closure to the families of Carolyn Sinclair and Lorna Blacksmith," said Smyth. "It was hoped subsequent information would be forthcoming to bring closure to the families of other victims that Mr. Lamb may have been involved in."

Shawn Lamb wasn't done talking. One day after resolving his high-profile case in court, Lamb was back on the phone from the Remand Centre with a *Free Press* reporter. Lamb claimed police were hoping to pin "as many as 80" homicides on him as part of a massive, Canada-wide investigation. "Their eyes lit up, bells went off. They thought they'd have everything in the past 30 years solved. They thought every murder, especially of an aboriginal person, was at my hands," Lamb said. Lamb said police showed him dozens of photos and lists of names of other young missing or slain women, hoping he would confess. They included local victims and those from other provinces.

He said the $1,500 police paid him was part of their desperate attempts to clear as many cases as possible. "I had admitted to these [two killings] without any inducement. But then after that, police went off the rails," said Lamb. Lamb said the money was deposited into his jail canteen so he could buy magazines, crossword puzzles, snacks and running shoes. And while he admitted being in a position of power over the police, he denied manipulating them or the victims' families. "I took responsibility for what I did do. As for the other stuff, I don't know. I guess police will have to go find the people who did it," he said.

FRIDAY NOVEMBER 22, 2013
It was the result many suspected was coming. And now it was official. The third, and final, homicide case against Shawn Lamb was being dropped. There just

wasn't enough evidence to link him to the death of Tanya Nepinak. The biggest obstacle was the fact her body had still not been found despite an exhaustive search of the landfill where it was believed she had been taken. Nepinak had last been seen Sept. 13, 2011 – the day court documents had alleged Lamb murdered her.

"In terms of the murder charge, based on the evidence to date and a careful reassessment of all of the evidence, the Crown has determined that there is no reasonable likelihood of conviction at this time," Crown attorney Sheila Leinburd told court. "Consequently, the Crown will be entering a stay of proceedings. Should new evidence be discovered, the case can be reviewed for possible future prosecution."

Lamb had always denied involvement in Nepinak's death. "There really was no evidence against him—there never was," defence lawyer Martin Glazer said outside court. "In my view, he should have never been charged. To this day, there is no evidence that it's a murder."

Nepinak's relatives expressed shock at the Crown's decision. Her aunt, Sue Caribou, said they were unaware of what had happened until contacted by the *Free Press* following court. "We had no clue," Caribou, the sister of Nepinak's mother, Joyce, said. "No clue this was going on."

Family members held a rally earlier in the week, angered by the fact Nepinak's case seemed to be ignored while Blacksmith and Sinclair's deaths were being wrapped up. "They didn't pay for my daughter; why didn't they do that?" Tanya's mother, Joyce Nepinak, said in reference to the controversial payment police gave to Lamb.

In his final jailhouse interview, Shawn Lamb also took aim at the Lorna Blacksmith and Carolyn Sinclair families, who criticized justice officials for cutting a deal with him. "I'm amazed. All of the family knew this was happening. They were all quite content. Then they all go in front of the cameras and sing a different song," said Lamb. He didn't stop there, questioning Sinclair's family for not submitting a victim impact statement to the court. "If you cared so much about her, you couldn't even take the time to write a victim impact statement? Come on," said Lamb.

He also bristled at suggestions he wasn't sorry for his actions. Lamb said he had no doubt he would have walked free if he'd chosen to reject a plea deal and go to trial. "There was no evidence against me except for me. I am the evidence," said Lamb. "I could have dragged this out for years. Step 1 is taking responsibility. Sorry is not enough. I can say it until I turn blue. It's not going to change what happened. Nobody wants to focus on my remorse, responsibility and empathy. [Regardless] of whether I would have walked or not, I took responsibility. If they don't want to hear that, that's their choice."

Lamb also commented about the lifestyle choices of his two victims, saying it was "really not their fault." "Even if these women are prostitutes, you can't blame that. That's how their issues evolved," said Lamb. "They're living a dangerous lifestyle. Some people get out of it with a minor scare, some with a major one, or some don't until they die."

Lamb also offered a grim prediction for those fearing he will return to society. "I'm going to be out in a decade," he said, vowing to get parole at his earliest eligibility date. "Oh yeah. I've got my release date marked down. I'll get out. I'm going to work to make myself a better person."

Shawn Lamb stopped calling me a few weeks after his sentencing hearing. In his final voice mail message, he ranted about how "pathetic" I was and claimed I had repeatedly twisted his words. To be honest, I was relieved the phone stopped ringing. I didn't believe a single word that came out of his mouth and truly felt like he was wasting my time.

Lamb had become a frequent caller to my Sunday-night radio show. It made for some truly surreal moments. One night, he called to ask my guest, Manitoba provincial court Judge Ray Wyant, a question about the criminal justice system. It wasn't until he was on-air that we recognized the voice. Obviously an accused serial killer asking a sitting judge questions on live radio isn't an everyday scenario. But Lamb relished it. On another occasion, Lamb wanted to tell listeners how a Quebec filmmaker making videos of models pretending to be raped and murdered was "cool." And then there was the time he told me how he thought Col. Russell Williams, convicted of brutally murdering two Ontario women and raping several others, "looked good" in pictures tendered in court of him wearing the panties of his victims.

There was no reason for him to be making these outlandish statements short of the "look-at-me" attitude he clearly possesses. I'm just glad he's finally been silenced and is where he belongs. And I'm glad at least a couple families have found the justice they were looking for.

CHAPTER 13

THE LOST SOULS

It is remarkable to think in this day and age of social media, where we are seemingly more connected than ever, that a person could die in complete obscurity and anonymity. Yet this sort of thing actually happens more than you might think. I've covered two tragic cases like this.

The first, involving a homeless man, took a remarkable turn after my initial story was published. The second, sadly, is still shrouded in mystery. I think about both of these people often. Not only about how they died, but more about how they lived. And what their sad stories say about us as a society.

MONDAY JULY 4, 2005
It must have been a horrible death. A homeless man, no doubt accustomed to being alone, fighting his own losing battle with a strap that somehow became entangled around his neck. His final, futile breaths came in the fading light of day, on a sidewalk in Winnipeg's popular, often-crowded Exchange District. It was a neighbourhood where he would often be seen pushing around a shopping cart that held his life's meagre possessions. Tragically, the bungee-cord strap that would strangle him was attached to the cart, a lifeline of sorts to ensure he held tightly what he cherished.

Police believed his death was a horrible accident caused when the man tripped and fell. Although there were no obvious signs of foul play, police were still awaiting autopsy results to confirm exact cause of death. "This is so very sad. He must have been very lonely," said Greg Stetski, who had seen his share of tragic tales while serving as executive director of the Union Gospel Mission just down the street from where the man died. Not surprisingly, police and medical officials had great difficulty tracking down someone, anyone, who cared enough about the man to know he'd died. No one had come forward to claim his body.

Stetski was saddened to hear about the difficulties in finding someone to notify about the death. "So many people lose family and friends, or are shunned by them, when you go in a certain direction," he said. Stetski recalled seeing the man regularly pushing a shopping cart in the area, but said he rarely stopped in for nourishment at the homeless shelter. He would often see others who clearly needed help, but refused to ask for it. "A lot of [homeless] people are embarrassed," he said.

Johanna Abbott, director of the chief medical examiner's office, said there were nearly 60 cases a year in Winnipeg where it was difficult to track down family members to notify them about a death. She said the number of lost souls who die in virtual anonymity is a sad reflection on society. Most involved deceased who were down and out, forgotten not only by the public but by their friends and relatives as well. Other cases involved people who were the last living member of their family and had no surviving loved ones. "Not very many cases end up where we can't find anyone at all to come forward," said Abbott. When all else failed, the Government of Manitoba would take possession of a body and ensure a proper burial occurred.

The Union Gospel Mission had a recent case where an elderly homeless man succumbed to illness. When not a single relative or friend could be found, the shelter sprang into action to ensure his death wouldn't go unnoticed. Led by Stetski, several people gathered at the mission for a funeral service to pay their respects to a man they never really knew, but refused to abandon even in death.

"He was not forgotten," said Stetski. Sadly, far too many others were.

SATURDAY JULY 9, 2005

His name was Fred Linton—and thanks to some kind-hearted Winnipeggers, the 47-year-old homeless man who died a horrible death on a city street would not be forgotten. It was a tragic end to a life filled with heartache and despair—from the shocking death of both parents at a young age to a lifelong battle with alcoholism.

Like many Winnipeggers, Kevin Sweryd was moved after reading about the man's death in the *Winnipeg Free Press* before he had been identified. "As a funeral director, I believe no life, whether you're the mayor of Winnipeg or someone pushing a shopping cart on the street, should go unnoticed," said Sweryd, who managed Bardal Funeral Home. "This just seems like one of those sad stories of someone who has slipped through the cracks of society." And that's why Sweryd had devoted time and energy to organizing a funeral service for a man he'd never met.

His idea had taken off beyond his wildest dreams following an incredible sequence of events.

It all started with a phone call two days earlier from Doris Linton, who identified herself as the aunt of Fred Linton. Doris Linton was calling from southern Ontario, where she lived on a farm with her husband. Winnipeg police had tracked her down after finding her name and address on a crumpled piece of paper found among Linton's belongings.

"She asked if Fred could be cremated, and if we could send the remains to her. I asked about having a service, but she didn't think anybody would come," said Sweryd. He began asking some questions about Fred Linton's life, and learned he'd spent several years working at a Winnipeg scrap metal business until he was let go in two months earlier.

Sweryd called Orloff Scrap Metal, and was surprised by the reaction of the employees. They were stunned and saddened by news of Linton's death. They wanted to know if there would be a service. They wanted to come. It seemed Linton, warts and all, had left quite an impression.

"I was his boss, but I guess I was also one of his closest friends," said owner Shelby Orloff. He gave a dishevelled-looking Linton a job six years earlier after he walked in off the street unannounced—then had the unenviable task of recently firing him when his battle with the bottle became too much. "His biggest demon was that he drank too much, and it became his relief from the world to get drunk," said Orloff. "He started coming in, and it was obvious he'd been drinking all night. But he was in denial. I felt very sorry for him, and tried very hard to keep him going with his day-to-day fight with society. But we didn't know what else to do."

Linton took great pride in his work—quickly progressing from a "lowly labourer" to a crane operator—but was drinking away all his earnings while living in a suite inside the Northern Hotel on Main Street, he said. "Even when he had a job, he didn't live too much better than an animal. He never bought new clothes, and he'd eat raw wieners all the time. We saw the lifestyle he had, and it was very sad," said Orloff.

Linton's life was on a downward spiral since the age of 13 when his mother was killed after his alcoholic father flipped his car in a drunken stupor near the family's Ontario home, pinning the woman underneath, according to his aunt. Three years later, Linton's father was found dead inside a car of suspected carbon monoxide poisoning. He was naked, along with a deceased young woman found beside him, said Doris Linton, 63. Linton and his younger brother, Kenneth briefly lived with Doris and her husband before hitting the streets to live on their own. Ken Linton had not been seen, or heard from, in many years, she said. Fred Linton moved to Winnipeg in his early twenties after suffering major head trauma in a car accident. "His head was split open, and he spent about six months in the hospital," said Doris Linton.

Fred never fully recovered, physically or mentally, and lived an isolated and clearly troubled life in Manitoba. His only connection to his family was with Doris, whom he would call nearly every weekend. "The calls stopped coming this year just after Easter.

He never called me on Mother's Day, which he always did. I was very worried. He would never give us a number to call him at," she said.

Even after losing his job, Linton continued to stop by his former employer at the corner of King Street and Sutherland Avenue on a regular basis. It was clear life had gone from bad to worse, as Linton had been evicted from the hotel for not paying rent and was out on the streets with his shopping cart. "He would come by, almost every day, and bring us scraps of metal he'd collected in his shopping cart. We'd give him a few bucks, but knew he was probably just using it to drink," said Orloff. Just days before he died, a secretary at the company began trying to set Linton up with some social help. But they would never see him again.

Doris Linton was now trying to get funds together to come to Winnipeg for her nephew's service. For Linton, as for most Canadian farmers, times were tough and money was tight. A small private service would be held the following month in Rosenorth, Ontario, where Linton would be buried in a family plot.

"One of the last conversations I'd had with him, he told me out of the blue that 'I want to be buried with Mom and Dad.' He broke down and cried," said Doris Linton. "I told him, 'Well, Fred. You better put my name in your wallet in case something happens.' And I guess he did. I always worried about him. At least I now know where he is."

TUESDAY JULY 12, 2005

At first he was a John Doe. Then some relatives were tracked down to give him an identity. And now the long-lost brother of Fred Linton had finally surfaced and reunited with his family after a *Winnipeg Free Press* subscriber recognized him as her newspaper carrier.

Ken Linton was delivering copies of the previous Saturday's edition in Fort Frances, Ontario, when one of his customers read him a story about the accidental strangling death of a man on a Winnipeg street. The subscriber said she recognized the name and immediately made the connection.

Ken, who had battled through his own problems and was illiterate, was stunned to discover his brother had died. "I always wondered about him, and never knew where to find him. Fred was supposed to come to my wedding nine years ago. He never showed up," said Ken. "I tried to call him at the hotel he was living at in Winnipeg, but he never called back. I don't even know if he got the messages, and I never heard from him again."

Equally shocked by Fred Linton's passing was his aunt. Until last week, Doris Linton had no idea what happened to the brothers, who were on their own in their teens. She had now gone from preparing for an August memorial service for Fred in their Ontario hometown, to planning to reunite with Ken for the first time in almost a decade. The pair had a tearful telephone conversation over the weekend.

"He told me he always thought I knew where he was, but I never did. I always worried Ken would end up the way Fred had," she said. Ken had turned his life around and was recently honoured for his volunteer work for speaking about fetal alcohol syndrome. He had also developed strong ties with a community church.

"Fred was the most marvellous guy, and he was always a survivor. It's so sad," Ken said. He came to Winnipeg to attend the funeral service.

Sweryd said his business received many calls from people with no connection to Fred Linton, inquiring about the service and even offering to make donations in his memory. "The [newspaper] article has done a world of good. It's helped reunite a nephew with the aunt who raised him and made it possible for a man to come and say goodbye to his brother."

SATURDAY APRIL 13, 2013

Somewhere under a pile of soon-to-be-melted snow at Brookside Cemetery was the unmarked grave of a mystery woman. Very little was known about her demise, which came to light the previous summer when a badly decomposed body was fished out of the Red River in Winnipeg. Even less was known about her life—not her name, not her age, not her place of birth or whether she had any living relatives or friends. It is the rarest of cases, an unidentified Jane Doe who had somehow lost her life without a single person coming forward to claim the body or offer information.

And the many lingering questions had Winnipeg police and the Office of the Chief Medical Examiner desperate for answers but open to the possibility she could forever remain buried in anonymity. "This person has lived on this Earth, they have made a contribution to society," said Gordon Holens, a sub-inspector and statistician with the Office of the Chief Medical Examiner. He had spent the past 10 months trying to find anything he could about the woman he had dubbed "Miss X." "You just don't see this very often," he said.

Information had been difficult to obtain since a resident who lives just south of the north Perimeter Highway bridge made the grisly discovery on June 15, 2012. The case was initially treated as suspicious because there was plastic wrapped around the remains. Police later determined it was likely debris that had become entangled and ruled out foul play. But other factors—such as when she died and how and why she died remained a mystery, as did anything pertaining to her identity.

Police took the unusual step last September of issuing a forensic sketch of the woman, along with photos of jewellery she was wearing when pulled from the water. The drawing of the woman was a facial reconstruction, not an exact likeness. She was believed to have been between 35 and 50 years old and about 5'5" with a slim build. She may have worn dentures. It was hoped the public plea for assistance would lead to a break in the case. But investigators were met with frustrating silence.

"We have to sometimes think outside the box. We were very hopeful and optimistic at the time it might generate some discussion and get someone to come forward. Unfortunately that hasn't happened," said police Const. Jason Michalyshen. "The investigators really take these matters very personally. They really want to bring some closure out of respect for the individual."

Holens said his office held the woman's remains until last October, then finally arranged for a brief funeral service and burial at Brookside. Predictably, nobody showed up. "We view it as a community service to try and make at least some reasonable effort to locate family," said Holens.

Holens had held his job for 13 years and said this was only the second case he could remember in which a person remained anonymous long past burial. He said there were typically about 70 cases a year in Manitoba in which a person whose identity was known died in relative obscurity and nobody would come forward immediately to claim the body. Usually about half are resolved quickly when a family member or friend is tracked down. The other half are given a service and burial similar to the one Miss X received last fall under the Manitoba Anatomy Act.

"Usually there is nobody going, or you can count the attendance in terms of one or two," said Holens, who does as much research as he can on the unclaimed person to plan a funeral that suits their religious background or even have them buried in the same cemetery as other deceased relatives. "But a lot of these unclaimed bodies, they chose to live that lifestyle, they like being on their own. And in some cases we'll find family and they just refuse to claim because of family dynamics that go on," he said.

Of course, there's no way of knowing what the family dynamics are in the case of Miss X. Winnipeg police had reached out to other jurisdictions, asking law enforcement to check their missing-persons' databases to see if there could be a match. Forensic sciences hadn't been able to offer much help so far.

"This case is not closed in our eyes by any stretch of the imagination," said Michalyshen. "Learning a bit about the history of this individual would certainly help us paint a better picture of what happened. We'd be taking quite a leap right now to try and say."

It is the type of case that can keep a police officer or medical examiner tossing and turning at night. Gordon Holens still can't shake lingering thoughts of the very first "John Doe" buried under his watch as he now tried to find answers in a similar case involving the unidentified woman he dubbed "Miss X." Holens said he often thinks about the anonymous man who was laid to rest about a decade ago in complete obscurity. He spent months trying to track down clues in the case only to be repeatedly met with frustration. Holens was only able to learn the following:

> The man appeared to be Korean, in his mid-30s and may have been financially well-off given the clothing and jewelry he was wearing. He came to Winnipeg and bought a one-way bus ticket at the downtown terminal. His final stop was Grand Rapids, about 400 kilometres north of Winnipeg.
>
> The man checked into a motel under a bogus name and paid cash. When he didn't check out the following morning, staff entered his room and found him hanging. He had committed suicide.
>
> "As it so happened, the Korean ambassador was in town at the time and we had him look at the body," Holens said. But they were never able to learn who the man was, where he came from or who he may have left behind. "He was probably running from something. I thought he may have been from the US," said Holens.

As of the deadline for this book, the identity of Miss X remains unknown. Her story is one that sticks with me far beyond the daily tales of despair coming from the court docket and police blotter. Winnipeg police and medical officials have continued searching for clues without any success. And so she continues to be a nameless victim of an unknown demise.

Hopefully, in the months ahead, the mystery of Miss X can finally be solved. Anyone with information is asked to call the police missing persons unit at 204-986-6250 or Crime Stoppers at 204-786-TIPS (8477).

Holens is also still searching for answers in his John Doe case.

CHAPTER 14

HORROR ON THE GREYHOUND

WEDNESDAY JULY 30, 2008
The mass email arrived at 9:21 p.m. from one of my editors at the Free Press, *Helen Fallding. The subject line read "Homicide Volunteer."*

"Someone decapitated on a Greyhound on highway past Portage la Prairie. Suspect barricaded inside the bus," it began. Helen explained that a reporter and photographer were on their way out to the scene from Winnipeg. But that this was clearly an all-hands-on-deck type of situation. "Anyone willing to head out there and help out?" she concluded.

My immediate reaction was that this must be some kind of a mistake. There was no possible way this could be true. Perhaps it was the result of some prankster phoning the newsroom, or some bizarre news tip. But a quick phone call to the news desk revealed it was deadly serious. The police scanner was buzzing with news of an incredible crime unfolding in the middle of the Prairies.

Naturally, the initial instinct as a justice reporter was to rush out there to cover it. But there was just one little problem: I was more than 700 kilometres away, in Minneapolis, Minnesota, on vacation with my family. It would be a couple days before I returned home *and found myself immersed in the case that quickly made international headlines.*

Years later, it remains the story I am asked to talk about most often. But words are often difficult to come by. It was an unspeakable tragedy on many, many levels.

TUESDAY AUGUST 5, 2008

He swayed back and forth, staring blankly at the floor and responding to a series of questions with audible grunts and sudden jerks of his head—up and down in the affirmative, side to side in the negative. The heavily shackled man showed no visible reaction as the Crown attorney read aloud some of the facts of his alleged crimes, even while some courtroom spectators gasped.

And then, quickly and quietly, he spoke for the first time. "Please kill me," Vince Li, 40, said inside the packed courtroom in Portage la Prairie, Manitoba.

Provincial court Judge Michel Chartier had heard and seen enough. Chartier agreed with the Crown's request to order a forensic psychological assessment for Li, saying there appeared to be serious mental health issues that could affect whether the Chinese immigrant was fit to stand trial. Li was facing a second-degree murder charge for what seemed impossible to comprehend: The decapitation killing and cannibalization of a complete stranger, 22-year-old Tim McLean, on board a Greyhound bus. The unprovoked slaying of the Winnipeg carnival worker just days earlier had prompted an outpouring of grief and outrage.

Dr. Frank Vattheur was set to meet with Li to try to get information to form an expert opinion that would determine if, or how, the case would proceed. If

Vattheur ruled Li wasn't fit to stand trial, that would effectively end the matter. Li would be sent indefinitely to a mental-health facility and held until, or unless, he was ever deemed ready to appreciate the legal process. The court case would resume at that point. If found fit to stand trial, the next issue would be whether Li was criminally responsible for his actions. Vattheur planned to submit an opinion on that issue as well. A finding of "not criminally responsible" would result in Li going to a hospital instead of prison. His release would be in the hands of medical professionals who would have the option of keeping him locked up and in treatment as long as they deemed necessary.

Crown attorney Joyce Dalmyn revealed full details about the circumstances surrounding McLean's killing. She did so at the invitation of Chartier, who wanted to know what her grounds were for seeking a forensic assessment. They weren't for the faint of heart.

Li had been exhibiting "bizarre and unusual behaviour" in recent weeks and months, including taking sudden bus trips to various cities in Canada for no apparent reason, Dalmyn said. Li had worked in the automotive department at an Edmonton Wal-Mart and delivered newspapers and flyers. The last day he was seen at work was Monday, July 28, two days before the deadly assault. His wife told an employer he had an "emergency" in Winnipeg and was coming for a job interview.

Dalmyn told court Li attacked a sleeping McLean for absolutely no reason as the Greyhound bus travelled down the Trans-Canada Highway near Portage la Prairie, stabbing him as many as 40 times while 36 horrified passengers looked on. He got McLean on the floor and then sat on top of him in the aisle of the bus, stabbing away with a large hunting knife, court was told. A passenger called 911 while the Greyhound driver pulled over at the side of the highway, allowing all the passengers to flee. The driver then locked the bus with just Li and a mortally wounded McLean inside.

Police rushed to the scene and surrounded the bus. Officers watched in horror as Li began carrying around McLean's severed head and appeared to be taunting them with it, court was told. Li said nothing to police, except to tell them at one point, "I have to stay on this bus forever," Dalmyn said. At one point, Li began cutting other body parts off McLean and was seen to consume some of them, she said. There were audible gasps in the packed courtroom at this revelation, including from several members of McLean's family.

"He appeared to be focused on his victim. He did not appear to be drunk or high," Dalmyn said. "This was a completely random attack. There's been no link established [between Li and McLean]."

Police elected not to storm the bus, waiting until Li smashed out a window and tossed a bloody knife and scissors towards them. He then jumped from the broken window, cutting his hand on the shards of glass, and was arrested, Dalmyn said. Police searched him and found several severed body parts, including an ear, nose and partial mouth, inside a plastic bag in his pocket. Police tried to interview Li but he refused to make verbal responses. However, he did softly mutter that he was "guilty" at least four times, Dalmyn said.

He had arrived from China in 2001 and found a home in Winnipeg, surrounded by a loving wife and caring members of the community who quickly took him under their wing. He soon found a job, vastly improved his English and enjoyed socializing with new friends at Sunday-morning church services, dinner parties and trips out to Falcon Lake. On the outside, life appeared to be very good for the new Canadian. Yet those who got to know Vince Li well soon recognized that beneath his friendly, polite exterior lurked something very troubling. "He was kind of a lost soul. It was as if he was always looking for something," said a member of a Winnipeg family which befriended Li—even having him over for Christmas dinner two years ago.

The woman and her family requested anonymity, not wanting to be deluged by other media covering the story. They were reeling over news of what Li had done. They had long suspected Li was battling mental illness, but he had refused repeated offers to see a doctor and get help.

"I think, in their culture, [the issue of mental illness] is kind of frowned upon," the woman said. She works in the mental health field and said it was obvious Li was struggling. "He was definitely schizophrenic, probably paranoid schizophrenic," she said. "He needed help but he just wouldn't get it."

There was the constant paranoia, a feeling that he was always being watched and that others might be out to get him. There were his bizarre, rambling stories that seemed to come out of nowhere. And there were the unannounced bus trips that would catch his wife by surprise—such as the time he hopped on a Greyhound headed to The Pas, later explaining that he wanted to look at some land he was thinking about buying.

"I don't think he actually had any money. This was probably just a symptom of his disease," the woman said. She recalled an unusual conversation with Li shortly after he got a red-light ticket in Winnipeg. "He started talking about how 'they were after me, there was nothing there,' " the woman said.

Li's illness soon began taking a toll on his marriage. He and his common-law wife Anna found a home in the Osborne Village area of Winnipeg shortly after coming to Canada. He got hired as a forklift driver with Midland Foods on Nairn Avenue, while she began working several waitressing jobs at Chinese-food restaurants in the city. The couple began occasionally attending church services at the Grant Memorial Baptist Church, which opened the door to other social opportunities. Li worked at the church and its attached schoolhouse as a night custodian for a time.

The woman said her father and stepmother took a liking to the couple and began having them over for dinner and, eventually, for visits to their Whiteshell cottage. "He was always a little bit quiet, kind of reserved. I think that's because he was self-conscious about his English," she said. However, Li eventually warmed up to the family. "We'd play cards together, dominoes, games like that," she said. But things took a turn about two years ago when Li suddenly left his wife and went to Edmonton. The woman said it was clear Li's wife was frustrated by her husband's erratic behaviour. She stayed behind in Winnipeg—continuing to work various jobs—but recently moved to Edmonton where Li had found work.

Members of Grant Memorial church had recently spoken with Li, apparently concerned about how he and his wife were doing. However, nobody predicted things would reach such a crisis point and climax in one of the country's grisliest murder cases.

WEDNESDAY AUGUST 6, 2008

It's located on the eastern edge of downtown Edmonton beside an elementary school, a sprawling two-tower high-rise that provides a spectacular view of the Saskatchewan River. The 20 floors of the north tower of Boardwalk Centre host a mix of residents, mostly seniors on the lower floors, low-income earners on assisted living above. The south tower, with a view of Commonwealth Stadium, had been a frequent home to players with the CFL's Edmonton Eskimos. But these days, nobody living in Boardwalk Centre was talking about football stars. All the buzz has been about the residents of suite 1612.

Vince Li and Anna had moved into the block about four months earlier—around the time Anna was believed to have come to Edmonton from Winnipeg to rejoin her estranged partner. Li was often seen by residents enjoying the swimming pool on the fourth floor. He would engage neighbours in short conversations during elevator rides.

"I remember one time, around June, we just talked about the weather, how nice it was," said Scott Arnold, who also lived on the 16th floor. "It seemed like he was keeping real weird hours, sometimes I'd see or hear him coming and going in the middle of the night."

Sightings of Anna were less frequent. And she rarely spoke to anyone in the building. "She seemed rather shy," said Arnold. Just days after her partner was accused of one of the most sadistic murders in

Canadian history, Anna was seen leaving her suite with a man believed to be a police officer. "She was wearing all black, with black sunglasses and a baseball cap. She was carrying a backpack," said Arnold.

He cheerfully wishes people a "wonderful day" at the end of his personal cellphone message. And yet it was becoming clear life was anything but wonderful for Vince Li, especially in the weeks preceding his attack on Tim McLean. His Edmonton employer, Vincent Augert, described how Li attracted attention at a recent company picnic with erratic behaviour that may have been a disturbing sign of things to come. Li was one of about 250 newspaper carries who showed up for the annual summer thank-you event on June 29—just a month before the deadly attack.

Augert caught Li standing alone near a newspaper vending machine that was being used as a target for a children's game that day. Li was hunched over, a blank look on his face, tilting his head and staring into the empty machine. "It was very strange. He was looking at it the way you'd expect a three-year-old would do," Augert recalled. "I went up to him and said 'Vince, it's just a newspaper vending machine. You know, you put money in it and get papers'." Li continued to display a childlike wonderment. Augert moved on, greeting others at the party, while Li quietly slipped away and left shortly after. Was it a sign of a serious mental illness, which some who knew Li have suggested he suffered from?

Augert said the incident was the first time he started wondering about Li's mindset. Until then, he'd been a model employee known for being efficient, well-dressed and able to juggle multiple paper routes without confusion. The two men would often meet for coffee at McDonald's—Li's choice—where he would always order a small coffee, black. Augert would offer to buy him food but Li always declined. "He was a good guy, I respected him, he respected me," said Augert.

He spoke with Li's wife by telephone after the man failed to show up for work during the previous week. Anna seemed confused by what was happening and made no mention during their last conversation on July 31 about the tragedy that had unfolded the night before. She just said Li had an emergency in Winnipeg but that she hadn't heard from him. Augert told her he would drop Li's July paycheque off at their downtown high-rise apartment. That cheque was now in the hands of police, who interviewed Augert about his involvement with Li.

"They're kinda stumped, to tell you the truth, as to why he would do that," he said.

Several patrons of an Edmonton casino said that Li was often seen gambling at the establishment—usually playing card games. Augert said Li would have only been making about $800 per month—before taxes—but wasn't surprised to hear he may have been gambling some of it away.

THURSDAY AUGUST 7, 2008

They had suffered in private while the entire world reacted in shock to their son's death. But now, on the eve of a funeral that threatened to turn into a three-ring circus, the parents of Tim McLean broke their silence. Carol and Tim deDelley, the mother and stepfather of the 22-year-old man, wanted to clear the air—especially with word that some members of the US-based Westboro Baptist Church were threatening to crash the service.

"I hope, however the funeral goes down, it's done with respect to Tim, that we are allowed to lay him to rest," said Tim deDelley. He said the days since learning of McLean's death had been a blur. "We're trying to deal what with happened here. We haven't even had a chance to mourn yet," he said.

Carol deDelley said she was frustrated by much of what has been written and said about her son's death—from sensational headlines and gory details to bogus claims made about the circumstances of the unprovoked killing. DeDelley also felt some people had been critical of the family's silence while so many others have been grieving publicly. "I haven't fallen off the face of the Earth. And I need to honour my son in this way [by speaking out]," she said.

The couple said they were taking a "wait-and-see" approach to the case against Vince Li. And they were refusing to get caught up in the furor that had seen Internet chat rooms filled with uninformed commentary and several special-interest groups try and capitalize on the tragedy for their own personal gain. They planned to follow the court proceedings closely but didn't want to make any comments on Li at this time. They described McLean, known to his friends as Timmy, as a "free spirit" with a big heart and passion for travelling the country while working at various summer fairs and carnivals.

TUESDAY SEPTEMBER 2, 2008
After weeks of relative silence, family members of Tim McLean were making quite the statement. A sweeping lawsuit had now been filed in which they condemned the actions of the federal government, RCMP and Greyhound following the killing of their son. They were seeking a total of $170,000 in general damages plus additional costs from the named parties but insist this has nothing to do with money.

"It's about accountability, responsibility for what happened to their son. It's about getting answers, so that his death might not be a total waste, that there might be some good to come from it," the family's lawyer, Jay Prober, told a packed news conference.

The McLean family didn't attend in person because they were too upset, he said. Prober and his colleague, Norman Boudreau, said the family "agonized" over the decision to go after the RCMP but ultimately decided it must be done. Their main source of concern was why police stood around the bus for nearly five hours while the killer beheaded, dismembered and cannibalized McLean in full view. They never stormed the bus, and the standoff only ended when suspect Vince Li tried to escape by jumping through a smashed window.

"How could this incident be allowed to continue for so long?" asked Prober. "We're told by the family they're not getting answers" from police. According to the statement of claim, "the RCMP failed to adhere to proper and established arresting procedures required by law... and knew or ought to have known that their acts and conduct amounted to a wanton disregard and/or total repudiation of the statutory duties incumbent upon members of the RCMP." By not taking action sooner, police "caused irreparable damage and injury" to the McLean family, "thereby allowing [the killer] to defile the body of the deceased."

The family was also taking aim at the Government of Canada, the minister of public safety and the minister of public health, saying they clearly failed in their duty to provide a safe environment for passengers on board that ill-fated bus. "You can go on a bus carrying a knife... but you can't get on an airplane with one," said Boudreau, saying proper regulation of bus safety is clearly needed. "People who take the bus are people who can't afford to take the plane. Why are these people subjected to having their safety being put in danger? Everyone should be offered the same security and safety. When is the Government of Canada going to put an end to this?"

They cited six other Greyhound incidents of violence—three from the past 18 months—which ought to have raised alarm bells. "It is clear that [the government] omitted and continues to omit putting in place safety regulations to ensure that similar violent incidents would be prevented," the lawsuit states. The family was making similar allegations against Calgary-based Greyhound Transportation Inc., which had repeatedly gone on record to say bus travel was safe. Prober said the fact a person can easily walk onto a bus with a hunting knife and attack a fellow passenger without any warning or provocation suggests that's not true.

The lawsuit claimed Greyhound had failed to install proper security measures such as metal detectors and bag checks and failed to provide adequate training to employees regarding passenger safety. Prober said the claim by Greyhound that such a system isn't feasible "doesn't wash" with the McLean family. "Hopefully Greyhound will be held accountable," he said. Prober said the family had talked about using the money to start up a scholarship in McLean's name.

MONDAY OCTOBER 6, 2008
It was being described as a significant transformation that had occurred while being lodged at a Winnipeg psychiatric ward. And now a medical expert was saying Vince Li fully understood his legal situation and was fit to stand trial.

"We are quite confident in his ability to instruct counsel," defence lawyer Gordon Bates told court. Doctors agreed Li clearly understood how the court system worked, the role of the various lawyers, the charge he faced and the potential consequences. With Li's current mental health no longer in question, the focus now turned to whether he should face criminal sanctions for the death of McLean.

"That's really the sole issue in this case," defence lawyer Alan Libman said outside court. "If someone commits an offence while suffering a disease of the mind and they don't know their actions are wrong, they can't be held criminally responsible."

Li did not appear in court but was said to be fully co-operating with his lawyers and officials at the PX3 ward at the Health Sciences Centre, where he had been held since early August. "Obviously now he's talking," said Bates. Li had also agreed to medication, he said.

Dr. Stanley Yaren has submitted a detailed report on Li's mental state following two months of intensive evaluation. Libman told court there had been no definitive finding with regards to an opinion on whether Li could be held criminally responsible. "We want him to get a fair trial, don't want to affect a potential jury pool," Libman said in explaining the need for public secrecy at this point. "This should be litigated in court and not the court of public opinion," said Libman.

THURSDAY OCTOBER 9, 2008

Carol deDelley was planning to fight all the way to Ottawa to ensure Li never tasted freedom again. Her calls for a "Tim's Law"—tough new anti-crime legislation that would also honour her son—had sparked a flurry of public debate. DeDelley said she believed that "if you voluntarily take an innocent life like what was done here, you should forfeit your own." She said in cases where there was absolutely "no doubt" about guilt, a murderer should either be executed or at least get life in prison, with no chance of parole.

"All I am attempting to do is bring awareness that our current laws leave huge gaps in public safety and are in need of amendment. Eventually, for my sake, I will have to forgive Mr. Li's horrific actions against my beautiful and loving son, Tim, and that forgiveness will be the next most difficult thing I will encounter in my life," she said. "In the meanwhile, however, I cannot just remain quiet and say or do nothing for fear that one day Mr. Li is released into society and tragically repeats what he has demonstrated he is capable of doing. Mr. Li should be medically and psychologically treated so as to remain aware of what he did to another human being and that is his punishment. But at the same time, he needs to be kept away from society because he is dangerous, as he has most graphically proven."

DeDelley said it was outrageous her son's killer would have the chance for freedom again, and she was angry there were no provisions in Canadian law to ensure the most dangerous criminals were at least guaranteed to be locked up forever.

TUESDAY MARCH 3, 2009

It was a mere formality at this point: Vince Li was going to be found not criminally responsible for his actions. Medical experts who had spent months examining Li on behalf of both the Crown and the defence had come to the same conclusion. Now the public was getting to go inside Li's brain as his high-profile trial began with the inevitable conclusion just days away.

Dr. Stanley Yaren told court he believed Li had a very strong chance to recover from the major mental illness and extreme psychosis that triggered the unprovoked killing of Tim McLean. He described Li as an otherwise "decent person" who was suffering from untreated schizophrenia and clearly out of his mind when he believed he was acting on God's commands to eliminate "the force of evil" by attacking the sleeping victim.

"He was being tormented by auditory hallucinations," said Yaren. "He believed Mr. McLean was a force of evil and was about to execute him. He had to act fast, urgently, to save himself. This wasn't an innocent bystander or stranger he chose to kill, but rather an evil force he was commanded to kill."

Li, wearing handcuffs and leg shackles, shuffled into the room led by several sheriff's officers, and was placed in the prisoner's box. He sat motionless, wearing a dark suit jacket, slacks and a light-coloured dress shirt.

"He didn't understand, in my opinion, that he was just killing an innocent bystander. He understood this was the only action he could take," Yaren told Court of Queen's Bench Justice John Scurfield. Once McLean was obviously dead from dozens of stab wounds to the back and chest, Li continued to hear voices demanding he attack the body, Yaren said.

"He was terrified, frightened, tormented. Mr. Li's fear, because of what he was being told through these hallucinated voices, is that what he perceived to be the evil being would come back to life, through some supernatural powers and finish him off. He was in a frenzy to prevent this from happening," said Yaren. He said Li had been co-operative and made significant strides since being hospitalized and medicated and could function again in the community—something Yaren admitted didn't sit well with most people, including the victim's family. "I completely understand the need for a sense of justice, of retribution. It would be in some sense easier if Mr. Li was an anti-social psychopath with a history of malicious behaviour, but he isn't that. He is, as I've come to know him, a decent person. He is as much a victim of this horrendous illness... as Mr. McLean was a victim. Don't hate the person. Hate the illness."

Yaren conceded Li's actions could not have been predicted, given that he had no prior criminal record or a violent history. Yaren described him as polite, humble and hard-working and not a "monstrous psychopath." "The man I described, without psychosis, would have had no reason to [kill McLean]," he said. He said Li began experiencing psychotic episodes around 2003, including a 2005 incident where he was picked up by police walking down Highway 401 in Ontario, believing he was "following the sun" after shedding most of his possessions. He was briefly hospitalized in Etobicoke, Ont., but received no follow-up after refusing to accept he had an illness or take any treatment, court was told. Yaren said there remained a stigma with mental illness that was difficult to overcome, especially for men.

"Our society as a whole doesn't have a lot of tolerance for people with a severe mental illness," he said. Yaren said Li was slowly beginning to realize what he's done but still didn't accept the fact he consumed some of McLean's body parts. "It may be he's blocked it from his consciousness... that it's just too awful for him to contemplate," he said. Yaren believed Li could make a significant recovery in the next few years under rigorous treatment and medication but was still suffering some delusions, including a belief he would one day be executed. "He is not 100 per cent out of his psychotic phase yet," he said. "But over time, as he recovers, he will have to come to terms with the awful things that have occurred."

He boarded the Greyhound bus in Edmonton just after midnight, leaving a note in the apartment he shared with his wife. "I'm gone. Don't look for me. I wish you were happy," Vince Li wrote, according to testimony heard at his second-degree murder trial.

Li—travelling under the bogus name of Wong Pent—had a one-way ticket to Thunder Bay. But he got off the bus in the early evening in Erickson, Manitoba.

He would spend the next 24 hours in the small town, most of the time sleeping and sitting on a park bench. Li also sold and burned many of his possessions. Li called Anna around 6 a.m. on July 30 but made little sense. "He was talking to her about the Yellow River in China," Crown attorney Joyce Dalmyn told court. Some of the conversation was in English, the rest in Mandarin. Li told Anna he would return home once he "set up."

He boarded the daily Thunder Bay-bound Greyhound that passed through Erickson later that afternoon, taking a seat near the front. A woman who got on with him later told police she thought Li was acting "agitated, somewhat distraught" while waiting for it to arrive.

"He was pacing back and forth, talking to himself in Chinese," said Dalmyn.

On the same bus as Li was Winnipeg resident Tim McLean, who was making his way home following a summer stint on the Canadian carnival circuit. At some point, police believe McLean smiled at Li and may have said a friendly "Hello." Following a rest stop outside of Brandon, Li moved to the back of the bus and sat down in an empty seat beside McLean, who was sleeping and listening to an iPod. Just west of Portage la Prairie, Li attacked McLean without provocation.

WEDNESDAY MARCH 4, 2009

Carol deDelley was prepared to watch her son's killer walk out of court headed for a hospital, not a prison cell. But the grieving mother was vowing to do everything possible to ensure Vince Li never experienced freedom again.

"I am absolutely terrified of him and his capabilities. I think he'd do it again," deDelley said after hearing a second straight day of disturbing court testimony. "I'm going to fight to keep everyone safe from him. "If it means going [to court] every year, I'll go every year. Instead of birthday parties, it'll be NCR hearings." DeDelley accepted the fact Li was mentally ill, especially after hearing testimony from two forensic psychiatrists. She also recognized an inevitable conclusion to the case.

"This is as close to beyond a reasonable doubt as you can get. There's no contradictory evidence here," Li's lawyer, Alan Libman, told Queen's Bench Justice John Scurfield during a brief closing argument.

Prosecutor Joyce Dalmyn said her department had a duty to raise the issue of criminal responsibility even though it is controversial with the public. "Almost every member of the public has said 'That guy is crazy, he needs to be locked up,'" she said. "The Crown can't ask this court to convict Li of second-degree murder when all evidence points to him being not criminally responsible. He was not able to appreciate the nature of his actions due to his delusional thinking. He was not able to determine right from wrong."

Dalmyn said it was also obvious Li was not close to being ready for release back into the community. "It's clear from the evidence called... Mr. Li, at this point and time, does pose a risk to the public and himself," she said.

Dr. Jonathan Rootenberg, a forensic psychiatrist who met with Li at the request of his lawyers, told court that he believed Li didn't know what he was doing on board the Greyhound bus. "He certainly didn't know it was wrong. He was quite psychotic during that time period," Rootenberg said. He said Li likely didn't view McLean as a human being as he attacked him. "He viewed the unfortunate victim as a demon. He believes it wasn't his hands doing that, but it was God's hands, through him."

He called Li a good candidate for treatment because he didn't have any history of substance abuse or anti-social disorders, which were often psychotic triggers for people who have schizophrenia. Rootenberg added that Li had responded well to medical treatment and therapy but would always have to be watched closely to protect against a relapse. "He is in the very early stages of being treated. He definitely represents a significant risk at this point," he said.

THURSDAY MARCH 5, 2009
Some had called for the return of the death penalty. Others had advocated something even worse. But in the end, a Manitoba judge said there was only one outcome to the tragic Greyhound murder case.

"Clearly there is a logical reason for the law, and indeed for society, to distinguish between persons who are sane and those who are not," Justice John Scurfield said as he found Vince Li not criminally responsible. "Persons who are profoundly ill do not have the mental capacity to intentionally commit a crime. The goal of criminal law is to punish criminals, not persons who have a severe mental illness," he said.

Li showed no emotion at the verdict and was quietly led away by sheriff's officers.

"These grotesque acts are appalling. However, the acts themselves and the context in which they were committed are strongly suggestive of a mental disorder. He did not appreciate the actions he committed were morally wrong. He believed he was acting in self-defence," said Scurfield. The judge said he believed Li still posed a "significant" risk to reoffend if he were to be quickly released or stop taking his medication. "No doubt that factor, together with Mr. Li's history of extreme violence, will weigh heavily on any future application for release from a secure institution," he said. Li would now be housed in a secure mental health facility indefinitely to continue treatment for schizophrenia.

"He is getting away with murder," McLean's older sister, Vana Smart, told said outside court. "He'll never have a criminal record. After the review board decides that he can be medically managed in the community, he can get a job in a daycare. He can cross the border. He'll never have this stigma attached to him... He will be able to pursue his life as he pleases."

The victim's father, Tim McLean Sr., proudly showed off a tattoo on his chest of his son's face and the words "Tim McLean Forever Loved." "Knowing that the killer might get out sometime soon is very hard. This isn't the right result. We'll do what we can to ensure nobody gets hurt again," he said.

Vince Li claimed it was inner turmoil that triggered him to briefly get off a Greyhound bus in western Manitoba only to resume his journey 24 hours later and brutally kill an innocent passenger he believed was an "evil force." Now, the young man who encountered the mentally ill Li in the community of Erickson was again thankful he escaped unharmed.

Darren Beatty, 15, said he was stunned by the evidence that emerged during Li's trial. "Now that I look back... that's pretty scary," said Beatty.

Li claimed God began commanding him to burn and sell many of his possessions—including a laptop computer he was carrying.

"I thought he was just hard up for money. I didn't realize he wanted to get rid of all his things," Beatty said.

Beatty first spotted Li during the evening of July 29 as he bicycled by, then again on the morning of July 30 on his way to work as a gas jockey at a local gas station. During his coffee break, Beatty eyed the computer lying out for sale. Li had placed it on the sidewalk with a sign saying $600 O.B.O. Beatty proposed paying just $100 for the laptop, then $50. Li said he wanted at least $70, but then dropped his price down to $60.

"Now that I look back, he was changing his mind really fast, from $600 down to $60," said Beatty, who went to a local bank, withdrew cash and returned to Li to buy the computer. Li shook his hand, and the deal was done. Li also tried to sell him a computer bag for $35, but ultimately gave it to him for free when the teen said he didn't have any more money. Beatty went home and realized he didn't have the password to open the computer. He returned to the bench and got it from Li, who told him if he had any other problems to come back and talk to him. Beatty learned of the crime the following day when RCMP officers who were retracing Li's steps found out about the computer sale and seized it from him.

Beatty said the computer contained resumes with the name Vince Weiguang Li at the top. There were also photos of fighter jets and female Chinese models, he said. The laptop contained school schedules, job resumes, emails written in Chinese and innocuous nature photos. Beatty was surprised to hear in court that Li had the murder weapon on him the entire time after purchasing it from a Canadian Tire store in Edmonton, apparently under God's orders. Beatty never saw the knife and said he's tried to not ponder what could have been. "I don't really want to think about it too much," he said.

MONDAY JUNE 1, 2009

It was the first step on his journey back into society. But fears that Vince Li could taste freedom almost immediately were quickly put to rest at his first annual review board hearing. Dr. Stanley Yaren told the provincial panel Li was still a risk to the public, and himself, and should be locked up indefinitely at the Selkirk Mental Health Centre. "I'm advocating the highest level of security possible," Yaren said in the much-anticipated placement hearing to determine Li's immediate future. "Not because I see him as an imminent risk, but because he hasn't been tested in a less-restrictive environment. He has been functioning in an extremely controlled and regimented environment." Yaren was the only witness called to testify.

The review board on his case had three options—immediately release Li into the community with no conditions, grant him a conditional discharge or keep him in a secured mental health facility.

Yaren said that Li had not had any "active psychotic symptoms" for the past 12 weeks. He was also willingly taking his medication and had shown some remorse for his crime, especially after hearing victim impact statements read aloud by his lawyers. "He was quite affected. We spent time with him over the weekend to ensure he was coping," said Yaren. "Now his thought processes are organized. He is no longer tormented by voices and he is beginning to understand what his illness is all about."

He said Li's typical day included plenty of quiet reading in his room, including a Chinese Bible he requested shortly after he was admitted. Li also enjoyed playing cards and watching movies. Yaren warned board members that Li would always be at risk for a relapse, regardless of treatment. And he said a psychotic episode "could be" as severe as the one he experienced while killing McLean.

McLean's mother, Carol deDelley, struggled to keep her composure as she read her statement aloud. "My heart completely shattered and I ached to the core of my soul," deDelley said about her son's death. She constantly thinks of the gory details and how "my son's lifeless head with vacant eyes was being tossed around that bus" by Li. Other family members, including McLean's stepmother and uncle, described a "waking nightmare" and ongoing trauma they were experiencing.

The Greyhound bus driver, Bruce Martin, filed a statement that was read aloud by his lawyer. He had not returned to work and said he constantly thinks about the horror he witnessed and the impact on McLean's family. "Sometimes I feel gut-wrenching pain," he wrote.

MONDAY MAY 30, 2011

It was two years later. And Vince Li was being described as a model patient making such rapid progress that his treatment team was recommending extended privileges that would eventually include escorted leaves outside the Selkirk Mental Health Centre.

"The treatment team has had absolutely no difficulties," Dr. Steven Kremer said at the third annual review board hearing. He said Li knows that going off his meds would "make him vulnerable to the deterioration of his schizophrenia."

There had been no breaches by Li with the previous year's ruling that saw him receiving outdoor passes twice daily from his locked forensic unit to walk on hospital grounds, provided there was a 3:1 ratio of supervision.

The decision was not without controversy and had prompted the provincial government to make several security upgrades, including designating 11 of the mental health centre's security people as special constables following 40 hours of special training and other requirements. Two special constables and a health centre staffer were required to accompany Li on his walks. The centre also had installed $400,000 in security equipment upgrades, including more video surveillance and access controls throughout the property. Kremer was now suggesting a 2:1 ration of supervision, which would gradually give way to 1:1. Kremer said Li would then be allowed to participate in group outings on the grounds of Selkirk in which one staff member would supervise three patients at a time. The next step would be escorted passes out of the facility.

MONDAY MAY 14, 2012

Forget the short, supervised strolls on hospital grounds. Vince Li was about to take his biggest leap yet as he made his fourth annual appearance before the Criminal Code review board. His treatment team was now making two major recommendations, neither of which the Crown opposed.

The first proposal involved giving Li extended privileges within the Selkirk facility, based on the rapid progress he was making while receiving medical care. In the past year, he had been allowed passes out of his locked forensic unit to walk on hospital grounds under the direct supervision of a peace officer. Now, doctors say he was doing so well with the daily 60-to-90-minute walks, he should be allowed general supervision like any other patient at the hospital.

The second proposal involved allowing Li to take 30-minute excursions within Selkirk away from the hospital, provided he was accompanied at all times by a peace officer and a nurse. His doctors said those passes could be extended by up to 15 minutes a week, provided there were no incidents and he continued to make great strides. The community would not be given any notice about where or when he would be let out. In fact, his doctors suggested the accompanying peace officers be allowed to wear ordinary clothes to avoid drawing attention to Li.

DeDelley attended this latest hearing wearing a white T-shirt bearing her slain son's photo. She said it now seemed inevitable Li would regain his full freedom in the near future and called it "ironic and ridiculous" that the mental health system that failed to properly protect society from Li was now recommending he slowly be reintegrated into society. "Letting him go puts the rest of the public at risk," she said.

Li's treating psychiatrist, Dr. Steven Kremer, told the review board Li was still on medication and experiencing no symptoms or hallucinations. He had been diagnosed as having a 0.8 per cent chance of violently reoffending in the next seven years, according to risk assessments done on him. "The privileges being asked for... would not place the public at high risk," Kremer told the board. "He has done very well. He has been a robust responder. He understands if he were not to take his medication, he would experience a deterioration."

Li had improved his English and taken several occupational therapy programs, including job training and meal preparation. Crown attorney Susan Helenchilde said she had no grounds to oppose the recommendations.

"The Crown may not be opposed, but I certainly am," deDelley said.

MONDAY FEBRUARY 24, 2014

Another year—and another major step. It was time to loosen the reins. That was the opinion of Vince Li's treatment team at his sixth annual review board hearing. Three key recommendations were made, and ultimately accepted by the panel. Li would now be allowed unescorted passes into the city of Selkirk, on an incremental basis. Currently, Li had allowed off-site only while escorted. He had taken more than 100 such leaves into Selkirk without incident, the court heard. Li would be allowed more relaxed escorted passes into Winnipeg. Currently, Li must be given one-to-one supervision. Dr. Steven Kremer recommended Li be placed under "general supervision," which would be one worker for every three patients. Li would be moved from a locked facility at Selkirk into a more relaxed, unlocked facility.

As usual, the Crown wasn't objecting to the recommendations. "Mr. Li has done everything that's been asked of him," prosecutor Susan Helenchilde told court. She conceded her department is in a difficult position given it represents the public and Li's actions were so brutal. "This is one of the most ghoulish tragedies in Canadian history," she said. However, Helenchilde conceded Li's best interests must be considered following his not-criminally responsible finding in court.

Kremer said Li knew the importance of taking his medications for schizophrenia and had shown great insight into what triggered the attack. Kremer said the only security concern as Li ventured out into the community was that some member of the public might attack him.

The Vince Li case had left the courtroom and entered the political arena. The federal government had recently introduced Bill C-54, the Not Criminally Responsible Reform Act, in response to Li's case. The bill would create a new category of high-risk offenders who couldn't be considered for release until a court agreed to revoke the designation. They would be individuals deemed an "unmanageable" risk in the community. They would not have a review of their status for three years, would not be given unescorted passes and would only get escorted passes under narrow circumstances. The law would make public safety the main consideration in such cases and ensure victims would be notified when the offender is released. The law could also be applied retroactively.

Advocates said the bill further stigmatized the mentally ill, incorrectly suggested the likelihood of reoffending was connected to the brutality of the crime and made people unnecessarily afraid of those who had a mental illness.

Federal Public Safety Minister Steven Blaney slammed the review board's 2014 decision and defended Bill C-54 in a news release. "The provincial decision to grant Mr. Li unescorted trips around town is an insult to Tim McLean, the man he beheaded and cannibalized. Canadians expect that their justice system will keep them safe from high-risk individuals," the release said.

The case further entered the political arena when Manitoba MP Shelly Glover and the Manitoba government took turns swiping at each other about Li's status. Glover blasted the provincial Crown attorney's office for not objecting to enhanced freedoms for Li. In an unusual move, Glover called for Justice Minister Andrew Swan to file a legal appeal of his department's own position on the controversial matter.

"The decision by the Manitoba government not to object to any of the recommendations made to grant Vince Li additional freedoms, including unescorted trips into Selkirk, is an insult not only to the family of

Tim McLean but to all law-abiding Manitobans. Our Conservative government is firmly calling on the province of Manitoba to immediately appeal this insensitive decision," Glover wrote in a news release that was distributed to media by the Prime Minister's Office, indicating it had approval at the highest level of government. Glover's demand drew a quick response from the province, which accused her of "playing politics" with a serious matter.

Dave Chomiak, speaking on behalf of Justice Minister Andrew Swan, said a provincial attorney general could not intervene in a review board decision. Chomiak, a former Manitoba attorney general, said the province had sent two letters to the federal government urging it to change the Criminal Code to make public safety the paramount issue in these types of cases. "Shelly Glover could easily go down the hallway, talk to her colleague in the cabinet [federal Justice Minister Peter MacKay] and have the law changed, as we recommended," he told reporters. "They have not changed this law. It is their responsibility to do so."

Then Glover issued a terse response to Chomiak. "The people of Manitoba deserve better protection. Unlike the Manitoba government, which has not lifted a finger while Mr. Li was released onto the streets of Selkirk, our Conservative government has moved to amend the law to protect Canadians from dangerous offenders found not criminally responsible," her statement said.

Chomiak said he understood some members of the public might be concerned. "If you're going grocery shopping at Sobeys or at Superstore in Selkirk, and you were to encounter him [Li], you would feel unsure of yourself," he said.

It was another bitterly cold day in the winter of 2014—one of the nastiest in Manitoba history. But the small group of men inside the Selkirk Bowling Centre didn't seem very concerned about the weather outside. Or anything else for that matter. There were plenty of smiles and laughs and mutual encouragement as the group of about six took turns picking up the ball, setting up and firing it down the lane. The cheers were just as loud when it knocked over a few pins as they were when it ended up in the gutter. A competitive men's bowling league this wasn't. The main objective was clearly having fun.

The facility was mostly empty, save for a couple of staff members from the Selkirk Mental Health Centre who were here to supervise this public outing. I'd also made my way inside and stood near the shoe rental counter, making small chat with the lone adult female employee. I'd come here acting on a tip to our newsroom and was trying to be as subtle as possible, telling the woman I was interested in rates for booking a children's birthday party. In reality I was looking for someone. And it only took a few seconds before I found him.

Vince Li was seated on the bench, patiently waiting his turn. He was on one of his regular escorted leaves, a low-key affair that residents of Selkirk were oblivious to. Li looked a lot more relaxed than all of the times I'd seen him in court. It's hard to believe this was the same man I watched years earlier say "Please

Kill Me" in court, the same man responsible for the horrors that occurred on the Greyhound nearly six years earlier. According to medical experts, it wasn't. Only time will tell if the public ever accepts that.

Meanwhile, the tragic fallout of this case continues, in ways perhaps we never would have imagined. RCMP Cpl. Ken Barker, who was one of the first police officers on the scene that night, took his own life in July 2014. Family members say he'd struggled for years with the effects of post-traumatic stress disorder. Although the 51-year-old saw plenty of awful things during nearly two decades of police work, his wife said the Li case was the "straw that broke the camel's back." Barker had been unable to cope with what he encountered on the Greyhound. And it only got worse as the years went on.

In Barker's memory, family members asked for tax deductible donations to be sent to either the RCMP Foundation (http://rcmp-f.ca/pub/donate) which supports families of the RCMP for PTSD awareness, or to Little Warriors, (www.littlewarriors.ca) a national group which helps prevent child sexual abuse.

CHAPTER 15

COLD WINTER, WARM HEART

Who doesn't appreciate a good love story?

When you spend your days immersed in the typical gloom and doom of the courthouse offerings, it can be difficult to find stories that could be considered positive, even uplifting. But every now and then, a little gem comes along that restores your faith in humanity. Even warms the ol' heart. Charles Gonsoulin fits into that category.

An RCMP media release came across my computer one frigid winter day in 2005, providing a few details about a very unusual arrest. An American man had been found shivering on a southern Manitoba golf course, apparently lost and confused. He had illegally entered the country at a nearby border crossing, although the reasons for that weren't released publicly. There was also mention of Gonsoulin suffering some injuries related to his exposure to the cold, but no real specifics.

I wanted to know more: Who was this guy? What had brought him here? What was his experience like? What was his prognosis? Nailing down those details provide to be a lot simpler than I thought. A few phone calls later and suddenly I had Gonsoulin on the phone, directly from his hospital room. The cop who found him also agreed to talk. It was the start of a beautiful relationship between a lovesick fugitive and a reporter—that would be me—who knew he had stumbled on to a great tale.

THURSDAY FEBRUARY 24, 2005

"I was a desperate man who found a desperate way to try and be with the woman I love." And that, Charles Gonsoulin said, was the best explanation for why he'd done something incredibly stupid. The 41-year-old long-time resident of Los Angeles, California admitted he could have easily died trying to sneak across the Canadian border as part of a poorly-thought out plan to meet up with a woman he'd fallen head over heels for—despite the fact they'd never actually met. It was love in the modern age, the result of an Internet friendship which quickly turned into something more serious.

Now Gonsoulin was sitting in his Morris, Manitoba hospital room, his severely frostbitten fingers wrapped in bandages, explaining to a reporter over the telephone just what he'd endured during four days spent wandering outdoors in the heart of a nasty Prairie winter. There was deep snow in North Dakota. There was even deeper snow in Manitoba. And then there was the cold. Oh, God, was it ever cold.

"I wasn't aware of what the weather conditions would be. It was a lot worse than I thought. It got to a point where I was giving up," said Gonsoulin.

The medical diagnosis would be "severe hypothermia." But Gonsoulin was likely headed for something much more dire—try D.O.A.—if not for an RCMP officer who came along at just the right time. "He is very lucky to be alive," said Cpl. Don McKenna of the Emerson RCMP detachment.

So how exactly did Gonsoulin, a self-employed mechanic, find himself near-death in a Manitoba snowbank? Well, for starters, there was that pesky little robbery conviction two decades earlier which meant Gonsoulin couldn't legally cross the border. So he decided to hatch a plan to get himself into Canada through more nefarious means. But it was safe to say that geography and environmental studies were not exactly his strong point.

Gonsoulin made his way to Pembina, North Dakota just fine. But that's where things fell off the rails. His plan was to sneak across the border, catch a bus and head to Quebec to meet the woman he said changed his life. They had met two years earlier in an Internet chat room for people with depression. Gonsoulin said the woman, Jennifer Couture, restored his will to live when he was at an extreme low point in his life. He needed that will to live as he struggled to stay conscious while battling the elements once he got across southern Manitoba—an approximately seven kilometer trek that apparently took him close to 100 hours on foot.

Gonsoulin was discovered by McKenna, who followed a trail of footprints on a golf course just outside Emerson. McKenna eventually found Gonsoulin wandering in the bush. "When I found him, he was babbling and incoherent. His hands were black and frozen solid. He didn't know who he was or where he was," said McKenna.

Gonsoulin's frozen body might not have been found until spring if not for some chance happenings.

First, a man reporting a traffic accident that day told McKenna he thought he spotted someone wandering around the golf course as he drove to the RCMP detachment. McKenna went just outside the town for a look, but initially didn't see anything suspicious.

"The golf course is closed, so I knew there wasn't supposed to be anyone on it. I started trampling through the snow for a closer look, and luckily we'd had some fresh snow because I saw some footprints," McKenna said. The officer quickly realized something was amiss when he found a pair of gloves along the trail of footprints. A few steps later was a duffel bag. Then another. "I went down a little embankment and there he was at the bottom," McKenna said.

Gonsoulin had shed some of his clothing and opened his jacket—a telltale sign that he was suffering from hypothermia, as victims often begin to feel a sense of warmth. McKenna called an ambulance and Gonsoulin was rushed to hospital. His first meeting with his cyberspace sweetie would have to wait. When released from hospital, Gonsoulin would be detained in custody to answer to a criminal charge of illegally entering the country. Once disposed of, he'd be deported back to the United States by Canadian justice officials.

"My past is coming back to haunt me," said Gonsoulin. He had been sentenced to five years in prison following a robbery conviction in 1984. Gonsoulin said he tried to enter Canada legally in 2004, but was turned away at the New York-Quebec border because of his criminal record. So he went home to California dejected but came up with a new plan to get into the country during conversations with Couture. "I had reached a point in my life, before we met, where I was very despondent and not really wanting to keep on living. I needed someone to talk to, needed someone to listen, and that was her," said Gonsoulin, a divorced father.

Gonsoulin said Couture was a single mother of little financial means and was unable to travel to California. He bought a bus ticket, which took him to Pembina, where he purchased some winter survival gear, including boots, two tuques, a parka, two sets of gloves, thermal socks and a compass. He also packed some trail mix and water, which quickly ran out. "I was told by some people that west of the Great Lakes, the winter hadn't been very bad this year," he said.

He picked the Prairies as his point of entry, believing Manitoba's border might be easier to sneak across because of the wide-open spaces and dense brush that could provide cover. "I was looking for the least amount of visibility possible," said Gonsoulin, who began eating snow but found it only made him thirstier and hungrier. Gonsoulin said he hadn't given up on his quest to be with his love, but admitted they would have to find a less dangerous way of arranging their first meeting.

MONDAY MARCH 7, 2005

"It's a love story with a very sad ending." Winnipeg defence lawyer Mike Cook, eloquent as always, summarized the plight of Charles Gonsoulin as he stood in a Winnipeg courtroom. It was the latest episode of this real-life soap opera which had made national headlines.

Gonsoulin had just entered a guilty plea to illegally entering the country. And Cook noted his client had lost much more than just an opportunity to meet his Internet girlfriend, Jennifer Couture, for the first time. Gonsoulin was also going to lose every one of his fingers, right down to the knuckle, along with several toes on his right foot. So much for a Hollywood ending to this bizarre international love story.

Wearing bandages on his feet and hands, Gonsoulin was seeking a discharge, which would not have registered as a criminal conviction in Canada. Cook noted his client just had one prior conviction—that damn 1984 robbery at an Arkansas Pizza Hut which had prevented him from coming to Canada in a much less dangerous fashion. A sympathetic provincial court Judge Tim Preston said it WAS clear Gonsoulin had suffered for his crime but still dished out a conviction in the form of a year-long suspended sentence. He said other people thinking of sneaking into Canada must be sent "a strong message." That would pave the way for Gonsoulin to be deported back to his home in Los Angeles.

"In his lifetime, he had only ever seen a dusting of snow. He tells me the coldest it ever got to in his lifetime has been 10 degrees," Cook told court. "He didn't really know there was any place on Earth that could be so cold and inhospitable."

Weeks later, doctors would amputate all eight fingers and several toes from Gonsoulin. And despite having to re-learn how to use his hands and even walk with major adjustments, he continued to be upbeat as he recovered in Winnipeg hospital awaiting deportation. Much of that could be attributed to the fact that he had spoken by phone with Couture, who would come to Winnipeg a few weeks later for that long-sought face-to-face meeting. "It's amazing. He's only got his thumbs left, but he is so positive thinking about the future. I truly admire the spirit of this man. He believes in his relationship," said Cook. "He believes in a happy future. He's such a unique individual, and I'm inspired by him."

The meeting did happen prior to mid-June, when Gonsoulin was finally released from hospital and deported. It was done in private, away from the prying eyes of media cameras. "While we know a worldwide interest has grown in wanting to know what has been going on with us as a quote-unquote 'story,' reporters are forgetting that very deep, powerful, personal, and... often very painful emotions are being lived day in and day out by the two of us towards the other," Couture wrote in an e-mail to The Canadian Press after the fact. Both she and Gonsoulin declined to give specifics of where their relationship might be headed as Gonsoulin was about to be shipped back to California. "We would prefer not to talk about it anymore. We're all talked out," Couture told the Canadian Press.

Gonsoulin had actually made one final plea to stay in Canada, citing "humanitarian grounds" during an appearance before Canada Border Services officials. He was denied. As always, Gonsoulin continued to look at his cup being half full. "I'm just a person who followed my heart, to do something I felt I really need to do, to catch my dream so to speak," he told the Canadian Press.

The love bug that came over Charles Gonsoulin was apparently spreading. Another convicted U.S. criminal—with a much more serious record than

Gonsoulin—was caught sneaking into Manitoba to meet a woman he'd fallen in love with over the Internet. Unlike Gonsoulin, he waited until the weather was a bit nicer to begin his trek through the province.

Robert Rowelson, 39, was arrested while walking down Hwy. 12 near Sprague. He pleaded guilty days later to illegally entering the country and was sentenced to 45 days behind bars. He was deported upon completion of his sentence.

"He wanted to come across the border to Winnipeg to meet the love of his life," defence lawyer Randy Minuk told court." This was an Internet romance that acted as an aphrodisiac and tempted him to do what he's done."

Rowelson had been released from prison in 2007 year after serving 11 years for manslaughter. He stabbed a man to death during a 1996 bar fight in Nebraska. Crown attorney Steve Christie said Rowelson first tried to enter Canada in February 2008 through the Sprague border crossing. He told officials he had no prior criminal record, but was quickly caught in a lie when they did a computer check. Rowelson was denied entry and told not to attempt another crossing.

On May 20, 2008, Canada Border Services officials got a tip that Rowelson had tried again and was successful. They notified RCMP, who found Rowelson just west of Sprague. He told police he'd snuck into Canada through the bush to avoid getting grilled by border guards. "He said he was coming to Winnipeg, but that he had changed his mind and was instead going to go to Alaska," said Christie. "He said he'd gotten a ride up to the border crossing by a guy named Dave in a brown car."

Provincial court Judge Ron Meyers questioned why Rowelson's Internet girlfriend didn't visit him in the US instead of him attempting another risky entry. "Why didn't he just say to her 'I was turned back, if you really love me, then join me down here'?" asked Meyers.

"He should have. But what can I say? Love makes people stupid," replied Minuk.

"Well, she's a very considerate woman," said Meyers.

I'd love to tell you Charles Gonsoulin ended up living happily ever after with the woman he risked life—and limb—to be with. But I honestly don't know. I kept in touch with Gonsoulin for a few years after he was deported, occasionally emailing him or enjoying a brief phone chat.

At one point, he had moved from California to a more central US state where he had family members. The idea was to be closer to Couture, who had made trips down south to see him. Gonsoulin had told me the relationship was going well and they were hoping to have a solid future together. But he admitted the distance between them was difficult, and nothing was guaranteed in life. But then he just seemed to vanish. I stopped hearing from him, emails suddenly weren't returned and the only phone number I had for him was out-of-service.

To this day, I often think about Gonsoulin. He was one of the most humble, charming individuals I've had the pleasure of meeting in my career. His positive attitude was infectious, especially considering the grim circumstances in which I met him. I couldn't help but feel a bit sorry for him, but also marvel at the lengths he was willing to go to chase something he felt strongly about. Isn't that a quality we'd all like to have?

I honestly hope he's doing well, wherever he might be these days. Perhaps he's off on another adventure, following his heart. I just hope he remembers to check the forecast ahead of time.

CHAPTER 16

TJ'S GIFT

It's every parent's fear—the late-night knock at your door, the grim-faced police officer on the other side, the news that your child is dead. Floyd and Karen Wiebe experienced that horror when their son, T.J., was murdered in January 2003. It's a case that sent shockwaves through the city, both for its brutality and the exposure it gave to a drug culture that continues to run rampant and destroy countless lives.

The Wiebes have become well-known throughout the city as advocates for justice. They have vowed to do everything they can to spare other children and parents from a similar ordeal. I'm proud to now call them friends. I spent much time getting them to know them while sitting in various courtrooms over the years covering the numerous hearings for their son's four accused killers. Outside court, I've been honoured to emcee their annual fundraising gala named in their slain son's memory.

This is their story.

MARCH 2005

They stood before the packed courtroom, looking their son's killer directly in the eye. Anthony Pulsifer sat stone-faced in the prisoner's box as they began to speak. At one point he appeared to be wiping tears from his eyes.

"My heart physically hurts so much I'm amazed it still beats," said Karen Wiebe. The Winnipeg schoolteacher described constantly being haunted at the horrific circumstances of the crime.

Trevor "T.J." Wiebe was just 20 years old when his life was stolen as part of a sadistic plot cooked up by his so-called friends. "How I wish I could hold him again," his mother said.

T.J. was lured out of his home, injected with a syringe, strangled with a shoelace, stabbed in the throat and left to die in a frozen field south of Winnipeg in January 2003. His body was found five weeks later as the snow began to melt. An autopsy revealed Wiebe actually died of cardiac arrest, likely from a combination of the attack and having ingested cocaine and crystal meth that would have increased his heart rate, Dr. Charles Littman told jurors.

A large photo of the victim, taken just days before he vanished, was set up in court for all to see. Pulsifer's lawyer, Randy Janis, had objected to it being allowed, saying it was prejudicial and would turn the sentencing into a "memorial service." But the judge agreed at the request of the Crown and family members who wanted everyone to see what they had lost.

"He was truly a special gift from God to us," said Floyd Wiebe, T.J.'s father. He described all of the milestones which would never come. "I shall not be able to dance at T.J.'s wedding," he said.

Four people had been charged in the senseless killing. Pulsifer was the first to be resolved, having just been found guilty of second-degree murder for his role in the attack. Pulsifer, 23, now faced a mandatory life sentence with no chance of parole for at least 10 years.

It had been a high-profile trial which provided a startling glimpse into Winnipeg's growing problem with crystal methamphetamine, a popular and highly addictive street drug. That was the drug with which Wiebe, his accused killers and several suburban friends were all heavily involved in both using and selling. More than two dozen witnesses had testified during the three-week case, including several friends of Pulsifer who, like him, were involved in the use of crystal meth.

Wiebe's so-called best friend was aware of a plot to attack him but did nothing to warn him—even when the young man asked if he was being set up just hours before he was brutally murdered. "They wanted to jack him, to put him out," Trista Hildebrand had told jurors during the trial. Yet she remained silent, and admitted she even helped the accused who had formed the plan by telling them about some of Wiebe's valuable possessions. "He asked me if he was being set up. I didn't really answer him. I told him just to come and pick me up after lunch," said Hildebrand, who had been arguing with Wiebe the day of his death. He never made their lunch date. Instead, Wiebe went with several men on the bogus premise of buying a car stereo system and never returned.

Hildebrand said her boyfriend—a youth co-accused who couldn't be named under the Youth Criminal Justice Act—was angry with Wiebe for apparently stealing marijuana from him. He also didn't like the time Hildebrand was spending with Wiebe. Wiebe, in turn, was angry with Hildebrand for recently moving into her boyfriend's apartment.

"I think he was just looking out for my best interests," said Hildebrand, who denied there was any romantic connection between herself and Wiebe. She told jurors that all of the accused decided to target Wiebe on January 5, 2003 in what she thought was going to be a robbery. She claims Pulsifer pulled out a "great big green-and-black knife." Hildebrand told the men Wiebe would likely be carrying a video camera, drugs and a few thousand dollars. "T.J. always had lots of drugs on him," she said.

Another witness described how Pulsifer had calmly confessed to murdering T.J. by choking him "until he turned blue" and then cutting his throat with a knife. "Anthony was going on about how he killed T.J. [Wiebe]. He was asking me if I'd ever seen the fear in someone's eyes. I kept telling him to shut up," Mallory Johnson told court. She told jurors the confession came just days after Pulsifer and two co-accused were openly talking about injecting Wiebe with a syringe. "They were trying to find the best way to kill T.J. They were asking me what they could put into needles," said Johnson.

After Wiebe was dead, Pulsifer spoke about his failed attempts at drugging the young man, Johnson said. "He said they tried sticking needles into his neck and it didn't even give him a headache. He said it didn't work so he had to strangle him with his bare hands," she said. "He just kept going on and on about seeing the fear in someone's eyes. It made me very uncomfortable." Johnson didn't say what type of chemical she believed they injected into Wiebe.

Johnson admitted she would smoke crystal meth as often as once an hour, and would sometimes be awake for six straight days because of the high she would get. Other young witnesses had also openly discussed their addictions to meth, along with other drugs, such as ecstasy, LSD and ketamine. Johnson told jurors she stayed silent about Wiebe's death and even helped dispose of evidence by dumping the accused's clothes in a dumpster along Portage Avenue. Johnson and her friend, Kelly Fernandez, say they were paid $37 and ordered to get rid of the evidence by Pulsifer and the other men.

But not everyone could keep the killing secret. Chantel Skehen, then a girlfriend of one of the accused, came forward to police days after reading in the newspaper about Wiebe's body being found. Skehen, 19, testified that Pulsifer and her boyfriend had confessed to her about the killing in early January.

"He told me they had done something terrible. He told me they had killed somebody, that Anthony had done it and he went along to make sure there was no evidence left behind," said Skehen. The two men were showing off several items they claimed to have stolen from the victim, including cash, drugs and a video camera. Skehen said they even played her a home movie on the camera that showed a young man she now knows to be Wiebe.

"[Her boyfriend] said that's the guy Anthony killed," she said. "They beat him, and Anthony said he choked him and mentioned something about cutting his neck." Pulsifer was "very calm and quiet" while talking about the killing, said Skehen. Both men claimed Wiebe was killed because "money was owed." Pulsifer then left the city a few days later to hide out in Calgary, she said.

In a four-hour videotaped interview with police, Pulsifer claimed he had no choice but to kill Wiebe.

He said he tried to warn his "friend" that there was a plot to murder him just moments before he plunged a knife into the young man's neck and left him to die. "I remember telling T.J. what these guys were trying to do to him. I told him to save himself, get out of the city," said Pulsifer. Pulsifer claimed Wiebe reacted to the news by lunging at him with a knife. Pulsifer said he had no choice but to defend himself by attacking Wiebe. Homicide investigators repeatedly confronted Pulsifer about the claim, saying it went against the evidence and "dishonours" Wiebe's memory.

Pulsifer's story changed dramatically from the start of the police interview, when he claimed he didn't even know who Wiebe was. He then later claimed to have "blacked out" and not remember any part of the killing before finally getting into specific details about two hours later. Eventually, Pulsifer told police the pair were friends and former schoolmates who got mixed up in Winnipeg's drug scene.

Pulsifer said two other drug "associates" decided they wanted Wiebe dead because of an ongoing dispute over stolen narcotics. Pulsifer and another man were then told to finish Wiebe off. The plan was hatched about three days before the killing, he said.

"We were forced to do this. We were threatened with our lives, our children's lives,'" Pulsifer told police. Pulsifer claimed the two men who orchestrated Wiebe's death wanted him to kill at least two other enemies, plus collect drug debts. "They said, 'You do this or you're next on the list,'" he said.

Queen's Bench Justice Perry Schulman now had the option of raising parole eligibility as high as 25 years.

Jurors who convicted Pulsifer were asked for their recommendation. They suggested making it 15 years. Crown attorney Brian Bell was seeking 20 years. "This was not a spontaneous act," Bell said in his sentencing submission.

Pulsifer apologized to the Wiebe family for his actions in a letter read aloud by his lawyer. He claimed he wasn't the "monster" everyone likely thought he was. "I have spent many days and nights thinking of everyone who has suffered," he wrote.

Schulman ultimately went with the jury's recommendation, raising parole eligibility to 15 years. "This was a brutal, senseless act which is difficult to comprehend," said Schulman. He noted that Pulsifer presented as an intelligent, polite and articulate man. "It's bizarre to realize that life was of so little value to the conspirators that the victim could have been anyone in the group for whom someone took a dislike," said Schulman.

Outside court, the Wiebes said they hoped what happened to T.J. served as a wake-up call to other parents about the city's growing drug problem. They told the *Winnipeg Free Press* the story of his promising life—and violent death—should send a chill up every family's collective spines.

"This is a real sad commentary on society. Parents and police have to get together to deal with the drug problem. Our generation of parents have been raised that if you do this and this and this, things will turn out a certain way," said Karen Wiebe. "But when two and two equal five, how do you deal with it? You just don't know how to fix the problem, how to get kids out of it."

Police and justice officials agreed that hard drugs such as crystal meth were becoming a major concern in the city. Crystal meth was an increasingly popular street drug that was commonly used in the club and rave scene for the high-end rush it produced. It could be smoked or snorted.

"If it can happen to our family, it can happen to anyone," said Floyd Wiebe. "Since T.J. was killed, we have had so many parents come up to us and say, 'You have no idea how close my kid has come to where T.J. ended up.'"

Wiebe's killing had struck a chord with many Winnipeggers, not only for the brutal facts which emerged during Pulsifer's trial but because T.J. didn't fit the typical stereotype of someone who would fall victim to the shady drug underworld. After all, this was a smart young man who grew up in the cozy suburb of St. Vital, had two devoted parents, two loving siblings and a large network of extended family and friends. T.J. had attended French-immersion classes at École St. Germain and Collège Jeanne Sauvé and then transferred to Glenlawn Collegiate, where he graduated in 2000 with an unblemished record. When he wasn't in class, Wiebe was often at the family cabin in Nopiming Provincial Park, where he snowmobiled in the winter and swam in the summer.

Wiebe's dream was to become an underwater welder, doing work on boats or oil rigs far from his Winnipeg home. He was already certified as a scuba diver and was enrolled at Winnipeg Technical College learning how to become a welder. Wiebe had first learned about scuba diving while on a family holiday in

Hawaii. But drugs began to change everything. And as hard as they tried, Floyd and Karen Wiebe were powerless to stop what became a downward spiral. The Wiebes described how their son's drug problem first surfaced when he got into a car accident in 2002 and police found him in possession of LSD and Tylenol 3. T.J. pleaded guilty and was given a $300 fine.

Wiebe began using crystal meth, then dealing the drug to support his habit. That put him in touch with several shady people—including all of those now accused in his death. "Everyone knew one another because of it," a police source had said shortly after the slaying.

The family had tried to intervene, and Wiebe had reluctantly agreed to attend a drug counselling program. He was killed the day before his first scheduled meeting. "That was taken away from T.J.," said Floyd Wiebe. "As parents, we were on top of everything we could be."

The Wiebes still faced a long legal road, as the other three accused remained before the courts. But they were adamant about ensuring their son's death wouldn't be forgotten. They wanted to make a difference. They had big plans.

MARCH 2006

He had certainly helped plot the grisly murder of T.J. Wiebe. But a Winnipeg jury was unable to reach a verdict on whether Dominic Urichen played a direct role in the killing. The result was a hung jury and mistrial on the charge of first-degree murder. Jurors spent two full days deliberating before telling the judge they'd reached an impasse. They did, however, deliver a guilty verdict on an additional charge of conspiracy to commit murder.

"The jury found that other people committed the murder and he did not actively participate in aiding and abetting it," said defence lawyer Greg Brodsky. The Crown asked for a 17-year sentence for Urichen.

"I loved my son T.J. from the day he opened his eyes until the day you closed them," Floyd Wiebe said while reading a new victim impact statement in court. He then walked past a poster-sized picture of his son that was on display in the courtroom and gave it a kiss. "The fact... people planned for my son to die is unfathomable. There is no reason T.J. should have been murdered. Every time I hear of the plan to kill him, I get sick to my stomach and go into a very dark hole." Wiebe said.

His wife, Karen, told court the killing and subsequent drawn-out legal process had taken a heavy emotional and physical toll on her family. She recently had back surgery to relieve stress-induced pain, while Floyd had suffered two heart attacks.

Urichen was ultimately sentenced to 12 years. It was a far cry from the life sentence he faced had he been convicted of the original murder charge.

"No time is enough. It won't bring our son back," Karen Wiebe said outside court.

A third accused had just struck a last-minute deal to resolve his case without going to trial. Chad Handsor was set to begin his first-degree murder jury case but admitted to the lesser offence of second-degree murder. At his sentencing hearing, he offered a sobbing apology for his role in the crime. He was given a mandatory life sentence and had his parole eligibility raised to 15 years—the same penalty given months earlier to co-accused Anthony Pulsifer.

Once again, the Wiebes directly confronted the killer in court. "What gave you the right to take my son's life? Every day I get to my office and say good morning to a photo of T.J. on my desk. That's not good enough. I want to be able to hug my son, to speak with him. But I can't," said Floyd Wiebe. Karen Wiebe described the constant nightmares she had of her son losing his struggle to live. "Do you see the fear that I see in my dreams?" she asked Handsor.

The victim's younger brother, Chad Wiebe, said he didn't believe Handsor was remorseful. "I saw you look at me in court one day and laugh. You killed my brother. Pleading guilty only says you didn't want to be convicted of first-degree murder," he said.

APRIL 2006

He was the alleged mastermind of a notorious murder. The three men he allegedly recruited to carry out the crime had already been sent to prison. But the 20-year-old Winnipegger wouldn't be going down with them. In a stunning decision, he walked out of court a free man after Queen's Bench Justice Joan McKelvey found him not guilty of first-degree murder and conspiracy to commit murder. The man, who couldn't be named because he was 17 at the time of the slaying, had managed to dodge a legal bullet by the slimmest of margins.

"There are clearly very suspicious issues... involving this accused. He had a motive. There was evidence, albeit from unreliable sources, that he set in motion the plan to kill T.J. Wiebe. However, there are huge gaps in the evidence," wrote McKelvey. "It is difficult, if not impossible, to determine what happened in this case involving this accused without making quantum leaps and speculating as to the nature and intent of the evidence. This difficulty is particularly enhanced given the haze of drug abuse under which all these young people operated."

McKelvey called Wiebe's killing "an act of extreme depravity and brutality." "He lost his life and has left a family and friends who mourn him on a daily basis. The tragedy involves not only the loss of life, but the milieu of drugs which overtook this group of young people," she said. "While I may believe or have suspicions that this accused had some part in the untimely death of T.J. Wiebe, I cannot be satisfied beyond a reasonable doubt."

The accused broke out in a huge smile while his father, a major executive at a high-profile Winnipeg company, hugged his wife and other family members. Wiebe's stunned family, friends and supporters—including relatives of several other recent Manitoba homicide victims—were angered by the verdict, shouting "Shame on you" and "Where's the justice?" towards McKelvey as she left court.

Floyd Wiebe said it was difficult to understand how the man who allegedly came up with the plan to kill his son could escape blame. "Society should be very scared. If the justice system was working properly, he'd go down like the other three," he said outside court. Wiebe noted that several judges had previously commented on the strength of the Crown's case against the youth.

"The evidence showed [the youth] planned this murder, supplied the weapons of death, received drugs afterward and even bleached the supplied murder weapon," Queen's Bench Justice Brenda Keyser said in her March 2004 decision to deny the youth bail.

"The evidence points the finger at [the youth], as the absolute main planner of this murder. It all started with him," said provincial court Judge Lynn Stannard in her December 2004 decision to order the youth to stand trial following a preliminary hearing. The youth was accused of recruiting Dominic Urichen, Anthony Pulsifer and Chad Handsor to kill Wiebe, whom he believed had stolen drugs from him. He may have also been jealous of Wiebe for being friends with his girlfriend, court was told.

"Without [the youth], T.J. would be alive. These three people were hired hit men who didn't even know my son. [The youth] did," said Floyd Wiebe.

The mother of the youth accused had testified how she was losing her grip on the drug-addicted teen in the months before the grisly killing. "He was very pale, always had dark rims around his eyes, was very skinny. He was always stoned," she told court. "He very rarely remembered much of what we talked about."

Pulsifer had previously told police in a videotaped statement that the youth accused had hired him to do the grisly job. However, the Crown's case against the youth took a major hit when Pulsifer retracted his entire statement at the youth's trial. He now claimed he and Handsor concocted a bogus story to implicate the teen.

Handsor claimed he played no role in Wiebe's killing, but implicated the youth when testifying for the Crown. However, he also admitted to dozens of lies in his original police statement. "Handsor's evidence cannot be relied upon. He is incapable of the truth. Handsor was caught in so many lies it would be dangerous to in any way rely upon his testimony," McKelvey said in reaching her decision.

Meanwhile, the Crown had tried to call the final co-accused, Dominic Urichen, but he had refused to testify. That led to him being cited for contempt of court—and slapped with an extra year behind bars in addition to the 12 he was already serving. Urichen blamed his silence on not wanting to be labeled a "rat."

"Compliance of the law isn't optional. And there will be consequences for failing to testify," McKelvey told him. "This was, without question, an interference with the administration of justice."

One that had greatly helped the alleged puppet master of the murder plot go free.

MAY 2007

They knew all about the horror of losing a child to drugs—and then to violence. And now they were planning to do everything in their power to prevent more families from going through a similar hell. In the years since T.J's death, the Wiebes had become strong local advocates on behalf of victims—opening up their home and cabin to other families of slain children and often sitting side-by-side with them during painful court proceedings. And now they were attempting to affect change on an even bigger scale with an ambitious fundraising effort. Their son's memory would be front and centre when the Wiebe's hosted the first-ever "TJ's Gift—A Gala Evening."

The goal was simple. The Wiebes planned to raise at least $40,000 which would go into sustaining The T.J. Wiebe Education and Awareness Fund, which was set up after their son's tragic death as a means of keeping his memory alive and steering others away from the dangerous lifestyle that reeled him in. The Louis Riel School Division had partnered with the Wiebes and would provide students access to the fund for peer education and drug awareness projects.

"We need to reach as many kids as possible," said Karen Wiebe. "We know kids will listen to other kids. And we can provide them with another vehicle for education," added Floyd Wiebe. Getting funding for a project—be it a school play, a lecture series or a science project—would come with a major commitment.

"They have to take a drug free oath," said Floyd Wiebe. "Now, I realize it's just a piece of paper they sign. But I truly believe that if a kid who's maybe 13 and signs that, and two years later is in a position [where drugs are present or being offered], well, maybe he or she remembers what they signed and it's another cog to make a positive choice," he said.

The Wiebes had been overwhelmed with support from family, friends and even complete strangers—both after their son was killed and when they recently launched their effort for the fundraiser. A Calgary resident, listening to Floyd Wiebe speak recently on a national radio show, called up and bought a corporate table for $1,000 simply as a kind gesture. Then there was the woman who approached Wiebe to speak of her own young son's struggles with drug addictions, and how he'd turned his life around by learning about what happened to T.J. Several *Winnipeg*

Free Press articles about the murder still hang in his bedroom.

"We do a fair amount of outreach these days," said Karen Wiebe.

DECEMBER 2012

It was always the toughest time of year, save for the anniversary of the day their son was murdered. Now Floyd Wiebe was sharing new insight into his family's loss. He wrote a powerful blog post which was published in the pages of the *Winnipeg Free Press*. It spoke of how the pain lingered, long after the final court case had ended.

> I recently attended the Manitoba Organization of Victim Assistance candlelight service. It's held at Christmas time, for families who have lost family members through homicide.
>
> MOVA is a club that no one wants to belong to. To be in a room filled with families that are like me is, well, indescribable, to say the least.
>
> There is so much emotion, so much pain and so many memories. We are all there because "someone" decided to kill a member of our family.
>
> Whether that "someone" is in jail for life without parole for 25 years, or served 15 months, or is having Christmas with his family because he was declared "not guilty," doesn't really mean anything. What does mean something is that we do not have our family members with us. No legal system or sentence will fill that void. It's not possible.
>
> When Christmas Day comes, there is an empty chair. Some families leave that chair empty at

the dinner table to remember the one missing. Some families reflect on memories at the table. Some don't talk about it at all because they simply cannot. Some families have stopped having Christmas altogether. There is no "right" way to do this. You do what your heart and emotions allow you to do.

The first two Christmases after my son died were spent in the Caribbean, as there was no way we could spend it at home with all the traditional festivities of fun, food and Santa. When the third Christmas came, my daughter said she wanted Christmas at home from now on, and that's all it took. My wife decided we needed a TJ Christmas tree, and for many years, we decorated it exclusively with angels and "TJ" decorations, ones that he made in school and church as a young child and the ones that he particularly liked. The one ornament that was always in front was the ball saying "TJ's First Christmas." They don't make balls that say "TJ's Last Christmas."

Unless you have lost a family member in this way, you can never understand what it is like. And I hope that you never can, because we don't want you in this club.

When I tell a stranger what happened to TJ, I sense a horror inside that person. I sense what they are saying to themselves at that moment and thinking of their own children. I do not sense an understanding. When I speak with a person in the club, I sense warmth, a connection like no other, a closeness and a sense that they know what it's like. You can even see it. At the candlelight service, we all realize why we are there and how we got there. We greet each other on common ground.

This year, the founder of MOVA, Darlene Rempel-Fillion, was guest speaker. It's been 28 years since her son Rob was murdered. Her voice broke as she spoke, she stopped to compose herself, and we all knew intimately what was going on in her mind. I remember thinking how raw that emotion was after 28 years.

As you can see, we do not "get over it." There is no closure, as people like to think there is. We do, however, move on, but we never get over it. We do laugh, a lot, and we still enjoy life, but it's a very different life indeed.

This is my 10th Christmas without my son. It seems like yesterday in so many ways. Merry Christmas to all.

MARCH 2013

The young man who allegedly cooked up the plot to kill T.J. Wiebe had walked free years earlier. Now one of the three men convicted for their role in the decade-old killing was about to regain his freedom. All of this despite the fact Dominic Urichen was hearing "command hallucinations" to stab strangers, had been deemed a high risk to violently reoffend and was found to have little understanding of how to cope in society and stay out of trouble. Urichen had now served two-thirds of his sentence, and the National Parole Board informed the victim's family Urichen was about to be set free on statutory release.

"It is not the fact that he is getting out of jail on parole. What I object to is that he has done absolutely nothing in jail for 10 years to rehabilitate himself," said Floyd Wiebe.

Urichen's parole documents included several references to him still showing little insight into his offences, wreaking havoc with staff and other inmates behind bars, and due to a diagnosis of paranoid schizophrenia, having violent hallucinations about going on a stabbing spree.

"Is this the kind of person that Canadians want walking around in their community?" Wiebe asked. "Obviously people have to be released slowly into the community so that they can reacquire what it is like to live in a community. But when he is having the exact issues that he had going into jail and 10 years later still has those same issues, does society not have more responsibility?"

In one paragraph, the parole board warned Urichen "has been incarcerated for many years and the contributing factors to your offending are still outstanding, suggesting that you will easily engage in drug use and association with negative peers, leading to a deterioration of your mental health, significantly increasing the risk you pose." The parole board did have the ability to suspend statutory release and keep Urichen behind bars until the expiry of his full sentence if they felt there was a grave risk to society.

Wiebe wondered why that wasn't being done in this case. "If this doesn't meet the criteria of keeping someone in, I shudder to think what it does take," he said.

The very first T.J.s Gift Gala ended up surpassing expectations and raised a total of $54,000. The annual fundraiser has been going strong ever since, *supplemented by other community efforts such as the "Rockin' for Choices" concert which sees thousands of local teens from dozens of schools pack into the MTS Centre to watch a Battle of the Bands combined with a positive, drug-free message. Life, of course, goes on. But the Wiebes have now dedicated their lives to helping other families avoid the kind of tragedy which consumed them. One only needs to check out their website—www.tjsgift.com—to fully grasp their efforts.*

In May 2014—while emceeing the eighth annual gala fundraiser event—I was moved by a speech from a young man who was perhaps headed down a similar road as T.J. He bravely got up before a crowd of strangers and told his story of how a murder victim he never met may have saved his life. About how hearing T.J.s story when Floyd Wiebe spoke at his high school made him re-consider his own choices in life: his increasingly chronic drug use, his negative peers. And how he was able to make a clean break from all of that. That young man graduated high school in June of 2014 and faces a bright future if he can stay on track. The Wiebes have heard many similar stories over the years. It's what motivates them to keep going. It truly is T.J.'s gift.